**Studia Fennica**
Folkloristica 10

The Finnish Literature Society (SKS) was founded in 1831 and has, from the very beginning, engaged in publishing operations. It nowadays publishes literature in the fields of ethnology and folkloristics, linguistics, literary research and cultural history.

The first volume of the Studia Fennica series appeared in 1933. Since 1992, the series has been divided into three thematic subseries: Ethnologica, Folkloristica and Linguistica. Two additional subseries were formed in 2002, Historica and Litteraria. The subseries Anthropologica was formed in 2007.

In addition to its publishing activities, the Finnish Literature Society maintains research activities and infrastructures, an archive containing folklore and literary collections, a research library and promotes Finnish literature abroad.

Studia fennica editorial board
Anna-Leena Siikala
Teppo Korhonen
Pentti Leino
Kristiina Näyhö

Editorial Office
SKS
P.O. Box 259
FI-00171 Helsinki

www.finlit.fi

Annikki Kaivola-Bregenhøj

# Riddles

Perspectives on the use, function and change
in a folklore genre

Finnish Literature Society • Helsinki

Studia Fennica Folkloristica 10

The publication has undergone a peer review.

VERTAISARVIOITU
KOLLEGIALT GRANSKAD
PEER-REVIEWED
www.tsv.fi/tunnus

The open access publication of this volume has received part funding via a Jane and Aatos Erkko Foundation grant.

© 2001 Annikki Kaivola-Bregenhøj and SKS
License CC-BY-NC-ND 4.0 International

A digital edition of a printed book first published in 2001 by the Finnish Literature Society.
Cover Design: Timo Numminen
EPUB: eLibris Media Oy

ISBN 978-951-746-019-4 (Print)
ISBN 978-951-746-576-2 (PDF)
ISBN 978-952-222-821-5 (EPUB)

ISSN 0085-6835 (Studia Fennica)
ISSN 1235-1946 (Studia Fennica Folkloristica)

DOI: http://dx.doi.org/10.21435/sff.10

This work is licensed under a Creative Commons CC-BY-NC-ND 4.0 International License.
To view a copy of the license, please visit http://creativecommons.org/licenses/by-nc-nd/4.0/

A free open access version of the book is available at http://dx.doi.org/10.21435/sff.10 or by scanning this QR code with your mobile device.

# Contents

FOREWORD AND ACKNOWLEDGEMENTS  7

1 INTRODUCTION  9

    The well-known riddles and sources  11
    The changing riddle tradition  14
    The contemporary riddle  16
    Riddles and other forms of folklore  25
    Trends in research  29

2 DEBATE ON THE BASIC ISSUES  38

    Riddle elements  38
    Definitions of the riddle  47

3 THE SUBGENRES OF THE RIDDLES  54

    True riddles  56
    Joking questions  57
    Visual riddles  62
    Wisdom questions  68
    Puzzles  70
    Parody riddles  72
    Literary riddles  75

4 SEXUAL RIDDLES  79

    Erotic teasing  81
    The use of sexual riddles today  83
    Sexual picture puzzles and spoonerisms  87

5 THE CONTEXTS AND FUNCTIONS OF RIDDLES  92

    Riddling situations  94
    Incidental riddling  96
    The traditional contexts and users of sexual riddles  101
    Riddle contests and organised games  105

Riddles as part of their context    109
The rules and restrictions governing the performance of riddles    113
The journey to Hymylä – the Finnish way of punishing
the poor riddlee    114
The functions of riddles and riddling    118
A contemporary case in Northern Ireland    123


6  THE EXPRESSIVE DEVICES OF RIDDLES    128

Ambiguity    130
Riddle metaphors    135
The culture-bound riddle metaphor    138
Riddle formulae    141
The international riddle model    143
The semantic formula    146


7  FROM IMAGE TO ANSWER    152

The relationship between the riddle metaphor and the answer    152
One image, many answers    153
Is it a case of guessing?    157
Arbitrary and conventional answers    159


8  THE FUTURE OF RIDDLE RESEARCH    163


BIBLIOGRAPHY    167

ABBREVIATIONS    174

INDEX    175

# Foreword and acknowledgements

Riddles are a voyage into the unknown. They are an invitation to embark on an adventure that either brings delight, amusement and gratification at discovering the right answer, or humiliation and vexation at being led astray. Few genres have such a long tradition, both oral and written, as the riddle. The first to record riddles were possibly the Sumerians, who were already noting them down in cuneiform in the fourth millennium BC. On the other hand, few genres have enjoyed such marked shifts in prestige as the riddle. Many celebrated writers and scholars have both invented and drawn inspiration from popular riddles; in the 17th century, they used riddles to produce poetry of distinction. The light contemporary riddle does not, by contrast, enjoy such high esteem, in most cases assuming the form of joking questions both in the oral tradition and in the media. Where the literary riddle produced exalted poetry fit for any occasion and company, the joking question is a witty, jesting, taunting, even vulgar gibe rooted firmly in the present. The riddle (its form, stylistic devices and even its content) has undergone transformation with the passing of time, but one of its primary functions – to entertain while at the same time posing a question requiring an answer – has remained constant.

The riddling tradition is almost too vast a field for a single researcher to explore. I will, in this book, be examining some of its basic characteristics and contexts, but I am only too well aware that many of them will remain beyond my reach. I personally have never been present at any occasion where riddles have been used spontaneously, because traditional riddling contexts have long been a thing of the past in Finland. My material is taken from the extensive archive collections of the Finnish Literature Society (SKS) and articles and publications by numerous colleagues. I am thoroughly familiar with the Finnish material, having worked in the archives of the Finnish Literature Society in the early days of my research career. In the case of the other materials I have trusted the expertise of my colleagues, who have either done fieldwork in cultures to which I have not had access or have drawn on the archive collections of their own countries.

There is a vast volume of research literature on the riddle: enough to occupy the scholar for a lifetime. It may perhaps sound somewhat surprising to write about a vision for the next basic treatise on the riddle in the foreword to a book, but I would nevertheless venture to do so, while at the same time pointing out that the best format for this treatise would, to my mind, be a research anthology in which each scholar would address his or her own particular field. This would do the fullest justice to different language and culture areas in a way no single writer can hope to achieve and at the same time throw light on the numerous subgenres and various dimensions of research.

All the Finnish riddles are given here first in their original language and then in translation. This will allow readers who do not speak Finnish to note, say, the use of alliteration, a stylistic device borrowed from oral poetry in the archaic Kalevalaic metre. By way of example I sometimes quote riddles from other language areas in their original language only, but also often solely in English if that was the language of the publication I consulted. – I assume responsibility for one problem posed by English: Finnish has only one, gender-neutral pronoun 'hän' for the third person singular (English she/he). Any reader who is irritated by the use of the English pronoun 'he' should therefore remember that to the Finnish speaker 'hän' could just as well be 'she' or very often an even wider category of narrators, tradition bearers, riddlers and riddlees: 'they'.

Now that this book is about to go to press, I would like to thank the many colleagues who have in one way or another assisted me with my work. Not all the good ideas suggested could, unfortunately, be taken up, and the responsibility for the ultimate decisions naturally lies with me. I wish to express my gratitude first and foremost to Professor Alan Dundes, who inspired me to undertake the project. He also encouraged me to carry on when I felt I had come to a dead end. The greatest expert on riddle tradition and research, he was able to give me a number of hints as to where to look in the literature. In 1988–1989, when I began exploring the research literature on riddles, I spent a year at the Hebrew University of Jerusalem, and there took part in a project entitled "Enigmatic Modes in Culture". I wish to thank the members of this project team for the fertile atmosphere for discussion. The collection of articles Untying the Knot (Hasan-Rokem–Shulman 1996) produced by the team was in many ways connected with my own research. I have received valuable comments on the manuscript from Carsten Bregenhøj, Lee Haring, Bengt af Klintberg, Ulf Palmenfelt and Fionnuala Carson Williams, who also placed the contemporary Northern Irish material collected by her at my disposal and helped me to understand its idiosyncrasies. Ulla Lipponen supplied me with both her own joking question collections and her expertise. Terttu Kaivola solved countless source reference problems for me and sought out books I needed. Roger D. Abrahams and Sirkka Saarinen provided answers to my questions, and Aki Arponen, Satu Apo and Arno Survo supplied me with additional material on subjects more familiar to them. To all of you, dear colleagues, I express my warmest thanks for your help. A special word of thanks is also due to Susan Sinisalo, the translator of many of my publications, to the Finnish Literature Society for agreeing to publish the book and to Päivi Vallisaari for her assistance at the printing stage.

Mustasaari, summer 2001

# 1 Introduction

The riddle is an astonishing genre: both dead and alive at the same time. Many 'true riddles' (such as "Kattila kiehuu kankaalla ilman puitta, tervaksitta. – Muurahaispesä."/"A kettle is boiling out on the heath, without wood, without fuel. – An Anthill." FR 284) are fast becoming no more than archive records of interest only to the researcher. Yet an old image may suddenly prove to be so viable that it is once again back in circulation on being attached to a topical answer ("Mikä se on kun ulkomailla höylätään ja lastut Suomeen lentelee? – Visa-kortti."/"What is it that is planed abroad and the shavings fly to Finland? – A Visa card."). Meanwhile wave upon wave of verbal wit flourishes in the tradition cultivated by children and young people ("Why did the elephant paint his toenails red? – To hide in the strawberry patch." Or: "Why did God create blondes? – Because apes never learnt to fetch beer from the fridge."). The joking question is another medium both for analysing a catastrophe ("Where did Christa McAuliffe take a vacation? – All over Florida.") or for acknowledging a tense political situation ("What is the difference between youghurt and Loyalists? – Youghurt has a culture."). The riddle confuses and amuses, it is a means of embarrassing anyone who does not know the answer or of winning the battle between life and death; of teaching norms or of commenting, with a twinkle in the eye, on a serious matter.

Riddles are known to have existed since way back in time, for the first documents date from thousands and hundreds of years ago and such countries as India, Palestine, Mesopotamia and ancient Greece. Most languages also have a word for riddles because as a genre riddles belong in all cultures to the archaic stratum of folklore. Sirkka Saarinen (2000) points out that these words "represent the emic category, i.e. tradition bearers' own classification".

The following may be proposed as a working definition of a riddle (for a discussion of riddle definitions see Chapter 2):

A riddle is a traditional, fix-phrased verbal expression containing an image and a seeming contradiction. It consists of two parts: an image and an answer, for example,

A house full, a yard full.
Couldn't catch a bowl full. – Smoke. (ER 1643 a)

Riddles clearly say something about the material culture of the community in which they are used. Nonmaterial phenomena are less frequently dealt with, though they are not unknown. The range of concepts occurring in riddles is rather limited, and the image and answer both have their own favourite motifs. According to the observations of Archer Taylor (1951:45) the motifs of European riddles are almost solely in the vicinity of the farmhouse and deal with the objects in a woman's world or a world as seen from the windows of a house. "Earthworms, chickens, milk and eggs, as well as household tools, are characteristic and popular themes. Yet even here the choice is extremely limited: dogs and horses are not often the answer to riddles, although often used as means of comparison. Cats or mice are virtually never used in either sense. European riddlers rarely allude to wild animals. It would be hard to find riddles for a stork, a bear, a fox, or a wolf, frequent as these creatures are in the folk story. Only a few fruits or vegetables occur as the themes of riddles."

Themes common and important in a culture may, on the other hand, be missing entirely from the answers to riddles. There is, for example, little mention in their riddles of the rice so important to the Filipinos, and Filipino riddles appear to be unaware of all major socio-political conflicts in the area (Hart 1964:66). Similarly, there is among Cheremis riddles not a single one about fishing and fishing tackle, even though fishing has been common in the Cheremis region. And although lime trees and oaks are common species in the Cheremis forests, they never appear as the answers to riddles. They are, however, to be found in riddle images. Sirkka Saarinen points out in her doctoral dissertation that some scholars reckon the reason for this is that limes and oaks were used as sacrificial trees in sacred groves. Their use as answers to riddles would, therefore, have been taboo. The more likely answer is, she feels, that a growing tree is not as a whole a sufficiently clear referent, even though parts of it may be popular answers. (Saarinen 1991:30–31.)

In the communities where the use of true riddles is a living tradition, new objects and methods are quickly taken up in riddles. Elli Köngäs Maranda made notes on the way the Lau of Malaita in the British Solomon Islands handled, by means of riddles, new commodities introduced by an alien culture (such as a truck, sugar, matches, aeroplane or axe). These riddles were by no means content to give a neutral description of the novelties and incorporated admiration implying that "Western technology is effective" (for example, "A small child carries a big man. – A chair."). But the riddles also indicated fear – "Western things are perishable" (for example, "A big men's house, very many men live in it. If they come out, they die. – Matches.") and direct criticism – "Western things are hard to acquire, lose their attractiveness or are dangerous" (for example, "A thing, when it hits a man, he dies. – A truck.") (Köngäs Maranda 1978:207–218.) In many parts of the Western world views such as this on the way of the world are nowadays presented by means of joking questions. Being easy to use, this genre has become a tool for expressing an amused or ironic opinion on, say, day-to-day politics, entertainment, sports or people. (See Chapter 3)

## *The well-known riddles and sources*

There are numerous ancient sources which refer to the popularity of riddles, among the most esteemed the *RigVeda* of India, the *Old Testament*, and some of the Icelandic sagas. Fragments of Mesopotamian clay tablets bearing texts recognisable as riddles have been discovered (Alster 1976). These riddles have a long literary history, since they were already being noted down in Sumerian cuneiform around 3100 BC. The *Talmud* and the *Koran* also mention riddles and their use.

The oldest riddle records are probably to be found in Vedic poetry, the oldest volumes of which were composed in the middle of the second millennium BC. For example, the eighth hymn of the *RigVeda* describes the chief deities in ten riddles. The following riddles describe the gods Soma and Agni:

> One of them is muddy brown, many-formed, generous, a youth; he adorns himself with gold. – Soma.

> Another descended refulgent into the womb, the wise among the gods. – Agni (Huizinga 1949:106).

The *Mahabharata* (300 BC–300 AD) in turn poses questions of the neck riddle type (cf. page 68), which often require answers of a moral or religious kind. The riddles are part of the narrative entity, as in the story of Yudhisthira and his four royal brothers who were dying of thirst in the forest. Spotting a pond, they began to drink from it, but the spirit of the pond, Yaksa, gave them permission to quench their thirst only if they could answer its questions correctly. They failed, and because they had nevertheless drunk the forbidden water, were punished with death. Yaksa's questions took the form of prasna or verbal puzzles, of which the epic is fond, and they fall into nine categories, one of which goes as follows:

> Still, tell me what foeman is worst to subdue?
> And what is the sickness lasts lifetime all through?
> Of men that are upright, say which is the best?
> And of those that are wicked, who passeth the rest?

By giving the right answers to all the questions put to him Yudhisthira was granted permission to drink the water and was finally able to bring his dead brothers back to life:

> Anger is man's unconquered foe;
> The ache of greed doth never go;
> Who loveth most of saints is first;

Of bad men cruel men are worst.
(Bhagwat 1943:11 and 1984, 524; Bryant 1990:15–16; for an analysis of Yaksa's Questions see Shulman 1996:151–167.)

Some riddles have become so familiar through publications that they are known by name. Examples are the riddle of the Sphinx appearing in the Boeotian myth, the riddle of Samson told in the *Old Testament*, and the Odin riddle from the Old Norse *Hervarar Saga*.

The Boeotian myth tells about a sphinx that was sent to the people of Thebes by way of punishment. The sphinx, which had "the face of a woman, the breast and feet and tail of a lion, and the wings of a bird" (Apollodorus 1967:347), took up residence on mount Phicium near Thebes and threatened with death any traveller who failed to solve the following riddle: "What kind of animal is it that stands on four legs in the morning, two in the day, and three in the evening?" (ER 47b) Many had already lost their lives before Oedipus put forward the explanation that the riddle referred to a man who crawled on all fours as a baby, stood on two feet as an adult and was forced to walk with a stick in old age. In reward Oedipus was given the kingdom and the wife of the dead king, who was in fact his mother. On hearing Oedipus's answer, the sphinx threw herself from the citadel.

The most famous account of riddling in the *Old Testament* is to be found in Judges 14, in the chapter where, during his wedding feast, Samson, a Jew, asks the Philistines what would appear to be an unanswerable riddle: "Out of the eater came something to eat; Out of the strong men came something sweet." The answer consists of two counter-questions: "What is sweeter than honey? What is stronger than a lion?" (Judges 14:14) He gives them seven days in which to find an answer, and the loser will have to pay the winner thirty fine linen wrappers and thirty gala dresses. The only one who knew the answer was, of course, Samson who, while in the wilderness, had seen a lion's carcass in which bees had made their hive, and Samson transformed this scene into a riddle. The Philistines, however, got Samson's wife to tell them the answer and the riddling ended in a bloodbath, for Samson killed thirty Philistines and gave their garments to the winners. The logic of Samson's riddle is only revealed on reading Judges 14, i.e. the frame story providing the necessary context. The riddle is partly prompted by the power struggle between the Israelites and the Philistines, which Samson hopes to win by posing a question that cannot be answered. But it also carries an erotic charge and struggle for power between a man and a woman. The scene of the events is the seven-day wedding feast of Samson and his Philistine wife. Samson refuses to reveal the answer to the riddle even to his wife, but consents on the seventh day because he cannot resist her seductiveness. In her fight for power, his wife uses weapons unfamiliar to Samson. The festivities end in enmity, and the riddle becomes a neck riddle: although the answer is correct, it is obtained in a way that could not be accepted and that led to the issuing of the death penalty. The first to suffer from the bloodbath are the Philistine kinsmen, but in the end the marriage between Samson and his newly wedded wife meets a tragic end. Samson's riddle has been seen as serving "as a challenge to privacy and autonomy. As long as it is not solved, privacy and autonomy are maintained, allowing one's social powers to exist. When the riddle is solved, privacy and power are gone." (Cohen 1996:303–304.)

The *Old Testament* also describes, in the First Book of Kings, a riddling match between King Solomon of Jerusalem and the Queen of Sheba. The Queen tested Solomon's wisdom by posing many "hard questions", but the reader is not told what these were. Further light is, however, thrown on the *Old Testament* story by the Midrash literature, *Midrash* meaning any of the Jewish commentaries and explanatory notes on the Scriptures, written between the beginning of the Exile and c. 1200 AD. One story in the Midrash of Proverbs poses four questions put by the Queen of Sheba to Solomon. Two of these are in the nature of practical tests, while the other two are clearly riddles in their imagery and structure: "She said to him: 'Seven exit and nine enter, two pour and one drinks.' He said to her: 'Surely, seven days of menstruation exit and nine months of pregnancy enter, two breasts pour and the baby drinks.' She said to him: 'What is /the case of/ a woman who says to her son: 'Your father is my father, your grandfather is my husband, you are my son and I am your sister.'" He said to her: 'Surely, the daughters of Lot say to their sons: Your father is my father, your grandfather is my husband, and you are my son and I am your sister.'"

The confrontation between Solomon and the Queen of Sheba once again displays an erotic charge and the tension between cultures so common in the *Old Testament*. These two characters have both fired the imagination of countless storytellers: Jews, Arabs and Christians alike. The Midrash literature stresses the destructively erotic, demonic and chaotic nature of the infidel Queen of Sheba compared with the wisdom of King Solomon and the superiority of the religion he represents. (Stein 1996:125–147.)

One of the most famous accounts of riddling in Old Norse literature is to be found in the medieval tale of King Heidrek in the *Hervarar Saga*. A contest is waged between Heidrek and the god Odin. The latter appears in the guise of an old man named Gestunblindi who had fallen out with the king. Tension thus accumulates between the riddler and the riddlee. King Heidrek has no difficulty at all in solving the riddles, which include the Odin riddle "Six legs, two heads, two hands and a nose. But uses only four legs as it goes. – A man on horseback." (ER 49)

There are many variants of the Odin riddle in Finland, too, and the following variant occurs in Swedish children's lore (Palmenfelt 1987:9):

> Vad har tre ögon, tio ben och en svans?
> – Den enögade Oden som rider på sin åttafotade häst Sleipner.
> (What is it that has three eyes, ten feet and a tail?
> – The one-eyed Odin riding his eight-footed horse Sleipner.)

Not until Odin poses a question in the nature of a neck riddle – "What did Odin whisper in Balder's ear, before he was placed on the pyre?" does the King realise he is competing with a god. The contest later ends with Odin being able to sidestep Heidrek's sword, but he is so incensed by Heidrek's behaviour that he orders his slaves to murder him (Bryant 1990:16–17.)

One thing all these ancient sources have in common is the fact that the riddles are framed by a narrative, and they come in a contest in which life is ultimately at stake (cf. Abrahams 1980). Meanwhile all these narratives provide cultural background information that helps to understand the imagery of riddles and their use.

## *The changing riddle tradition*

The material in this research represents numerous manifestations of the riddle tradition in various communities. The main emphasis is on the analysis of true riddles and their use, but I shall also be dealing with the various types of riddle, in Chapter 3.

The oral riddle tradition has in the past few decades undergone radical change. Riddle metaphors are inexorably tied to their cultural context, and this has proved the downfall of the entire genre. This has been the case throughout the Western world, where the technical revolution and industrialisation were a rapid process. True riddles are an integral part of the conceptual and fantasy world familiar to the people making their living from farming and its parallel occupations. The riddle metaphors are related to the objects, methods and animals known to all the riddle users. In its day the homogeneous material culture contributed to the emergence and use of a uniform riddle tradition. Spotting the semantic fit between the riddle image and answer was a pleasurable experience. But the images are not always comprehensible to someone from another culture. The riddle tradition never caught up with the change in material culture and thus did not renew accordingly, so that it gradually became a culturally alien tradition. Leea Virtanen (1977:77–78) describes the situation thus: "Spinning, churning, seine fishing, and ploughing changed into strange work, while, for example, a still, pothooks, baker's spit, carding combs, sieve, quern, quill pen, the runners of a sleigh, knapsack, scythe, millstones turned into strange articles. Central heating and electric lighting took the place of the fire burning in the oven or the forked stick for holding fir torches, not to speak of innumerable other changes: it was no longer taken for granted that there were lice in people's hair, porridge was not eaten from the same bowl, a pig no longer entered the living room, everyone learned to write (while before: 'Kylvää ken taitaa.', 'Let him 'sow' who can')." The images of riddles began to sound strange and old-fashioned as customs and living conditions changed. My colleague Ulf Palmenfelt is, I believe, right in saying (during a conversation I had with him in 1997) that the "urban, modern mentality" associated riddles, like fairytales, with the old, backward agrarian society and accordingly turned both genres into children's lore. Marked riddle language was another reason why riddles began to seem unnatural in the tradition of those peoples where the language of tradition differs significantly from the everyday spoken language.

Some riddles are, however, so neutral in their images that they could have retained their vitality. The following images connected with the observance of nature and travelling by water do not, for example, sound old-fashioned even to the modern ear:

> Puuropata kankahalla kylän lapset ympärillä. – Kusiaispesä.
> A pot of porridge out on the heath, the village children all around.
> – An anthill. (FR 822,
> ER 1193 paragraph 1)
> Kesät keikkuu kenollaan, talvet norkkuu nokallaan. – Vene.
> Backwards arching, it rocks in summer, it loafs on its nose in winter.
> – A boat. (FR 312)

But even riddles of this kind likewise declined with the overall true riddle genre. The riddle language, which in Finnish might often be in Kalevalaic metre and rich in metaphors, was difficult to manage, which meant that impromptu improvisation, for example, was not easy in a riddling situation. Some riddles incorporating new motifs proved clumsy and unworkable (see also Hart 1964:44, Krikman 1995).

In the course of a collection made in Finland in 1966 many active users of the riddling tradition in their youth gave their views on why the riddling tradition went out of use. Their opinions revealed some subtle factors contributing to the change in culture. The following informant was born in 1912 and takes a broad look at factors influencing the life of tradition:

> The reason why interest in the old-fashioned riddles ceased is to my mind education. When I was a child, there were none of the pastimes there are today. Ordinary families did not even have books, apart from the obligatory ones like the *Catechism* and an *ABC Book* and religious ones like the *Bible*. Very few people older than me have been to elementary school. Before I started school, I borrowed school books from others to read for fun. So the old began to fade into the background. Even when I was a pupil there, the school had a lending library where the pupils could borrow books either for themselves or for the folks at home. People began to take newspapers more. These were read carefully and their subjects were discussed. Then came the societies, the youth association, small farmers' association, countrywomen's association, study circle. These all came between 1925 and 1935. Then there were sewing circles in winter at least twice a week. Almost all young people belonged to something. Every society had an entertainments committee, and so on. All of a sudden the printed word thus began to gain ground. The unwritten book of the people faded into the background, forgotten, outdated.(SKS. Helmi Laiho AK 9:112.1966)

The accounts often also mention the radio and later TV, which spread in the 1960s. "People no longer needed to think things up for themselves, because everything was there ready and waiting. Anything that was old was inferior and had to be pushed aside. People began to be 'refined', even their very speech, and they sometimes went to ridiculous extremes in trying to 'speak proper'. " (ibid.) An example of the confrontation of the riddling tradition and the spread of the mass media is to be found in the Philippines, where certain small local radio stations broadcast a programme in the 1950s based on riddles sent in by listeners. In return, the contributors received a small fee. The best riddles were chosen from the 30–50 sent in every week and presented on the programme. This was a real competition, in which the winners received prizes. The programme yielded relatively few innovations, but riddles were invented on such subjects as the radio, telephone, television, motion pictures, the typewriter, motorcycle, and a post-war brand of soap. The resulting riddle did not always satisfy the best expressive norms for the genre: "Riddles about recent innovations often are clumsy in concept and awkward in composition, suggesting recent origin, lacking the polish gained by age and frequent repetition. An example will illustrate: 'You cannot get fire from Mr. Edison's light. – Electricity.' " (Hart 1964:43–44.)

Once the metaphors characteristic of riddles and the worldview reflected in the tradition have become strange to the users of riddles, the tradition no longer has a sounding board. More than anything it has, however, been influenced by the change in the community's interests, lifestyle and values. Ways of spending the leisure hours have changed and people prefer other forms of entertainment rather than true riddles. There is no longer any point in asking old true riddles; they do not amuse, and neither do they arouse people's curiosity. One reason for this may be that the metaphors and answers are no longer relevant in the modern environment with its surfeit of material goods and external stimuli. Another reason is the verbal clumsiness of the riddle images. They are no longer arresting, so they are forgotten.

## *The contemporary riddle*

While these major changes have been taking place, folklorists have documented the subsequent life of the riddling tradition in an urbanised milieu. They have observed the fashionable waves of riddles rapidly spread via the mass media throughout the Western world. The most popular riddles have been joking questions, in which the teller of the joke presents both an image in question form and an answer. Jokes are specifically young people's tradition, though children do still know riddles. (Sutton-Smith 1976:113.) Joking questions are based on stereotypes permitting endless variation. In the first wave came the elephant jokes (cf. joking questions, Chapter 3) that spread through the college students in the USA in the 1960s.

After the elephants came ethnic riddle jokes, the second main category of riddle of the joking-question type. These are targeted at both ethnic and other minorities and are often highly racist. The target for ethnic riddles was, in the USA, most often the Polish immigrants. The Polack jokes were often crude, and either the Poles were depicted as simpletons who did everything wrong, or the point of the jest was aimed at their dirtiness or their lowly position in society. (For example, "What do you get if you pour hot water on a Polack? – Instant shit." Davies 1990:85.) Sometimes dirt and stupidity are linked together in ethnic jokes. Of course, there is no proof that the Poles are any less hygienic than their fellow citizens in America.

(Davies 1990:89, 308.) It has subsequently been argued that the Poles acted as a channel for letting off the aggression that could not be openly aimed at the Afro-Americans (Dundes 1971:186–203).

In the Nordic countries, too, one of the most incredible phenomena of sick humour is the Negro jokes that have been part of the oral tradition since the early 1970s. This type of riddle is markedly racist and aggressive, such as:

> What's the difference between a Negro and a barrel of shit? – A barrel.
> Why are there holes in Negroes' coffins?
> – So the worms can come out and vomit.

Other themes include stereotypical ideas of how Negroes look and act. In Sweden schoolchildren thought the Biafra, Jew and Negro jokes were both funny and cruel. Their popularity lay in the fact that they were shocking and daring. Most of the children did not, however, subscribe to the racist views of Negroes represented by the jokes. According to studies made by Bengt af Klintberg (1983), the Negro riddles popular in Sweden and the other Nordic countries did not appear in publications printed in the United States, nor were they openly told. According to the archives, however, they were indeed known in the States and had found their way to Sweden with young people visiting the USA. It is difficult to even guess why, in the Nordic countries, which have no black minority, Negro jokes do sometimes turn up from time to time. Are they an indication of fear of the alien, of latent racism (both highly familiar and sometimes openly manifest in the Nordic countries) or merely of a desire to play with a topic felt to be taboo?

In addition to the oral tradition and to the press, the literary channels used to spread this genre include calendars giving a joking question for each day of the year. *The Truly Tasteless Joke-a-Date Book 1994* clearly reveals the subjects popular in the early 1990s.

Some ethnic minorities in the USA – such as African-Americans, Italians, Irish and Poles – find themselves featured in the calendar every month, the Jews, Mexicans and Chinese slightly less often. The questions seem to follow set stereotypes (for example, the drinkloving Irish: "How can you tell an Irishman in a topless bar? – He's there to drink.") and to propagate them. Also in the limelight are gays and lesbos, blondes, hookers and WASPs, who also merit a joking question every month (for example, "What's the WASP recipe for chicken soup? – Bring a pot of Perrier to a full boil..."). As its name suggests, the calendar also contains some truly tasteless jokes, on such themes as dead babies.

The vogue in 1994 seemed to be for Somali jokes, which likewise appeared every month. Let us take a closer look at them (the date on which the joke appears is given in brackets):

> Why do Somalis give such good head? – They'll swallow anything. (22.1.)
> What's this? (Hold up a blank piece of paper.) – A Somali menu. (17.2.)
> What's black and has cobwebs? – A Somali's asshole. (15.3.)
> What's the fastest animal in the world? – The Somali chicken (date 16.4.)

> What do you call a Somali with five dogs? – A caterer. (15.5.)
> What's so great about getting a blow job from a Somali?
> – You know they'll drink every drop. (16.6.)
> What do you do if you suffer from bulimia? – Propose to a Somali. (17.7.)
> What do you call a Somali with a stubbed toe? – A three iron. (13.8.)
> What do you call a Somali with a dime on his head? – A nail. (2.9.)
> What do you call a Somali with buck teeth? – A rake. (23.9.)
> Why did the Somali have a mouthful of dirt?
> – He was training to be a javelin. (17.10.)
> How do you know when a Somali is pregnant?
> – You can see the baby. (17.11.)
> What's this? (Hold up a comb.) – 100 Somalis carrying a canoe. (16.12.)

Somalis were a topical theme, both because of the tragic war raging within their country and, in particular, because of the unsuccessful peace-keeping operation. Like Biafra jokes, the themes of these joking questions underline the catastrophic nature of the situation, though one might even expect a more biting tone due to the humiliations suffered by the American troops. The Somalis stepped into the vacuum vacated by the Iraqis, but the point of the joke is different. It would be interesting to know, as regards the spreading and preservation of tradition, whether the tradition propagated by the calendars is also oral tradition, or whether it then becomes oral tradition.

Jesting aimed at a minority has sometimes turned into neighbour humour even passing very incisive comments on the local inhabitants or people from a neighbouring country. The Canadians joked at the expense of the Newfoundlanders ("Why did the Newfie move his house two inches? – He was trying to tighten his clothesline." Davies 1990:14), in Denmark the point of the riddle joke was aimed at the residents of the second largest city, Århus ("Do you know why Århusians have so many scars round their mouths on Mondays? – It is because they have been practising eating with a knife and fork on the Sunday." Davies 1990:166), the English laughed about the stupid Irish, the French about the Belgians ("How do you recognise a Belgian in a submarine? – He's the one with a parachute on his back." Davies 1990:20), and vice versa. (af Klintberg 1983, Kaivola-Bregenhøj 1974.)

In Sweden, where Negro jokes nevertheless vanished almost entirely from 1975 onwards, jokes about stupid Norwegians took their place. The aggression could also be presented in the form of a joke, such as:

> Brain surgery is so far advanced in Sweden that you can even change someone's nationality. If you remove 1/3 of a Swede's brain you get an American. Well, there was one man who wanted an operation but the surgeon made a mistake. He removed 1/2 of his brain. Just as the surgeon and his colleagues were wondering what to do, the patient sat up and said, "Hej, jag är Håkan från Norge!" [Hi, I'm Håkan from Norway!]
> (SKS. Ulla Lipponen KT 489:11. 1976)

The butt of the joke is close at hand, a group well known. To the riddler, the group represents the periphery, but at the same time a culture dependent on his own. As Christie Davies points out (1990:313), its members are not viewed "as a clearly separate, alien people in their own right, but as possessing an imperfect, 'stupid' version of the joke-teller's own culture."

The aggressiveness of the humour was on a par with that of the Negro jokes, but it was easier to target a kindred people living next door than black people living far away of whom very few had any personal experience. Both are, however, examples of a joke fad that spread right across the Western world. (Communication from Bengt af Klintberg, 1994). In 1975 this playful aggressiveness between Sweden and Norway developed into a "war of jokes" by the newspapers *Vb* and *Expressen*, with the two neighbours supposed to be vying with one another to see who could fire the most jokes, often of an ethnic nature, at one another. Reimund Kvideland (1983) reckons that this cycle of jokes belongs to the same category as the Århus jokes in Denmark, East Frisian jokes in Germany, and the Polack jokes popular in America.

Joking relations often grow up between different professions and at work and can be maintained by means of joking questions. One student made a collection of jokes attached to viola players. In form, these riddles are typical joking questions (cf. Chapter 3) such as:

> How do you know a man's a gentleman?
> – He knows how to play the viola but doesn't.
> How do you rescue a viola player who has fallen through the ice?
> – You don't.
> Why can't a viola player catch aids?
> – Even a virus has some sense of pride.
> What's the difference between a viola and a violin?
> – A viola burns for longer.

The reason for the jokes was, in the opinion of the student collecting them, that the viola was for a long time at a disadvantage because almost no solos were written for it. It was even said that a viola player is just an unsuccessful violinist. This special status has enhanced viola players' in-group spirit, which in turn further strengthens the flora of joking questions: "We can be proud of the viola jokes because no other section of the orchestra can boast such a large collection of jokes. Violinists are rightly resentful of the fine kindred spirit prevailing among viola players" (Puurunen 1992:24).

One rather special genre of tradition consists of the jokes of riddle or question-and-answer pattern that spring up after a major accident or world catastrophe. These often come in the form of cycles that spread both orally and via the media. Once the issue they concern fades from the news, the tradition vanishes, making room for another cycle. The oldest joking questions in this catastrophe tradition tell about Jews exterminated by the Nazis during the Second World War, such as: "How many Jews can you fit in a German car? – Four in the seats and thirty in the ash tray." (Bronner 1988:123). Alan Dundes and Thomas Hauschild (1983) have called this type of joking question the "Auschwitz joke" and are slightly perplexed by the popularity of riddles of "the Jew ashes" type that seem to be such a living tradition all over Europe and the United States. Sick jokes about Jews may pop up as a result of a programme on television, for example, such as:

"What's the difference between a pizza pie and a Jewish person? – A pizza pie don't scream when you shove it in the oven." (Barrick 1980:444).

Catastrophe jokes about such events as the Holocaust always arouse strong emotions and questions as to why they are told, and whether it is right to present or publish them. I fully agree with Dundes and Hauschild (1983:249) who say, "Nothing is so sacred, so taboo, or so disgusting that it cannot be the subject of humour. Quite the contrary – it is precisely those topics culturally defined as sacred, taboo, or disgusting which more often than not provide the principal grist for humour mills." But not all catastrophe jokes are expressions of racism connected with Jews, since most ethnic minorities in the United States, for example, have to bear the brunt of cruel, crude humour. In the case of children's tradition it is above all a question of drawing the line between the permissible and the impermissible and temporarily violating this line by means of tradition. And is racism really the only issue? It seems to me, at least, that these catastrophe jokes revel in horror and revulsion in the same way as certain urban legends, the tellers and listeners of which enjoy crossing the border of the permissible.

The war in Biafra in 1968 and the resulting famine led to a new joking question cycle in which the leading character was the starving black Biafran who weighed scarcely more than a ping pong ball: "What's the difference between a Biafran child and a ping pong ball? – 5 grams." Among the tellers of the riddles were Scandinavian schoolchildren who had watched the TV reports of the famine. These catastrophe jokes raised a laugh, but many people protested that such humour was neither right nor funny. (af Klintberg 1972.) The hunger jokes tinged with black humour were later associated with other starving nations, such as the Ethiopians. The war in Biafra and the resulting famine that killed about two million civilians was, however, the first crisis to attract worldwide attention in the media. The starving Biafran child came to symbolise hunger. Catastrophe jokes are presumably here to stay, but the target group is changing all the time. Not all catastrophes spawn an international joke tradition. There were, for example, no signs of the war in Kosovo in Finnish children's lore in 1999 (communication by Ulla Lipponen, who read through hundreds of contributions from children).

The American spaceship Challenger exploded on 28 January 1986, killing seven astronauts. One of them was Christa McAuliffe, a teacher allowed to join the space flight in order to be able to report it later to schoolchildren. Most of the joking questions that sprang up after the disaster picked on her specifically in, for example, the school tradition:

> How do you know that Christa McAuliffe wasn't a good teacher?
> – Good teachers don't blow up in front of their class. (cf. example p.9; Bronner 1988:129–130.)

Challenger jokes began to appear at least as soon as two-and-a-half weeks after the disaster. According to observations made by Bill Ellis (1991), they spread in two waves, the second of which was marked by the arrival of considerably grimmer jokes than the first. They included images like those quoted above of the astronauts' bodies cast by the explosion all over the state. Jokes spring up as the public grieving process nears its end, to be replaced by a complex mix of emotions in which there is room both for grief but also for anger. Some have interpreted the telling of such jokes as a therapeutic means of expressing the feelings of horror and of sharing them with others. Why, then, are jokes not invented and spread immediately after a catastrophe? Another explanation for catastrophe jokes is said to be that people get tired of mulling over disasters and that the jokes "evoked closure – that is, they were quite consciously attempts to be the last thing said about a topic" (Ellis 1991:117–118).

The shipwreck claiming some 850 lives on the way from Estonia to Sweden in autumn 1994 likewise set up a wave of catastrophe jokes. In Finland the first joking questions appeared as black humour and were told by workers for the shipping company in an attempt to relieve their distress and the pressure they suffered in dealing with clients. Later, questions such as these spread among children and young people:

> Miksi Estonian katpeenille ei voi antaa joulukalenteria?
> – Hän avaa kaikki luukut etukäteen.
> Why can't you give the Captain of the Estonia an Advent calendar?
> – He opens all the windows beforehand. [Finnish has the same word for window and hatch in this meaning.]
> Mikä on virolaisen merikapteenin motto? – Luukut auki Eurooppaan.
> What's the motto of an Estonian sea captain? – Windows open on Europe.
> Miksi kaikki ruotsalaiset kuolivat Estonian laivaonnettomuudessa?
> – Koska homobaari oli pohjakerroksessa.
> Why did all the Swedes die in the Estonian sea disaster?
> – Because the gay bar was on the bottom deck.

Very many of these joking questions are either language- or culture-specific. (cf. Chapter 3) The second of these three, for example, contains an allusion familiar to those acquainted with Finnish literature to the 1930s strivings to "open the windows on Europe", while the last is a typical product of neighbourly humour.

The tradition attached to the Estonia was a typical fashionable vogue: the first jokes found their way into the Folklore Archives of the Finnish Literature Society just before Christmas 1994, little over two months after the disaster, and by the following autumn the subject had more or less been forgotten (details of this tradition from Ulla Lipponen). Jokes emerged as news of the disaster began to spread (Smyth 1986:243). This observation coincides with one made by Bill Ellis, who says that as time passed, "...the jokes became less fresh in the informants' minds. Later collections surveyed memories of an event, rather than a living phenomenon" (Ellis 1991:115–116). People turn their attention on new topics, and the jokes told only yesterday become stale.

The international nature of catastrophe tradition is also manifest in individual joking questions, because they can be applied to numerous situations simply by changing the name of the main character. The following question familiar from the Christa McAuliffe tradition was also attached to the captain of the ill-fated ship the Estonia:

> What were Christa McAuliffe's last words home?
> – You feed the dog and I'll feed the fish.

Similarly the "Jew-ashes" pattern is observed in the following joking question:

> How do you get six Indians into a Mini?
> – Five in the front and Mrs. Gandhi in the ashtray.

This riddle comes from Northern Ireland, where it was heard soon after the murder of Prime Minister Indira Gandhi.

Only some catastrophe joking questions spread all over the world, while others, such as the Challenger or Estonian ones, tend to be limited to the region affected by the disaster (Handberger 1995:12).

The modern riddle is also an excellent medium for the expression of political views. A good example are the Iranian riddles that sprang up in 1987 while American diplomats were being held hostage in Teheran, and the Iraqi riddles which spread in America during the Gulf War of 1993. They have the same bite as the ethnic riddle jokes in describing the stupidity and cruelty of the Iraqis. Some old riddles have been effectively recycled: simply adapting the nationality and the answer of an old riddle to a topical context is sufficient to produce a new, serviceable variation:

> How many Iraqis does it take to change a light bulb?
> – Four – one to unscrew the bulb, one to kill the house owner and two to carry the television out.
> How can you get 45 Iraqis into a telephone kiosk?
> – Tell them the kiosk is NOT theirs.

In just the same way the joking question is, for the Palestinians, a harmless means of letting off steam about the Israelis, or of telling what the Russian thinks of the outlook for Communism in 1992. Try as I might, I have not been able to locate any examples of such Palestinian joking questions, though I know they have been part of the living tradition.

The joking questions criticising the Soviet regime draw on all the tricks at the genre's disposal, playing on the ambiguity of words or the practical politics of everyday life. Some of the jokes are so closely tied to their language and culture that they lose their impact in translation. The next four can, however, be understood even by someone with little knowledge of the culture:

> What is a rubber truncheon? – The beating heart of the party.
> With whom does the Soviet Union have a common border?
> – With whoever it wants.
> Why did a Soviet delegation visit Finland?
> – To find out how to live in harmony with a big neighbour in the east.
> What is your attitude to the Soviet Union?
> – Like that to my wife: I love her but fear her.

Following the downfall of the Soviet Union, oral tradition such as this began to appear in print as well. I was given these examples by my colleague, Arno Survo, who translated them into Finnish for me.

In Chapter 5 dealing with the functions of riddles I shall be talking about joking questions found in Northern Ireland by which people give vent to the pressure built up by the prolonged political tension.

Children's lore also provides an insight into a country's domestic policy. In addition to providing mere amusement, the joking question is a means of expressing even barbed opinions. Urho Kekkonen (1900–1986), for many years President of Finland, is a regular character in children's lore ("Mikä oli Kekkosen lempilaulu? – En etsi valtaa, loistoa."/"What was Kekkonen's favourite song? – I seek not power or glory."; a Finnish Christmas carol), but Martti Ahtisaari, who was President 1994–2000, also received his share ("Miksi Martti Ahtisaarella on vyö, jossa on eri maiden lippujen kuvia? – Jotta housut pysyisivät ylhäällä."/"Why does Martti Ahtisaari wear a belt showing the flags of different countries? –To keep his trousers up."). The point of the jokes is appreciated by anyone who knows that Kekkonen, who remained in power for many years, sought power and glory both at home and abroad, and that Ahtisaari went on numerous state visits abroad during his term as President. When the first woman President, Tarja Halonen, was installed in Finland on 6 February 2000, I received the following President joke within two days from Ulla Lipponen's network:

> Mitä tapahtuu Mäntyniemessä maaliskuun alussa?
> – Pingviini lähtee pois ja Pinokkio tulee tilalle.
> What's going to happen at Mäntyniemi [the President's official residence] at the beginning of March?
> – The Penguin will go out and Pinoccio will come in.

This joke is speared at the ample figure of the outgoing President and the prominent nose of the incoming one. I also heard that various jokes went the rounds by mobile phone throughout the election campaign.

Political events of the early 1990s in Finland featuring in such jokes include the presidential elections, the floating of the Finnish markka, the recession and economic revival, joining the EU, and the negotiations with the Soviet Union over the return of Karelia ceded to the Soviet Union as a result of the Second World War.

There are some foreign news events to be found in the children's joking question tradition of the early 1990s: the collapse of the Soviet Union and the accompanying economic straits ("What do Russia and the United States have in common? – You can't buy anything with roubles in either, but dollars can buy you anything."), the Gulf War, the US presidential elections, and Princess Diana (Lipponen 1995:211–214), who became the subject of joking questions even before her death.

Joking questions are a tradition that may be heard in, for example, the casual conversations in the soap operas and other TV series made for international distribution. As a result, they quickly spread from one country to another and over linguistic borders. Light entertainment on the radio favours this easy way of raising a laugh; in the phone-in competition for "the worst joke in the world", for example, all the entries were of the joking question type. This can also be discerned in the world of postcards. Various types of greetings card exploit the surprise effect of familiar formulae by placing a riddle image on the front and the answer inside, such as:

> 1. Danish birthday card:
> What do you have in common with a bottle of old port? – You both improve with the years. Hearty congratulations!
> 2. Swedish birthday card:
> Birthday riddle: It's made of rubber, comes in different sizes and is good to have in bed. What is it? – A hot water bottle. Congratulations!
> 3. American Halloween card:
> A Halloween riddle: Know why the mummy's always in such a foul mood? – If you hadn't had sex in 3000 years, you'd be in a foul mood, too! Happy Halloween!

Advertising agencies have spotted the selling power of a joke/riddle that is on everybody's lips. What is more, the models of expression in joking questions are so simple that they can always be used to produce more questions. In 1993 the Swedish State Railways advertised its "Central Line" as follows:

> What do the Central Line and a down coat have in common?
> – They're both warm and cosy in winter.
> What do the Central Line and a Ferrari have in common?
> – They can both do 160 kph with ease.

As riddles these advertisements fail in the sense that they lack a joking point and their surprise element is very tame. The familiar formula nevertheless makes people remember them.

The expressive devices of modern riddles are more limited than those of traditional true riddles, and their distribution and use differ from those of the old tradition. The jokes and jests nowadays presented in the form of a riddle are an indication of the way the generic borders shift. Riddles and jokes have the same tendency to make use of and to depend on ambiguity, though they use it in different ways (Hamnett 1967:382). Although true riddles have for the most part vanished from the oral tradition, some of the features characteristic of the genre have remained: the desire to ask, the desire to mislead the listener who has not yet spotted the unexpected link between the image and the answer. All sorts of jests, crazy humour, joking questions and riddle parodies are just some of the forms of tradition that fill a gap in the cultural context in which we live. The riddle cycles are a form of entertainment and, at the same time, they question the contemporary values and norms reflected in them. They prove that riddles are a living genre capable of adaptation and of meeting the challenge of the times.

## Riddles and other forms of folklore

The joking questions quoted prove that generic borders are created by scholars, but that living tradition changes and seeks both different forms and contexts. In communities with a living tradition the performing contexts of different genres are by no means separate events, for they frequently overlap. Many of the accounts of the use of riddles (for example, Herskovits & Herskovits 1958:55, Abrahams 1983:272, Haring 1985:176–177) demonstrate that riddling and storytelling are usually parts of the same event. Narrative elements may be enhanced in riddling situations, and it is possible that consecutive series of riddles could fulfil roles similar to those of individual narratives in such sessions (Evans 1976:186). Genres may also be linked together because they are contrastive and activate participants in different ways. In situations in which children use traditional genres, spooky stories and short riddling sessions have been found interspersed. Whereas stories make the strange familiar, riddles make the familiar strange; stories permit one narrator to keep charge of the situation and force the others to inactivity, whereas riddles draw all participants into highly active roles. (McDowell 1979:133.) The genres performed on the same occasion supplement one another and may, in addition to providing entertainment, communicate a shared message.

The narrative and the riddle intertwine in a unique way in the genre known as dilemma tales. These tales are a form of prose narrative culminating in either a question or an argument that provides an opportunity for discussion, argument or the search for a solution. Sometimes the answer is provided by the teller, at other times by the listeners. The following example comes from the Wolof tribe in Africa and is included in William Bascom's anthology *African Dilemma Tales:*

> Three youths came to a huge river. The first split the water with his sword and reached the other bank with dry feet. The second unrolled a band of cloth and made a bridge on which he crossed over. The third shot arrow after arrow, each striking the other so that it formed a wooden bridge over the river. Which is the most cunning? (Bascom 1975:119.)

Unlike ordinary riddles, finding the answer is in dilemma tales less important than the argument itself. Using this criterion, the border with closely-related genres can be drawn as follows: "riddles are to be answered; arithmetical puzzles are to be solved; dilemma tales are to be resolved" (Bascom 1975:12).

The relationship between the riddle and other genres of folklore has aroused considerable interest in a number of researchers. Numerous comparisons have been made of the riddle and the proverb, and the structural and stylistic similarity between them is indeed obvious. Roger D. Abrahams has made a detailed analysis of the characteristics of the genres and begins by emphasising the points they have in common: "Proverbs and riddles are short forms; both use a sentence as their linguistic frame. Both use the devices of poetry as the stylistic basis of their linguistic organizations: rhythm, balanced phrasing, rhyme, metaphor, and assonance. Both are descriptions whose referents must be inferred through the aptness of their elements" (Abrahams 1968:149). The differences are, however, clear. Although both genres usually consist of two or more elements or traits, in the proverb "the combination of elements of description sets up an image or idea in an immediately meaningful and dynamic *Gestalt*." In the riddle, however, the elements are so combined that the *Gestalt* (or "implicit pattern " Abrahams, personal communication, July 2000) is impaired until the referent has been stated. The tasks of the genres, and the way they function, which Abrahams calls their strategy, also differ, because as a rule the proverb clarifies and instructs, whereas the riddle confuses and entertains. (Abrahams 1968:151–152.) The difference between the genres can be summarised by means of the following definition: "If a riddle is an overt question with a covert answer, a proverb is an overt answer to a covert question" (George B. Milner in Köngäs Maranda 1976:129–130). Even if it is a play on words, it does throw some light on the differences between genres. The proverb does, however, often appear on comparison to be too serious, and its humorous and ironic sides tend to be overlooked.

The relationship between the riddle and the proverb cannot, however, be fully determined without examining the contexts in which they are used. Abrahams (1968:151) describes their contexts as follows: "Proverbs exist in a conversational context in which there must be a clear relation between description and referent; otherwise the strategy of the proverb fails. Riddles, on the other hand, are found in the permissive atmosphere of the riddle session in which the relation between described traits and referent must be blurred to carry out the intent of the riddler." This does indeed apply in most cultures. Reports from African folklore communities nevertheless stress that fixed phrased sentences acting in some contexts as proverbs may in other contexts appear as riddles (Hamnett 1967:385, Kuusi 1969:305–311, Glazier 1976:214, Haring 1985:174). Similar cases have also been reported in Turkey (Basgöz 1972:656). In such cases the researchers have ended up by speaking of riddle proverbs (Kuusi op, cit., cf. Harries 1971:389 "proverb riddle"). To give an example: the image of the Ovambo riddle "One finger cannot catch a louse. – One person cannot do all the work." is known in Madagascar as a proverb (Kuusi 1974:68–69, Haring 1985:174). Some riddles of the Bantu Sotho people, in view of their form and contents, could well be transposed into proverbs (Hamnett 1967:385). The same correspondingly applies to proverbs that could well serve as riddles. In Madagascar there is a structural similarity between these two genres, since countless metaphoric sayings have been collected as proverbs in which two sentences almost identical in structure are juxtaposed on the question-and-answer pattern of the riddle (Haring 1985:174–175). The result may be a pair of sentences whose parts appear to be unrelated until closer examination reveals subtle connections. The following example is from the Anang of South-Eastern Nigeria: "A single vine does not fill forest", which evokes the reply, "A single coin that falls makes no sound" (Messenger 1960:225–226). The same sentence pattern also recurs in the images of many riddles. Since in

Madagascar both the question and the answer to a riddle or a closely-related genre could be presented by one and the same person, the difference between the proverb and the riddle has almost completely vanished. Such a close affinity is unknown in Western tradition, since the images of genres, their function and use are, despite the stylistic devices, remote from one another.

An example of the interesting coexistence of a riddle and a proverb is also to be found in the Babylonian Talmud. Galit Hasan-Rokem (1974) demonstrated that the same motif (H 1054 in Thompson's index) can be found in different manifestations in a folktale, "The Clever Peasant Girl" (AT 875), riddle and proverb. In the tale the girl is faced with a typical dilemma, this time of how to appear before the king undressed and dressed at the same time. Different tale variants offer different solutions, but one is the expression "Undressed and naked, and wears shoes" presumably known as a proverb. Since shoes are only a part of dress, the riddle contained in the tale can be solved. The article by Hasan-Rokem (1974:936–940) presents an interesting perspective and a challenge to examine how well-known motifs occur in the genres of different cultures. Hasam-Rokem herself points out that the relationship may, as in this tale and proverb, be of a structural nature, but it may also be genetic, because in some cases the same text is known both as a proverb and as a riddle.

The interest in riddles was in previous times partly derived from an attempt to use riddles as mythological research material in order to throw light on obscure myths (Taylor 1951:2, Kuusi 1956:181). André Jolles (1930:129) regarded the myth and the riddle as inverse phenomena: "the myth is an answer implying a question; the riddle is a question demanding an answer". Elli Köngäs Maranda (1978:208) analysed the relationship between the myth and the riddle while fieldworking among the Lau in Malaita. The contexts and users of the genre differed. The myths were sacred and helped members of the community to understand why things are as they are. Riddles, on the other hand, were neutral, and they questioned the order of society. There was a clear division of labour, not connections, between the genres. Others have, however, observed that there is a link between myths and riddles that is particularly marked in the case of cosmogonic riddles. Linda Sadnik (1953:171) considers that the images of Bulgarian and Macedonian riddles are founded on ancient mythological fantasies. Views have been assimilated from other cultures, and they have taken root in popular thinking and gradually faded to become traditional views of nature. Those riddles which have both a cosmological and a profane explanation are in Sadnik's opinion in most cases of cosmological origin. Matti Kuusi nevertheless urges caution in interpreting riddles and has reservations about Sadnik's cosmological conclusions when applied to, for example, riddles that have a profane solution everywhere else in the world. Finnish riddles are rich in mythological metaphors, such as "Tapio's money", meaning furs, "Tapio's bull" (Tapio here referring in these metaphors to the male main spirit of the forests) or "the devil's elk" as a euphemism for a tree that has been felled, and "the skin of a hundred-horned ox" to mean birch bark. Such metaphors indicate that mythological concepts were at one time more common as metaphors than they are today. Riddle images and their explanations have become far more profane over the past hundred years. The images as such are not, however, always any help in the study of folk belief, since they are often stereotypical clichés such as those found in Kalevala-metric poetry. The purpose of these clichés is to act as misleading allusions in riddle images. Sometimes the image may, however, carry a concealed hint connecting it with a charm such as:

>    Iski tulta Ilmarinen, välähytti Väinämöinen. – Ukontuli.
>    Ilmarinen struck fire, Väinämöinen flashed.
>    – Lightning. (FR 162. Also in incantations, SKVR VII, 1418.)
>    Mytty mättähän takainen, kiekura kiven alainen, kieko kannon juurinen.
>    – Kärme.
>    Bunched up behind the hummock, curled up under a stone, a disc at the foot of a stump. – A snake. (FR 638)

These riddles only mean something to the riddlee familiar with the fire and snake charms. Because of their intertextual link, they are wisdom questions requiring special knowledge. Some riddles may, on the other hand, require special cosmological knowledge on the riddlee's part. In the following riddle there is a barely-disguised glimpse of the Finnish pagan god of thunder:

>    Pien ukko rautasaapas, astuu kivistä kattuu, kiven vuorta vongottaa. – Aatra.
>    Little old man iron boot, walks along a stony street, plods up a rocky hill.
>    – A plough. (FR 750)

Cosmological images may, on the other hand, be concealed in concepts that appear highly mundane, for such objects as old bowls, chest lids, sieves and baskets may, in the vocabulary of riddles, be founded on the ancient image of the heavens forming a hemispherical vault above the earth. (Kuusi 1956:181–185.) The old metaphors are, however, part of the joint linguistic heritage to such an extent that no explanation can be demanded of the riddler. Lyndon Harries (1976) reports that in recording riddles in Tanzania he tried to ask why, in the riddle "A big cooking-pot and a big basin. – The sky and the earth.", precisely these details were used as if they belonged to the same logical category. The explanation he received was that a cooking-pot is round like the sky, and a bowl shaped like a saucer is the earth. Harries was not entirely satisfied with the answer, though he was not primarily seeking a mythical explanation but the riddlees' sense of the semantic fit linking the concepts. He did not, however, continue his questioning for fear of spoiling the riddle.

The skilful riddler may improvise riddles for occasional use by drawing on his familiarity with the riddling tradition and by borrowing suitable images from other genres. A suitable image matters more than the genre from which it is taken. Turkish riddles, for example, have been devised by transforming folk songs, anecdotes, folktale formulae, and the poems of minstrels. For example:

Riddle:

It comes tumbling and mumbling from the mountain. It finishes beans and chick peas. – Hail.

The source of this riddle is the following song:

It comes tumbling and mumbling from the mountain
It ruins beans and chick peas
O my sister watch yourself
The little mouse became a girl-chaser. – A mouse.

Riddle:

That is a lie, this is a lie, a snake swallowed the elephant, it mounted the donkey and took the camel on his lap, is this too a lie? – A lie.

This riddle is in turn taken from the following folktale formula:

This is a lie, that is a lie, the snake has swallowed the elephant. Hey, the one who mounts the ant has taken the camel on his lap, "Did you see my water buffalo which fell out my saddle bag?"

A riddle such as this was usually made up under pressure during a competition, and the answer is either a new innovation or an abstract concept. If the source of a new riddle is a proverb, the answer may be the topic of the proverb. (Başgöz 1972:663–667.)

## *Trends in research*

The theories and methods employed in the study of riddles are clearly influenced by the general trends in research at the time. The approaches are, roughly speaking, of two types: either scholars have examined the genre as a form of verbal art with its own contentual, structural and stylistic features and circulation, or riddles have been regarded like all folklore as a form of cultural communication with clear communicative goals and functions, and links with both their milieu and their users. The former approach incorporates a comparative and structuralistic view, the latter questions arising in the course of fieldwork on the contexts, functions and users of folklore.

Two of the most distinguished advocates of the comparative research method are Antti Aarne and Archer Taylor. Antti Aarne (1867–1925) won international recognition as an expert on folktales and riddles. He was a loyal representative of the historical-geographical school, he trusted its potential and applied it in all his research. The historical-geographical or "Finnish" method was developed by Julius and Kaarle Krohn out of philological text criticism and aimed to determine the history of a product of folklore: where, in what form, and when, say, a Kalevala-metric poem or a folktale had come into being and how it had travelled further afield. This school took its name from the fact that its protagonists investigated the temporal and spatial transformation of folklore. The primary goal of the research employing the historical-geographical method was to uncover and reconstruct the invariant behind the variants. Every effort had to be taken to ensure that the material was as complete as possible: all the Finnish variants of a poem, for example, or if the research disposition so demanded, all the available international variants. The extensive source criticism often also included the laborious task of locating a folklore recording. The research material was arranged according to region. Once the geographical distribution of a poem, for example, had been determined from its recordings, it was thus possible to see how the poem varied from one region to another. The research could then proceed by means of detailed comparison towards its ultimate goal of determining the protoform of the item in question. (Krohn 1918 I:38–40.)

By the time he embarked on his study of riddles, Antti Aarne was already famous as a folktale scholar, thanks to his numerous folktale monographs in the FF Communications series and his *Verzeichnis der Märchentypen* (FFC 3) – an index of folktale types – published in 1910. Aarne's interest in riddles was possibly aroused above all by a desire for methodological experimentation, since this period in his research began with a paper given in 1916 in which he stressed his wish to prove that the geographical research method is just as applicable to the study of riddles as to any other genre of folklore (Aarne 1916:57). For four years he concentrated on writing papers on riddles and published them, mostly in German, as volumes 26–28 in the FF Communications series, *Vergleichende Rätselforschungen* I–III.

Antti Aarne (1918:19–34) began his study of riddles by exploring, in the spirit of Kaarle Krohn and Axel Olrik, the epic laws by means of which it is possible to analyse the various transformations manifest in riddles, as in other genres of folklore. In the case of riddles the transformation laws concern the expansion of the image by elements that did not originally belong to it (individual words or complete lines), and correspondingly contraction, which is in most cases the result of forgetting. Changes are further caused as some general concept is given a special meaning (for example, in riddles signifying an egg, a house becomes a church or a monastery), or as some object or thing adapts to local conditions (change in things, objects and names). Changes may derive from one another, or the original features are conducive to change. The quest for alliteration and rhyme brings about changes, likewise the law of opposites. Most important of all are, however, changes in the original meaning, so that one riddle may give birth to numerous different ones.

In his riddle research Aarne began with the answer and picked out riddles known internationally as the object for his analysis. He examined 11 riddles in all, or rather, as Archer Taylor put it (1951:6), patterns of riddles. He published in Finnish his analyses of riddles meaning an axe, fire and smoke, a magpie and an egg (Aarne 1917), in German riddles denoting writing or a book, the year, a human, a two, three or four-footed being, a cow, a rider and horse, and a wingless bird (Aarne 1918–1920).

Each of the miniature monographs observed precisely the same scheme. Let us take as an example the riddles denoting writing or a book, which Aarne approaches via the internationally-known image "A white field, black seeds" (see ER 1063). This riddle is known not only in Europe but also in Asia, Africa and America. The oldest known variant appeared in France in the 15th century in a publication entitled *Adevineaux amoureux*. There are no examples of this, but Aarne presents the following French variant:

> Blanc est le champ, /white is the field/
> noire est la semence, /black are the seeds/
> l'omme qui la semme, /the man who sows/
> est de tresgrant science. /possesses very great knowledge/
> (Rolland 1877:106, cf. Aarne 1918:35)

Aarne picks out examples according to his own preferences to illustrate the variation of the image in different language areas. The varying elements are both adjectives (for example, the Lithuanian riddle "Ein ehrbares Feld," /a modest field/ "eine wunderbare Saat." /a wonderful seed/ "Was ist das?" / What is that?/) and nouns (for example, the Latvian riddle "Eine weisse Wiese," / a white meadow/ "schwarze Rinder," /black cattle/ "für einen klugen angenehm zu weiden." /for a clever, pleasant person to herd./). The metaphor of a field may even change into snow, yet all the images share the white colour hinting at the answer (for example, the Vote riddle "Auf den Schnee hat man Saatkörner gesäet." /Seeds are sown on the snow./) The riddle metaphor may acquire local colour, as in the Argentinean riddle in which the neutral field is replaced by the pampas (for example, "Pampa blanca," / white pampas/ "semillas negras," /black seed/ "tres toros" /three bulls/ "y una tambera" /and a dairy cow/. (Aarne 1918:35–73.)

The extensive research material of Antti Aarne would allow the researcher of today to debate, for example, how much variation to accept in the "same" riddle.

Aarne did not quote his entire research material, but he always gave a precise presentation of it in his lists of variants arranged by country. Let us take a small example from the section of the catalogue containing references to versions of the riddle "a white field, black seed" in the Romance language area (Aarne 1918:43–44):

It appears from the catalogue that Aarne discovered 8 versions in Spain (RE), all of which are to be found in the Lehmann-Nitsche anthology. Examples 5 and 8 are located in the province of Catalonia, versions 6–7 on the island of Mallorca. France (RF) yielded 10 versions from different parts of the country and published in many sources, Italy (RI) 7 and Romania (RR) 6. The list gives only the source references and number of variants in accordance with the custom at that time. Aarne analysed examples in conjunction with his research texts. This material is taken from publications, but Aarne also used archive material whenever it was available. In addition to Europe, the same catalogues give the sources of research material for Asia, Africa and America, though only little material is, admittedly, known for Africa and America. By making geographical catalogues and

*Picture 1*

> **RE.** Spanier 1—4. (Lehmann-Nitsche, R., Folklore Argentino I. Adivinanzas Rioplatensis 1911, Nr. 560 S. 428). — **5.** Katalonien (Ders. Nr. 560 S. 428). — **6.** Mallorka (Ders. Nr. 560 S. 429). — **7.** (Ders. Nr. 560 S. 429). — **8.** Katalonien (Ders. Nr. 560 S. 429). — **RF.** Franzosen 1. Ober-Bretagne (Sébillot, P., Littérature orale de la Haute-Bretagne 1881, Nr. 40 S. 310). — **2.** Dol-de-Bretagne (Revue des traditions populaires XIX 1904, Nr. 34 S. 168). — **3.** Saint-Malo (Ebenda XVI 1901, S. 518). — **4.** (Mélusine, recueil de Mythologie, Littérature populaire . . . . par H. Gaidoz et E. Rolland I 1878, Nr. 14 S. 255). — **5.** Ille-et-Vilaine (Revue des traditions populaires XX 1905, Nr. 80 S. 508). — **6.** (Rolland 1877, Nr. 250 c S. 106). — **7.** (Petsch 1899, S. 136). — **8.** Dordogne (Rolland 1877, Nr. 250 a S. 105 = Petsch 1899, S. 136). — **9.** Lüttich (Revue des traditions populaires VII 1892, Nr. 38 S. 153). — **10.** Ober-Bretagne (Ebenda V 1890, S. 296). — **RI.** Italiener 1. Sizilien (Rolland 1877, S. 106 = Petsch 1899, S. 137). — **2—4.** Ebenda (Pitrè, G., Indovinelli, dubbi, scioglilingua 1897, Nr. 739 a—c S. 226—227). — **5.** Rom (Zeitschrift des Vereins für Volkskunde VI 1896, Nr. 1 S. 276). — **6.** (Ebenda VI 1896, Nr. 62 S. 281). — **7.** Wälsch-Tirol (Schneller, Chr., Märchen und Sagen aus Wälschtirol 1867, Nr. 20 S. 255 = Petsch 1899, S. 135). — **RR.** Rumänen 1—2. (Revue des traditions populaires VII 1892, S. 505, 1—2). — **3.** (Ebenda XII 1897, S. 25). — **4—6.** (Ebenda XIII 1898, S. 117, 1—3).

examinations, the researchers of the historical-geographical school sought to determine how variants observe the laws of thought and fantasy. They also aimed to unearth the original form of a folklore product — in this case a riddle (Aarne 1916:57).

Since riddles often have an extension, Aarne compares oral and literary sources in order to determine whether the extension was originally included in the riddle. He is extremely adept in the use of sources but is nevertheless forced to admit that in this case he does not have a sufficient number of literary manifestations of the riddle. Having made his comparisons, Aarne comes to the conclusion that the shorter version is the original one. Various extensions are a result of the changes in meaning of the riddle and depend on whether the riddler wished to denote writing (for example, the Serb riddle: "White field, black seed, a wise head that sows." cf. ER pp. 804—805.) and reading (for example, the Bulgarian riddle: "A white field, black seed, it is sown by hand and harvested by mouth." cf. ER p. 805.), or the difficulty of reading and writing (for example, the Russian riddle: "A white field, black seed. He who sows it has knowledge." cf. ER p. 804.). This riddle appears to have originated in Europe and from there spread to other parts of the world. The oldest literary source does not, however, yet reveal the time at which the riddle was born. At the end of his analyses Aarne further tries to determine how a riddle metaphor or formula may be varied in similar riddles; he did not yet use this terminology, however.

Antti Aarne was able to accumulate a vast corpus of material as the basis for his analyses, even though he complained of the difficulty of gathering material in the turbulent years of the First World War. He was also well acquainted with the scholarship available in his own day. As a scholar he made a precise, careful and clear analysis of large numbers of variants. His research approach was, however, marked by the formalism and limitations of the methods. He was not interested in any new or divergent view on, for example, the relationship between variation and the oral communication of riddles, the use of riddles, or the significance of global comparison, since he faithfully adhered to the well-tried folkloristic method of the times. In a way this method possibly exhausted its user: by the time he had completed his laborious analyses of the 11 riddles, Aarne's intellectual curiosity had been satisfied or even satiated and he was ready to move from riddles to the study of ancient poems, just as he had previously abandoned folktales in favour of riddles.

The studies of Antti Aarne tie in with not only the historical-geographical method but also with the comparative school then at its height. As manifestations of this other scholars, too, made analyses of the world history of a single riddle. To this end they chose riddles with a wide distribution the analysis of whose numerous variants posed fascinating problems to be solved. August Wünshe's study of the riddle referring to a year ("A Tree with Twelve Branches", ER 1037–8) appeared as early as 1896, to be continued a couple of decades later by Antti Aarne (Aarne 1918–1920:74–178). The comparative research model still seemed relevant in 1941, as demonstrated by the analysis by William A. Kozumplik of the concept of "the seven and nine holes in man" in riddles and literature (cf. ER 1101). The oldest known riddle variant using the metaphor 'hole' is Persian (c. 300 BC), but numerous examples of it are known in modern times. The metaphor appears in riddles in two different versions, such as:

> A block with nine holes. – A man.
> A lump with seven holes. – A person's head.

The first of these refers to the nine holes in the human body, the latter to those in the head. By studying the variation on the image and answer, the distribution, age and origin, and the probable users of the different versions of the riddle, Kozumplik was able to prove convincingly the history of the concept of holes in man. The oldest occurrences of the metaphor are Oriental, and the use of the image spread from India to Europe. Determination of its origin and age are further assisted by the fact that the metaphor 'hole' or its synonym, such as 'gate' or 'door', occurs not only in riddles but also in the sacred and profane texts of various cultures. For example, in the narrative *The Thousand and One Nights* the physician asks the old woman on the 449th night how man was created. Her answer in part is:

> There were created for him /Adam/ seven doors in his head, viz., the eyes, the ears, the nostrils, and the mouth, and two passages, before and behind.

Nine holes in the body appears on comparison to be the original version, and the riddle containing this metaphor belongs properly to adults. The metaphor of the seven holes is more recent and is particularly favoured in riddles by children. The simplest variations on the riddle are Asiatic and East European, while the more elaborate forms are West European.

Analysis of a single riddle and the dimensions of the metaphors presented in it does, if successful, make interesting reading, but it is of no great significance to the genre as a whole. The comparative analyses are, however, carefully executed and contain interesting material. They should perhaps be read not only as landmarks of their era but also on the assumption that the information on distributions and variations is an indication of the users of riddles and their preferences.

Comparative study required a command of the materials and knowledge of riddle variants and brought out the need for publications. The new approach resulted in many great collections of material, such as the publication of French riddles by Rolland (1877), German ones by Wossidlo (1897), Russian ones by Sadovnikov (1901) and Argentinean ones by Lehmann-Nitsche (1911).

The text-oriented comparative research approach persisted right up to the 1950s. The most distinguished of its later proponents was Archer Taylor (1890–1973), whose classic collection *English Riddles from Oral Tradition* appeared in 1951. Even in his previous articles Taylor was already paying considerable attention to the importance of collecting and publishing riddles; he was also interested in their distribution and in the spreading of the oral riddle tradition. In his article "Problems in the Study of Riddles" (1938) Taylor claimed that riddle research had three tasks: collection, descriptions of their stylistic peculiarities, and the history of their origins and use. He himself focused mainly on collection, the work *English Riddles* being a magnificent manifestation of his scholarship. Many of the chapters in the book are in fact small-scale monographs in themselves and delve deep into the history, distribution and variation of individual riddles. Taylor's work proved the importance of publishing and pointed the way for others to follow. A good example of the continuation of the Taylorian tradition and of systematic riddle collection and publication projects is *Bilmece: A Corpus of Turkish Riddles* edited by İlhan Başgöz and Andreas Tietze and published in 1973. This anthology contains 12,200 riddle variants in all. The introduction deals with problems of classification and analyses the expressive devices of Turkish riddles. Arranging material for publication is indeed always a challenge that cannot be dismissed. In most cases the publishers observe the model of Archer Taylor and classify riddles according to image content (see p. 41). Other solutions are the decision by Basgöz and Tietze to arrange the material according to the answers, or to list riddles in alphabetical order according to the first meaningful word, as in *Arvoitukset, Finnish Riddles*. All the methods need to be supplemented by indexes to bring out the affinities within the genre (for example, riddles with the same answer, the same cliché opening, a common metaphor or metric pattern). The publication is at the same time a research project.

Another proof of Archer Taylor's erudition is *The Literary Riddle Before 1600*, published in 1948 (cf. the chapter on the literary riddle, page 75). His works have continued to be pillars of riddle scholarship even though the trends in research have changed. As regards method, Taylor did not add anything new to riddle research.

The growing collection and study of riddles soon created the need for a bibliography. Here again Archer Taylor was to act as a pioneer in editing the first riddle bibliography, appearing in 1939 in the FF Communications series. The next, and so far the most recent international bibliography was that of Aldo Santi in 1952. Laurits Bødker and his Nordic colleagues produced *The Nordic Riddle: Terminology and Bibliography* in 1964, listing the relevant Nordic literature and all the terms used in the Nordic countries. For some terms they were able to point out correspondences and analogous forms in the English and German riddle terminology. The consolidation of all the terms under comprehensive superordinate concepts is, however, far from complete and the book reports primarily on the invention of new terms and the scattered terminology.

A clear change of direction came about in riddle research as in folkloristics in general in the 1960s. There had already been signs that something was happening prior to this. In 1949 William Bascom, in his article "Literary Style in Yoruba Riddles", had turned his attention to analysis of the stylistic structure of riddles – something that had been virtually overlooked by the comparativists. The article by Robert A. Georges and Alan Dundes entitled "Toward a Structural Definition of the Riddle" (1963) provided a new starting point for research in pointing out the morphological characteristics of riddles. I shall be discussing this article and its far-reaching effects on scientific debate on the riddle genre in Chapter 2, along with the work of other scholars approaching riddles from the structuralist aspect.

Other articles written in the 1960s set a number of trends that were later to prove interesting and guided research in a new direction. Suffice it to mention just a few examples here, but I shall be returning to them in later chapters in a more suitable context. Thomas Rhys Williams demonstrated in 1963 the way the riddles of the Dusun tribe of Borneo differ from those of Europe in their use, performance and functions. John Blacking (1961) and Kenneth Goldstein (1963) analysed the use and functions of riddles both in the Venda people of Africa and in Scotland. Don V. Hart (1964) made an extensive anthropologically oriented study of riddles, their users and the functions of riddling in *Riddles in Filipino Folklore*. Ian Hamnett

(1967) saw riddles as vehicles for the expression of native cognitive categories. These examples indicate that the study of riddles was expanding dynamically into new and previously uncharted fields of knowledge: the performance, contexts and users of the genre, its functions and meanings. But all the scholars I have mentioned had one thing in common: their analyses were all based on personal fieldwork.

The majority of the fieldworkers headed for Third World cultures, and Africa in particular. Some of them spent many months in the field, such as Don V. Hart in 1950–1951 and again in the Philippines in 1955–1956, Gwladys Hughes Simon 1951–1953 in Ceylon, Thomas Rhys Williams spent 1959–1960 in North Borneo, and Elli Köngäs Maranda almost two years 1966–1968 in the British Solomon Islands. The list does not end here (see Evans 1976). Many of the scholars were able to relate riddles and riddling to the total culture, because they learnt the language, the social and cultural systems. Their field reports provide extremely valuable and varied information to which I shall be returning later on: strategies of guessing and/or knowing the answer (Chapter 7), the use and contexts of the riddle tradition (Chapter 5), and the functions of riddles and riddling (Chapter 5). The reports of these scholars offer us a living encounter with tradition milieux otherwise inaccessible to us. We learn how riddles were used, and above all about their users. Riddler, riddlee and riddles are the focal point of the present study, too, and not researchers, even though these often occupy a conspicuous position as the suppliers of information.

The very discarding of the text-oriented aspects cast a shaft of light on the behavioural entity in which the riddle image and answer are part of wide-ranging interaction between the two parties involved. Attempts have been made to illuminate this relationship from various angles. For example, an experimental collection of riddles proved that the success of the venture was influenced by both the interviewer's expectations and the suitability of the location. The interviewers who had an idea that their interviewee was well versed in the riddle tradition collected more riddles than those who were assigned either a completely neutral or a negative attitude. The gender of the interviewer, and his/her previous experience also appeared to be of significance. The result was further influenced by whether the room used for the interview was suitable for the face-to-face exchange of information. (Fine & Crane 1977:517–524.)

Research into the use of folklore has broadened the perspective considerably, and scholars are now breaking free from, for example, the Euro-American ethnocentrism of which they have been accused in riddle classification (Williams 1963:100, Hart 1964:24). Riddles are a highly international genre known in the majority of cultures. But is the genre native to all cultures? Debate has waged longest over whether the tradition of the American Indians is native, or whether the riddles used by them are a loan from the surrounding cultures. Archer Taylor came to the conclusion that the riddles contained in the Huro ceremony dating from 1639 were indigenous, likewise the Ten'a riddles from British Columbia. Some Central and South American collections also appeared from Taylor's analysis to be native. (Taylor 1944.) Charles T. Scott continued the investigation in the 1960s and obtained interesting additional information from fieldworkers at the Summer Institute of Linguistics. The majority of them had never before encountered riddles in their linguistics researches. The affirmative responses in turn produced more material from the American Indian languages. The majority of these riddles appear to be either totally unrelated to riddles found elsewhere in the world, or the alien influences manifest in them are slight. This at least proves that the practice of riddling among the American Indians is not as uncommon as the anthropologists studying the Indians have long believed. (Scott 1963.) The result is of interest further in that there are few other cultures in which such a detailed attempt has been made to determine which part of the tradition is native, and which is borrowed.

The long fieldwork periods spent by scholars among alien cultures have proved that the riddle genre does not have a universal structure, content, performance or functions, but that it is bound to a specific cultural use and performing context. Roger D. Abrahams (1968:156) demonstrated that riddles are part of a broader entity in comparing traditions representing urban American subcultures, the Bantu Venda, and communities in the British West Indies. He says: "Riddles are equally formulaic, competitive, confusing, and witty, but they fit into the life of the group and disclose its values and expressive habits in widely varying ways."

I have in this study allowed for these "widely varying ways" in that almost all the examples could be supplemented by further evidence from one or more other cultures in which riddles, their uses and functions are slightly different or even in direct opposition. Anyone wishing to concentrate on one single culture, such as local African traditions, will have to select his sources from the appended bibliography. The transformation of tradition and the wealth of variations may come as a surprise even to scholars working with peoples and cultural areas close to one another.

# 2 Debate on the basic issues

The brief "traditional riddle" of crystallised form would appear at first sight to be astonishingly simple: it has only two parts, one functioning as a question, the other as its answer. The impression of simplicity is further enhanced by the fact that "riddle" is, in many languages, a term used in common parlance. The history of riddle research nevertheless reveals that the term denoting or defining each part of the riddle is by no means undisputed. For the "answer" was for a long time overlooked in the process of definition, despite its central role in the riddling situation. Different elements, going by a variety of names, have, by contrast, been sought and specified for the question part.

This chapter will be taking a look at ways of naming and defining the essential elements of the riddle and the consequences of various approaches. No conclusive result has been achieved, since researchers seldom rely on the definitions of others; rather, they usually begin by criticising them and formulating their own. I shall be returning to the formulae for verbalising the question part of the riddle in Chapter 6, and to the relationship between question and answer in Chapters 6 and 7.

## Riddle elements

Debate on the elements of riddles has proceeded on two fronts. First a basic terminology has been created for research by naming the two components making up the riddle entity. Scholars most commonly speak of a "(riddle) image" and "answer", but the statement presented to the riddlee may also be called a "question" (Haring 1985), a "proposition" (Scott 1965) or a "precedent" (Harries 1971); in the last of these cases the answer is called a "sequent". In using the general term "answer", I here refer to the word or words following the riddle image which the riddler accepts as correct. In this book, the answer part is always separated from the riddle image by a dash (–).

More extensive is, however, the debate surrounding the image, which in a true riddle consists – despite its brevity – of many sorts of elements. The image in most cases stands in a metaphorical relationship with the answer. It usually contains both an element aimed at misleading the riddlee and details that prove the answer true (for example, "Lies at the edge of the field in summer, shows the way in winter. – A road sign." Saarinen 1991:164). Or else it proves to be a metaphorical description once the answer has been revealed (for example, "An old man with grey hair on his stomach. – A pumpkin." Blacking 1961:9). Sometimes the image is, however, no more than a literal description (for example, "Wha' lives in de river? – Fish." ER 98, Taylor 1951:697–698, Georges and Dundes 1963, Saarinen 1991:175; this riddle does not actually satisfy the criteria for the genre, even though Archer Taylor approved it for his collection). The way the elements are defined varies from one scholar to another, likewise the reason for wishing to define the position of elements in the image.

The idea that the image contained elements made its appearance in riddle debate as a result of the doctoral thesis *Neue Beiträge zur Kenntnis des Volkrätsels* published by Robert Petsch in 1899. By examining the elements Petsch set out to analyse the stylistic structure of the riddle. He accordingly identified the following five elements: 1) introductory frame, 2) denominative kernel, 3) descriptive kernel, 4) block element, and 5) concluding frame. Petsch used the term "normal riddle" to denote a riddle containing these five elements, as in the example: "(1) In meines Vaters Garten (2) / In my father's garden/ Seh ich sieben Kameraden, / I see seven friends / (3) Kein ein, kein Bein, / Not one of them / (4) Kann niemand erreichen / Can anyone reach /. (5) Wer dieses kan raten / To whoever can solve this /, dem will ich geben einen Dukaten / I will give a ducat /, Wer dieses kan denken / To whoever can fathom this out /, dem will ich einen Louisdor schenken / I will give a louis d'or. – Siebengestirn / The Pleiades/." The term "normal riddle" was not a happy choice in that Petsch's material contains few riddles in which all five elements are present. Either one or both of the frame elements is often missing, and even more frequently the block element (Petsch 1899:49–50). There is no denying that the elements do not by any means always appear in riddles as independent, clearly distinct units; instead they overlap. The following Finnish riddles may serve as examples:

> Kun ottaa niin enenee, kun panee niin vähenee. – Aidanrako.
> Take away, it increases, put back, it decreases.
> – A space in a fence. (FR 712)

> Perintös syö ennen kun maailmaan tule. – Mato herneen palvoss.
> It eats its inheritance before it comes into the world.
> – A worm in a pea pod. (FR 732)

At other times the border between the elements is clear, as in:

> Perhe syö, pöytä laulaa. – Sika imettää porsaitaan.
> The family eats, the table sings. – A sow suckling piglets. (FR 731)

The nature and number of elements differ greatly from one culture to another. Petsch himself later abandoned his attempt at the mechanical breakdown into elements (1917:77).

Some sixty years ahead of the structuralists, Robert Petsch was already moulding the thinking of later scholars. Of the terms launched by him, "descriptive element" subsequently became established in the terminology of riddle research through articles by Archer Taylor (1943) and Robert A. Georges and Alan Dundes (1963), and "block element" is likewise used both as such (for example, Lieber 1976) and as, for example, "negative element" (Taylor 1943). It may also be called "an unresolvable opposition" (Green & Pepicello 1978:5). But some of the research ideas put forward by Petsch have also survived. Among other things, his observation on the countless ways in which different elements can be combined is to be found in, for example, the analysis by William Bascom of variation of the riddle image (1949).

The terminology proposed by Robert Lehmann-Nitsche (1911) likewise concerns image analysis. He regards as the basic substance the element of the image designed to mislead the riddlee, and as supplementary material the description leading to the solution. Similar classifications were put forward by Lehmann-Nitsche's contemporaries C.W. von Sydow (1915) and Antti Aarne (1917).

The analysis of elements has in riddle research tied in with the analysis of the image structure, the ultimate aim of which has sometimes been to arrive at a definition of the genre (for example, Taylor 1943 and Georges & Dundes 1963). This analysis has at the same time thrown light upon the steps the riddlee takes in proceeding from the image to the answer. On the other hand constant and irreducible basic elements have been used as the units for comparing riddles representing different cultures (Raa 1972:97–98). Not all scholars have been entirely successful in proposing a precise definition of the basic element or unit for study, and some have not even attempted it. Robert A. Georges and Alan Dundes have aimed at a clear definition and propose as the minimum unit for their structural analysis the descriptive element consisting of a topic and a comment. The topic is "the apparent referent; that is, it is the object or item which is allegedly described". Comment, on the other hand, is "an assertion about the topic, usually concerning the form, function, or action of the topic". A riddle has at least one descriptive element, as in "Twenty-fo' horses" (topic) "set upon a bridge" (comment) (ER 507). (Answer: "Teet' in yer gum".) On the other hand an image may contain several such basic elements. (Georges & Dundes 1963:113.) The topic is in practice what Lehmann-Nitsche and Aarne call the basic element and the comment comes close to the supplementary element. The topic and comment operate at the syntactic surface level of the riddle (Green & Pepicello 1979:9), and the descriptive element is a syntactic entity, a statement, which in its fullest form consists of a topic and a comment, i.e. a noun clause and a verb clause (Saarinen 1991:11). The topic may also be omitted from the surface structure, as in the riddles that describe the characteristics of the referent without actually naming it ("Was ist das, es macht bou bou bou, will immerfort fallen und geht dann fort. –Ein dürres Blatt, das der Wind fortträgt."/"What makes bou, bou, bou, is always about to fall and then goes away? – A leaf blown away by the wind." Peuckert 1938:180, several examples in Chyet 1988). Sometimes the image may be a mere comment, as in "Musta ja pehmeä, märkä ja makea. – Naurispaistikas."/ "Black and soft, wet and sweet. – Fried turnips." (FR 611).

The definition of elements would not in itself have much to offer riddle research had it not been a step towards taking a new look at the structural pillars of the genre. True, the identification of elements does also arise in the system commonly used in riddle anthologies and based on the use of the central hidden image. The riddles in some publications are in fact often grouped according to whether the latent image is, for example, a human, animal, plant or object, or whether the riddle metaphor describes the answer by an expression indicating form, function or operation. This classification is based on the system created by Lehmann-Nitsche in his collection (1911) *Folklore Argentino I. Adivinanzas Rioplatenses* and developed by Archer Taylor in *English Riddles from Oral Tradition* (1951). The important thing about this system is that riddles that describe their object in the same way are placed close to one another, even though the answers differ. Taylor's main subdivisions are descriptions of 1) something living, 2) an animal, 3) several animals, 4) a person, 5) several persons, 6) a plant, 7) a thing. In addition to these are descriptions which include enumerating 8) comparisons, 9) details of form, 10) details of colour and 11) characteristic acts (Taylor 1951:3–4). Countless anthologies and research materials have since been edited and presented according to Taylor's model. Sometimes these classifications are, however, rather forced, since Taylor's culture-oriented system is not applicable to, for example, riddle images that are not in line with the Anglo-Saxon tradition, or to material displaying a wealth of onomatopoeic or sexual riddles.

The identification of image elements led to analysis of the relationships between them: another new turn in riddle research. Significant in this respect was the article by Robert A. Georges and Alan Dundes (1963), in which they were the first to make a serious analysis of the image at the level of structure. The focus in the analysis model on the contrast of descriptive elements was not in itself anything new, since the basic essence of the image was already captured by Aristotle in saying, "The very nature indeed of a riddle is this, to describe a fact in an impossible combination of words " (*The Poetics*, Ch. XXII). William Bascom (1949:4) also took this as his starting point in reducing Yoruba riddles to the basic form "an enigma presented by two statements which appear to be mutually contradictory, incongruous or impossible". But Bascom's analysis was strictly confined to the registering of the linguistic schemes of riddles, and he needed a grand total of 29 stylistic patterns in order to classify the 55 riddles in his material. "Positive" and "negative" elements dominating the riddle image have also been pointed out in seeking a general definition for the riddle (Taylor 1938, 1943). What was new and revolutionary in the article by Georges and Dundes was their attempt to define the riddle genre via structural analysis of the elements occurring in the image. It was their aim to arrive at a definition of the riddle that would distinguish it from all other genres.

Georges and Dundes tried to determine the structural categories by means of which all true riddles could be classified. They therefore divided riddles into two general categories according to whether they contained oppositional or non-oppositional descriptive elements. The former contain a semantic opposition between at least two descriptive elements. Three types of opposition are to be found in English riddles: 1) the antithetical contradictive opposition ("What goes to the branch and drinks and don't drink? – A cow and bell." ER 247), 2) the privational contradictive opposition ("Something has an ear and cannot hear. – An ear of corn." ER 285), and 3) the causal contradictive opposition ("What goes to the mill every morning and don't make no tracks? – The road." ER 181). Non-oppositional riddles are in turn either 1) literal ("Wha' live in de river? – Fish." ER 98) or 2) metaphorical ("Two rows of white horses on a red hill. – Teeth." ER 505). In the former the riddle referent and the topic(s) of the descriptive element(s) are identical, while in the latter they are different (Georges & Dundes 1963:113–116). The first of these categories requires closer definition, since otherwise it is difficult to regard questions belonging to it as riddles. Sometimes the genre context may permit illogicality as well, since the performing situation, and the telling of riddles in series, may supplement and rectify structural faults in the texts.

Through their article Georges and Dundes sparked off an extremely lively debate that went on for years. The article is a clear milestone along the road towards modern folkloristics, and despite the widespread criticism it has received, it is still one of the classics of riddle research. The criticism of the principles applied, represented most forcefully by Charles T. Scott (1965 and 1969, see also Green & Pepicello 1979), is levelled at the nature of the minimum unit (descriptive element) isolated by Georges and Dundes: is it ultimately structural or not? The question was also raised of whether or not the definition of the genre was successful. Lee Haring (1974:294) notes that the structural scheme proposed by Georges and Dundes may be more useful as a classifying device than for definition. The reason is probably that the definition concentrates only on the image and does not make any allowance for the answer. On the other hand some scholars (Evans 1976:168) have been forced to claim that the model proposed in the article does not satisfy the need for classification within the genre itself. This is probably because in analysing the opposition within the basic element Georges and Dundes paid no attention to the other properties of the riddle. Michael L. Chyet (1988) has successfully made a few additions to the concepts of Georges and Dundes and proved their serviceability in analysing riddles from the Arabic-speaking area.

Internal contradictions are the most important part of the technique of confusion inherent in the construction of riddles. Roger D. Abrahams demonstrated that opposition is only the most salient of four techniques by which the "implicit pattern", as he described the term *Gestalt* when I asked him in 2000, presented in the riddle question is impaired. Abrahams describes these techniques as follows:

1. Opposition – *Gestalt* is impaired because the component parts of the presented image do not harmonise ("What has eyes but cannot see? – A potato." ER 277)
2. Incomplete detail – not enough information is given for proper – *Gestalt* to be made (i.e., for the parts to fit together; "What is white, then green, then red? – A berry growing.")
3. Too much detail – the important traits are buried in the midst of inconsequential detail, thus "scrambling" *Gestalt* ("As I was crossing London Bridge I met a man who tipped his hat and drew his cane, and now I gave you his name. What is it? – Andrew Cane.")
4. A false *Gestalt* – details are provided that lead to an ability to discern a referent, and thus call for an answer, but the answer is wrong. This answer is often an embarrassing, obscene reference. This technique is most common in catch riddles. ("What goes in hard and smooth and comes out soft and gooey? – A piece of chewing gum.") (Abrahams & Dundes 1972:131, Abrahams 1968:151–152.)

In most cases these techniques make the image indecipherable, and Abrahams thus goes on to say that the successful riddle is a description whose referent cannot be guessed. (See Chapter 7, Arbitrary or conventional answers)

One of the instigators of the widespread debate was Elli Köngäs Maranda, who in 1971 published three articles dealing with riddles (1971a, b and c). The most significant thing about these articles was that in them Elli Köngäs Maranda diverged from the research tradition concentrating solely on the image. She stressed (1971a:191–192): "My most important initial decision was to study the interrelations between the two parts of the riddle, the image and the answer." It nowadays seems incredible that the riddle had not, prior to this, been conceived of in the research sense as an entity in which the image and answer are interrelated. Admittedly Antti Aarne (1917:8) stressed that the answer exists before the image and provides the basis for it. The approach allowing for both of the basic riddle elements may justifiably be termed folkloristic discourse (Köngäs Maranda 1971a:195, Scott 1965:69).

Elli Köngäs Maranda identified the different elements of the riddle image and the logic of the answer as follows, taking as an example the Finnish riddle "Yksi sika, kaksi kärsää. – Pohdin."/"One pig, two snouts. – A plough." (FR1199), the structure of which she presented in tabular form:

*Picture 2*

| TERMS | | PREMISSES | | |
| --- | --- | --- | --- | --- |
| | | CONSTANT | VARIABLE | |
| GIVEN | A pig (I) | has snouts (II) | two (IV) | IMAGE |
| HIDDEN | A plough (V) | | one (III) | ANSWER |

I the given term, which is the signans of the metaphor, the core of the riddle image,
II the constant premise, which is true of both the signans (given term), and of the signatum (the answer),
III the hidden variable, which is recalled to notify the answerer that something is amiss with the statement of the riddle image, that it cannot fit (because the number of a pig's snouts is one, not two). By definition, this element is never made explicit, thus, in terms of the uttered statement, it always appears as zero,
IV the given variable, which in turn serves to point at the direction of the answer. This is the condition under which the metaphor holds true, and
V the hidden term, the signatum, i.e., the answer.
I, II and IV are "recited" by the person who poses the riddle; III is recalled by the answerer to evoke V, which he "recites". (Köngäs Maranda 1971a:198–199.)

Köngäs Maranda regards as the most vital feature of her riddle structure the variable premises, or clues, since the hidden variable (III) is known to be true in relation to the given term (I), and when it is replaced by the given variable (IV), the answerer understands that it refers to the hidden term (V), i.e. the answer. The basic structure of the riddle would thus appear to provide a model by which the competent riddlee may proceed towards the answer. But surely the riddlee has to be familiar with the culture and the answer in order to be able to distinguish the constant premise from the variable? What is more, any element whatsoever may be conceived of as the premise (Saarinen 1991:14), and the elements are said to owe more to logic than to an understanding of real riddles (Harries 1976:322). Since not all the elements of structure are always present in the riddle image, it is impossible not to doubt Köngäs Maranda's claim that the reasoning always takes place in the order I–II–III–IV–V.

In speaking of riddles Köngäs Maranda distinguishes two categories. The first is the metaphorical riddle in which there is congruence between two groups, i.e. between the characteristics and premises of the given and hidden terms, as in the riddle " Mikä /puu/ juuritta kasvaa? – Ihminen."/"What / tree/ grows without roots? – A human being." (FR 204) This riddle incorporates two truisms, "a tree has roots" and "a human being has no roots" (Köngäs Maranda 1971c:129). The second category consists of paradox riddles involving an intersection between two groups, such as in the riddle "Toista neuvoo, itse ei tiedä mitään. – Virstan patsas eli maantien viitta."/"Gives advice to others, himself knows nothing. – A road sign." (FR 1043) The riddle rests on the truism "gives advice that (he) himself knows". Paradox riddles are also known as negations of truisms, and metaphorical riddles a cross between two truisms. (Köngäs Maranda 1971a:199, 216.)

Köngäs Maranda's theory is, however, contradictory in that in explaining metaphorical riddles she makes allowance for both the image and the answer (two truisms), but in defining paradox riddles she concentrates on the image only. Even a metaphorical riddle can be made paradoxical: "What is a tree but grows without roots?" The truism would then be "a tree has roots". The fundamental difference between the two riddle categories is not that they are metaphorical or paradoxical but that in one of them the referent is given a metaphor, "tree", and in the other its characteristics are merely described. (Sirkka Saarinen, personal communication 1992.)

Elli Köngäs Maranda's theory on the logical structure of the riddle got an enthusiastic reception and scholars were eager to apply it to non-Finnish materials, too (for example, Haring 1974 and Harries 1976). The analytical model has not, however, proved suitable for riddles that do not contain any seeming contradiction, because it is then impossible to find a hidden premise. Nor is it as a rule possible to find the elements identified by Köngäs Maranda in riddles containing onomatopoeia (Harries 1976:321–322, Saarinen 1991:14).

In making the answer part of the riddle discourse Elli Köngäs Maranda examined the relationship between the image elements and the answer. The term included in the image ties in with the term in the answer (Köngäs Maranda 1971b:54), and the metaphor grows out of their juxtaposition. One important observation as regards the conformities of the riddle language is that these terms belong to opposite categories, such as animate – inanimate, cultural object – part of nature, human object, etc. The most popular analogy seems to be between human beings and cultural objects ("Akka loukossa, sata hammasta suussa. – Luuta."/"A woman's in her nook with a hundred teeth in her mouth. – A broom." FR 16), while plants are never compared to plants, humans to humans, or animals to animals (Köngäs Maranda 1971a:214–216, Kaivola-Bregenhøj 1978:53–54).

Along the lines of linguistics, Köngäs Maranda used the term kernel riddle for the riddle in which a feature of two categories is combined in its simplest form (Köngäs Maranda 1971c:138). She calls this feature (such as growing linking trees and humans) the common function of the two terms compared. As new common functions are found for the terms, the riddler can present a "transformation", a new yet related riddle. Transformations are of four types: specification (for example, trees of a certain type are compared to a woman), generalisation (for example, the death of a human and a tree is compared regardless of sex), inversion (for example, drawing a parallel between deciduous trees/women and coniferous trees/men), and reversal. The last of these types occurs in riddles when, for example, trees are used as a metaphor for humans ("Pihlaja pyhällä maalla, pyhä lehti pihlajassa. – Raskas vaimo."/"A rowan on a sacred hill, a sacred leaf on the rowan. – A bride." FR 754), and conversely humans may be used as a metaphor for trees ("A mamselle growing on top of a hill, her hair down over her shoulders. – A birch tree.") (Köngäs Maranda 1970 and 1971b:54–55.)

In linguistics the concept of the kernel sentence first made its appearance in the work *Syntactic Structures* by Noam Chomsky (1957). By this is meant an elemental sentence acting as a kernel that can be derived using simple phrase structures. All the other sentences in the language can be formed from kernel sentences by means of transformations. The concept has later been used metaphorically, and the "kernel riddle" proposed by Köngäs Maranda could be conceived of loosely as the elemental unit of riddles. It has, however, quite rightly been asked on what grounds it is possible to claim that a certain riddle is a kernel riddle and others transformations of it. Transformations are in fact extensions of a metaphor, "for example, extending the comparison of trees to human beings to include comparisons of limb trees to human appendages: leaves to hair, for example" (Pepicello & Green 1984:82–83). Köngäs Maranda has cleverly chosen her examples to support the transformation types she proposes. But one example is not convincing, especially since the metaphor built on the comparison of trees and a human being is rare in Finnish riddles. A more credible result could be achieved by studying the use of transformation types in riddle performance situations in which new riddles are improvised in addition to the familiar ones. But although Köngäs Maranda's idea, and especially her terminology, have been criticised, this does not detract from her observations on the diversity and – at least in the light of her examples – the regularity with which the riddle genre exploits its imagery.

The relationship between the basic riddle elements – image and answer – has been closely analysed in a study produced partly in reply to the claims made by Elli Köngäs Maranda. The debate has, among other things, concerned the meanings that are shared by the image and the answer and known as a "semantic fit" (Scott 1965:74, Harries 1971 and 1976). A semantic fit may exist between the image and the answer even though the surface structure of the image varies considerably from one riddle to another, as in the following riddles, in which the answer is an egg:

> My mother's house has no door. –
> Roundness, with no mouth. (Harries 1976:323)

The unique nature of the relationship between the riddle image and answer has also been expressed by the concept of ambiguity occurring at all levels of language (see Chapter 6). These basic riddle elements generally seem to belong to different categories (for example, + and – animate, for example, "*Mies* mäellä seisoo, rautahousut jalassa. – *Heinähanko.*"/"A *man* standing on the hill, iron trousers on his legs. – A *pitchfork*." FR 434). The only exception to this are the riddles in which both the image and the answer bear the feature + animal. This is then a subcategory (for example, "Pikku pukki, kippakuono kivivuorta kiipeääpi nahkahousut jalassa. – Tupasirkka."/ "Little billy, bent snout, climbs up a stone mountain wearing leather breeches. – A cottage cricket." FR 764) Matti Kuusi (1974:12), using Ovambo riddles as his material, characterised the relationship between image and answer, noting that the image and its answer must on the one hand display sufficient contrast yet on the other hand a certain analogy. In a class all of their own are the riddles in which there is no link at all between the image and the answer (for example, "Take some of it? – The state of a person who knows no riddles." Kuusi 1974:58), or the answer is a new enigma rather than an answer to the given metaphor (for example, "One day I went to Nairobi and wondered. – I saw a rat putting a piece of stiff porridge on his head." Haring 1974:205).

The elements of a riddle have also stimulated debate as to whether the person to whom the riddle image is posed is really expected to guess the answer, or whether the link between the image and the answer is closely regulated by tradition (for example, Haring 1974, Ben-Amos 1976 and Lieber 1976; see also Chapter 7). The debate has also asked why an image may carry several answers, and how different things and functions are associated in people's minds.

## *Definitions of the riddle*

A definition of the riddle may be sought for a number of research purposes and needs, such as analysis of the use of metaphor, classification of the content and stylistic devices of a riddle, the structuralistic identification of folkloristic genres, or the description of a riddle in a performing context. Although scholars debated the basic elements of the riddle for a long time without making any reference to the answer, the answer is nevertheless always inherent in definitions of the riddle. I shall here be limiting myself to the main definitions that have added something new to the identification of the inherent features of the genre.

The first well-known definition of the riddle was made by Aristotle in his work *On Rhetoric* (Bk. III, Ch. 2), in which he calls attention to the similarity between the riddle and the metaphor: "Good riddles do, in general, provide us with satisfactory metaphors: for metaphors imply riddles, and therefore a good riddle can furnish a good metaphor." The same link with the metaphor is evident in certain other definitions, too (such as Paris 1877, Potter 1950). The second recurring line of thought stresses the irreconcilable contradiction occurring in riddles, a feature that was likewise noted by Aristotle: "The very nature indeed of a riddle is this, to describe a fact that in an impossible combination of words (which cannot be done with the real names for things, but can be with their metaphorical substitute...)" (*On Poetics*, Ch. XXII). (Georges & Dundes 1963:111.)

The history of research into the riddle nevertheless reveals that definitions have followed fast upon one another as scholars have attempted to crystallise the inherent characteristics of the genre in the clear form called for in a definition. Their task has not proved easy. Archer Taylor wrote in 1938 that riddle research was still at its beginning; publications of material were needed in order to determine the stylistic peculiarities of riddles and the history of the origins and the use of riddles (Taylor 1938:1). A few years later Taylor (1943:129) proposed the following definition, which he limited to the most common type of riddle, the true riddle: "The true riddle or the riddle in the strict sense compares an object to another entirely different object." Taylor was thus content merely to mention the opposition between the riddle image and the answer, emphasising "the surprise that the solution occasions: the hearer perceives that he has entirely misunderstood what has been said to him." Taylor took as an example the riddle about Humpty Dumpty, in which an egg is likened to a man sitting on a wall:

> Humpty Dumpty sat on a wall,
> Humpty Dumpty had a great fall,
> All the king's horses and all the king's men
> Couldn't put Humpty Dumpty together again. – An egg. (ER 738)

Taylor goes on to say: "Only the queer fact, which is contradictory to the usual nature of man, that he cannot be cured or put together again after falling gives notice that we are not listening to an incident from life; in other words that we are being asked to guess a riddle." In 1951 Taylor used the same definition and arguments in his work *English Riddles* (Taylor 1951:1). Having identified the positive and negative descriptive elements contained in the riddle (Taylor 1943:130), he continues his analysis of true riddles by saying that "a true riddle consists of two descriptions of an object, one figurative and one literal, and confuses the hearer who endeavours to identify an object described in conflicting ways."

In their article "Toward a Structural Definition of the Riddle", Robert A. Georges and Alan Dundes worked on the well-founded claim that folklorists had not yet succeeded in defining the riddle in concrete and specific terms. Taylor's attempts to define the true riddle had been considered to cover too narrow a field. The positive and negative descriptions on which "true riddles" were founded did not always correspond to the material. In the following riddle, for example, the positive element is not metaphorical as might be expected:

> When it come, it does not come;
> when it does not come, it come. – A rat and corn. (ER 945)

On the other hand Taylor's definition was too loose, for there are many riddles in the *English Riddles* anthology that do not satisfy his criteria for a true riddle. The following riddle, for example, does not contain the positive and negative elements required by his definition:

> My fader have a horse, Go everywhere he like.
> – A pumpkin vine. (ER 419)

As mentioned before, the next riddle is a literal description with neither the metaphorical element nor the block element demanded by Taylor in the manner of Petsch:

> Wha' live in de river? – Fish. ER 98

Georges and Dundes set out to find a definition that was broad enough to include traditional texts while at the same time narrow enough to exclude other materials whose morphological characteristics indicated that they were specimens of another genre (Georges &Dundes 1963:113). For their method they chose structural analysis, because in their opinion the definitions based on content and style had proved inadequate. This has been clearly demonstrated by, for example, Than Sein and Dundes 1964. The choice of minimum unit for analysis was then important; like Petsch and Taylor they called this the descriptive element. Georges and Dundes thus modified their definition of the true riddle to read: "A riddle is a traditional verbal expression which contains one or more descriptive elements, a pair of which may be in opposition; the referent of the elements is to be guessed."

Georges and Dundes did not express any reservations on the applicability of their definition to riddles representing different cultures. This is understandable, since they were dealing with riddles in English representing Anglo-American culture. Like many structuralists, they possibly believed in the possibility of global genres and their definitions, because they began their article by saying: "An immediate aim of structural analysis in folklore is to define the genres of folklore." Once the genres of folklore have been defined, it will be possible to solve "the interesting problems of the *function* of folkloristic form in particular cultures" (Georges & Dundes 1963:111; the italics are mine). From the global level it is thus possible to shift the perspective to individual cultures. On the other hand Georges and Dundes do look beyond the generic borders in pointing out that a given structural pattern can be found in different genres (Georges and Dundes 1963:111).

Drawing the line between different genres according to their basic elements seems in general to have been important to the structuralists. This coincided with the more lasting interest in genre analysis emerging in the 1960s, the primary goal of which was the exhaustive classification and identification of oral tradition. A third scholar analysing the riddle tradition from a structuralist point of view was Charles T. Scott, who pointed out that the early definitions were marked by a tendency to "tell us nothing about how the riddle qua genre is formally distinct from other literary or folkloristic genres within cultures" (Scott 1965:15).

Scott regarded the analysis of Georges and Dundes as a serious attempt to define the riddle as a genre. He did, however, take an extremely critical attitude to the basic unit of analysis, the descriptive element, which despite all attempts by scholars does not operate at structural level. Since the same basic unit was also used in the definition of the proverb, the only difference remaining between these two genres was that the riddle had an answer. The result was unsatisfactory, since no distinguishing factor between the genres was achieved at structural level. (Scott 1965:17–19.)

Scott had the same goal in mind as Georges and Dundes, i.e. classification of the riddle structure. In *Persian and Arabic Riddles* (1965) he tried to isolate, define and classify linguistically the stylistic devices used by the riddle. As a result he arrived at the following definition: "A riddle is a unit of discourse consisting of an obligatory proposition slot filled by an utterance $p$ and an obligatory answer slot filled by an utterance $a$" (Scott 1965:69). The key word in this definition is discourse, and the fact that the proposition permits the possibility that it is not necessarily a question at the surface level of the riddle. Roger D. Abrahams and Alan Dundes (1972:143; see also Chyet 1988:278) in turn considered this attempt at definition unsuccessful though nevertheless important in trying to isolate sufficient linguistic features of riddles to define the riddle as a folkloristic genre.

Abrahams and Dundes themselves no longer aimed at a structural definition in their general treatises but placed the emphasis on the function of riddling: "Riddles are questions that are framed with the purpose of confusing or testing the wits of those who do not know the answer" (Abrahams & Dundes 1972:130).

In an article written a few years later Scott (1969) modified his criticism of the definition proposed by Georges and Dundes, extending it to their analysis of topic and comment and claiming that since this analysis yields different results at different levels, it is not successful. Of this criticism W.J. Pepicello and Thomas A. Green note (1984:79) that, though credible, it is based on a false premise, because Scott misinterpreted the topic-comment analysis.

The definitions and the criticism of them prove just how difficult it is to make simultaneous allowance for all the levels relevant in the definition of the riddle – and possibly riddling, too. No wonder some feel that the different definitions leave behind an unsatisfactory impression, especially since "they seem to lead to a cul-de-sac, to a situation where they tell us nothing really new about riddles but only criticize and refine previous definitions" (Evans 1976:169, see also Burns 1976:141). We may well wonder why none of the scholars seeking a definition of the riddle has begun with the answer, which is the point from which the entire riddle process begins. The whole idea in devising a riddle is, after all, to hit upon an object, animal or phenomenon familiar to all that can be described in the riddle image using a metaphor that both confuses the listeners and gives them a hint as to the answer. This aspect does, however, make a fleeting appearance in the theorisings of Lyndon Harries (1971:391), who stresses that in the African riddle "the items in P /image/ are put into correspondence with the items in S /answer/ on the basis of the identifications of common features and situations which the riddler believes they share."

Other aspects may on the other hand be added to the analysis. The Russian scholar Ju.I. Levin makes due allowance for both the semantic and the pragmatic aspect in analysing the structure of the riddle. Viewed from the semantic angle, the riddle can be defined as a text in which the denotate is an object that is not clearly mentioned in the text. From the pragmatic angle, however, the function of this text is to get the riddlee to name the object-denotate. Furthermore, the text does not need to give an exhaustive account of the object. (Levin 1973 and 1987).

The numerous field trips made by folklorists, anthropologists and philologists among alien cultures in particular gradually made scholars aware of the fact that a difference did indeed exist between the ideal types and natural genres in the case of the riddle, just as occurs with many other genres. The idea of a global definition of the genre began to look impossible as research showed just how narrow the definitions were. Studies in many African cultures revealed that a number of genres and their cultural tasks are nowhere near the same in Africa as they are in Europe (for example, Haring 1974:205 demonstrates the types of riddles that cannot be defined according to the structural scheme of Georges and Dundes). Ruth Finnegan

(1977:15) was well aware of the problems surrounding genre analysis: "One also has to accept that the whole idea of a 'genre' is relative and ambiguous, dependent on culturally accepted canons of differentiation rather than universal criteria."

A good example of a purely cultural definition of the genre is the analysis by Lyndon Harries (1971) of the factors to be allowed for in defining the African riddle. He stresses that "any definition of the riddle genre in Africa must, therefore, include the following criteria: (1) opening formula, (2) binary construction and (3) a semantic relationship between P and S". Each of these criteria is relevant in the African tradition. The opening formula is not the stylistic element described by Petsch but a crystallised statement opening the riddle session and indicating the transition to riddle discourse. The binary construction refers to the two immediate constituents of the riddle, the verbal utterances represented here as precedent /P/ and sequent /S/. The semantic relationship between P and S in turn means that they have shared semantic features. (Harries 1971:383–388.) Harries finally arrives at a tentative definition of the African riddle that allows for the criteria he lists as follows: "The riddle in Africa is defined as a unit of discourse distributed within a matrix of longer discourse introduced by a verbal formula, and internally composed of two speech units with shared semantic features and therefore a common application" (Harries 1971:393). This definition seems to work when applied to an ethnic genre, especially since each of the criteria is given careful deliberation and explained to the reader. The new thing about this definition is that it views the riddle as part of a broader discourse, and it is therefore possible to pick out its connection with both the social and the linguistic context.

Some scholars regard genre definition as a waste of time. One such scholar was Elli Köngäs Maranda, who pointed out that people seem to be able to recognise a riddle without any difficulty. On the other hand, "any a priori definition would be theoretically mistaken, since what we want to study is the 'classes of phenomena', i.e. domains, established by the participant of the culture". (Köngäs Maranda 1971a:191.) Köngäs Maranda is here clearly referring to a 'natural' (i.e. real or emic) genre which the tradition expert has no difficulty in recognising. From the point of view of research it is, however, necessary to establish agreed nominal genre terms for use in analysis and identification. Such terms may either be contrived or correspond to the genres recognised and named by the tradition experts. There may be links and continuity between nominal and real genres, and scholars may act as a bridge in combining their empirical observations with more abstract genre systems. (Honko 1980.)

It is also apparent that there are, even within the confines of a single culture, so many different types of riddles – structured and unstructured, irreal and real, metaphorical and lifelike – that it is impossible to arrive at a universal definition (Saarinen 1991:161, see also Ben-Amos 1992:23–26). We are thus faced with a familiar problem: choosing the level of abstraction of an operational, global genre definition appears to be an insuperable problem.

The only scholar to clearly emphasise the social function of the riddle is Dan Pagis. While not actually stating his intention to define the riddle as a genre, he begins his article by saying: "Every proper riddle must fulfil two conditions: the first is its social function as a competition between the riddler and the riddlees; the second is its literary form, which must be difficult and enigmatic, yet containing the clues needed to decipher it." Only the combination of these two conditions can produce the true riddle. Pagis points out that the social function is not restricted solely to situations involving face-to-face contact, since he also sees it as including the riddling situation between an author and reader. (Pagis 1996:81.) The type of text that can be presented as a challenge depends on the riddler, though the competent riddler would be unlikely to make a false choice precisely because the social nature of the situation makes it imperative to adhere to the communally approved practices.

Other views on defining the riddle have been put forward by W.J. Pepicello and Thomas A. Green in their book *The Language of Riddle, New Perspectives* (1984:13–14). Pepicello and Green set out to examine riddles as "verbal art from a linguistic perspective" and "to build toward a characterization of the genre as an integration of formal linguistic and culturally aesthetic strategies". They are not satisfied with the previous results of riddle research (Pepicello & Green 1984:73–89) and subject them to polemic criticism.

In attempting a definition of riddles, Pepicello and Green underline that in no culture, and especially so in English, do riddles go unanswered. Like Köngäs Maranda, they further stress that within their own context riddles are always questions requiring an attempt at an answer, even if the statement is not at surface level a question. They come to the conclusion that riddles are "conventional questions of various sorts that must be answered". "Conventional" is indeed a good modifier, though it does not exclude all non-riddles. They then go on to dismiss the term 'true riddle' in the case of a riddle such as "When is coffee like the soil? – When it is ground." A riddle such as this is usually regarded as a catch question, but in the opinion of Pepicello and Green it has just as much right to be called a true riddle as the riddles quoted by Archer Taylor. This claim is inconceivable and futile: why upset the classification observed by scholars for decades within the genre? Conventional terminology of an ideal type acts as a means of communication between scholars and helps them to conceive the field of real genres. What is more, Pepicello and Green cannot manage with the concept true riddles alone and have to resort to the concept of metaphorical ambiguity. They are thus forced to prove implicitly that true riddles really do differ from other riddles.

Like their predecessors, Pepicello and Green find themselves confronted with the fact that not all traditional questions are riddles. Making an exhaustive list of non-riddle questions is likewise a hopeless task, but Pepicello and Green do mention as examples catechetical questions and the closely related "zen *koan*", the answers of which are learned, clever questions demanding special knowledge, neck riddles, and joking questions, which permit their performer to deliver a punch line.

Pepicello and Green summarise the attributes of the folk riddle as follows: "We see first that the riddle form is based on the question and answer format. Moreover, it is potentially solvable from the information included in the question if the riddlee is able to determine the witty devices for confusion employed to frame the riddle. In turn, we see that the information necessary to discern the witty devices is to be found entirely by virtue of participation in a cultural system (i.e., shared language, world view, and tropes). Finally, the riddle act must, like all folklore, have a conventional locus within a particular tradition and within a performance context." (Pepicello & Green 1984:85–88).

Although Pepicello and Green speak of a definition, they are in fact content merely to list the distinguishing features of the genre to be allowed for in a definition. This does, however, have the advantage that they are able to give a more wordy account of the inherent features of the genre than their predecessors. They do not succeed in saying anything new about the structure of the riddle image or the relationship between image and answer; on the contrary, these aspects of the genre receive very little attention. On the other hand they do in many ways place their description of the genre in its cultural and performance context. This is an extremely good solution. It permits on the one hand culturally-specific genre classifications and on the other hand an insight into the complex interaction between question and answer.

Not a single riddle definition has yet gone into general circulation, and many a scholar has felt the need to express terminological reservations and to create a personal definition of the riddle within the context of the culture under study. All the definitions do, however, have one thing in common: it is difficult and futile to detach them from the material and research context to which they apply.

# 3 The subgenres of the riddles

The concept of "riddle" embraces both those traditional verbal expressions most commonly known as "true riddles" and a number of different subgenres appearing under different names. Riddles can be posed orally, in the form of drawings, gestures, and even drumming or tableaux (Burns 1976:157, Bhagwat 1943:71). Most of the publications of material, such as Archer Taylor's *English Riddles* (1951), concentrate on true riddles, and such riddles mostly form the substance for the chapters of this book. The bulk of the research literature deals with the distribution, age, structure, style and use of true riddles.

We cannot, however, claim to know all about the riddle tradition unless we also deal with its subgenres. The contemporary oral riddle tradition cultivated by children and young people is represented by joking questions on the borderline between the jest and the true riddle. As a matter of fact, however, some true riddles have indeed proved their viability, such as the following one signifying money and already mentioned in the collection *Aenigmata Fennica* (Ganander 1783); it has merely acquired a new answer: "Mikä se on kun ulkomailla höylätään ja lastut Suomeen lentelee? – Visakortti."/"What is it that is planed abroad and the shavings fly to Finland? – A Visa card." (Lipponen 1995:207). But new marginal forms draw their formulaic and other expressive riddle-like devices from other subgenres. The most striking difference between the true riddle and, for example, joking questions is that in the former the image violates the norm, and in the latter the answer (Bregenhøj 1988:181). The latter overlap with the discourse or other speech and the riddler in most cases provides the answer himself.

How should this recent riddling tradition be classified and named? The classification criteria may, for example, be determined according to the age group involved. Brian Sutton-Smith has demonstrated that 80 per cent of the children in a group of four-year-olds present questions and answers that may, in view of their nature, be called "pre-riddles" ("Why did the man chop down the chimney? – He needed the bricks."). By the time children reached school age the popularity of this type had fallen to seven per cent, and adults would not even consider pairs of questions and answers such as this as riddles. Schoolchildren in turn tend to ask riddles based on a homonym

("Why did the dog go out into the sun? – He wanted to be a hot dog."). The relationship between image and answer comes as an anticlimax and this type of riddle is called an "implicit reclassification (homonymic riddles)". (Sutton-Smith 1976:114–115.)

What makes the riddle genre difficult to describe as a whole is the fact that its subgenres are, with the exception of the large group of joking questions, small categories occurring only infrequently, and are not readily commensurable. The list of all the names encountered would be a long one. Researchers have hastened to give a name to any new subgenre they have discovered, and the result is a considerable jungle of terms in which it is often difficult to trace the links between concepts. An example of this is the lexicon *The Nordic Riddle* edited by Laurits Bødker in 1964 and presenting the terms used for various concepts in the different Nordic languages. Only seldom do the terms correspond to one another, and it is rare for them to have an unambiguous counterpart in English or German. An example is, say, the Swedish term *kuggfråga* (test question), "recited in order to test the sagacity of the person interrogated". The item contains crossreferences to the Swedish terms *doktrinärgåta* (from doctrinaire, *gåta* = riddle), *lärogåta* (from learning, teaching) and *problemgåta* (from problem). These crossreferences in turn raise even more terms. This classification is based on the studies by the Swedish riddle collector Fredrik Ström, but examination of the term as used by a larger number of writers would broaden its application. The corresponding terms in English are clever question, conundrum and witty question, in German *Scharfsinnsfrage* (Bødker 1964:42).

The same ambiguity can, however, be discerned in the English terminology. The main reason for this is that riddle subgenres have not yet been subjected to exhaustive investigation. Archer Taylor, for example, in the foreword to his *English Riddles* (1951:1), identified not only true riddles but also the neck riddle, the arithmetical puzzle, the clever question with its several types, and the conundrum or witty question, the collection and study of which he postponed to a later date. Mark Bryant, in *Riddles Ancient and Modern* and his *Dictionary of Riddles* (1983:14–16 and 1990:6–8), recognises the conundrum, charade, syllable riddle, logogriph, literary rebus, catch and pictorial riddle in addition to the true riddle. The variety of names may in part be due to the fact that no comprehensive terminology exists in the vernacular (for example, Basgöz 1972:659). For example, the Tambunan Dusun tradition recognised the conundrum and the clever question as well as the true riddle, "however, general distinctions between the true riddle form, clever questions, and conundrums appear not to be perceived by the Dusun." (Williams 1963:99.) This observation is not culture-bound and applies elsewhere, too. Nor is any distinction made between subgenres in the contexts in which riddles are used, although the formulae, metaphors and riddle contents may influence the types of riddle sequences put forward at a riddling session.

Recognising riddle subgenres is a matter of classification and would do well to begin with some general principle. One such approach is to examine the relationship between the image and the answer, i.e. to decide how the riddle is solved. The main distinguishing feature of the true riddle is that the image is regarded as containing sufficient information for the riddlee to guess the answer. This may be expressed more bluntly by saying that true riddles are "enigmatic questions in the form of descriptions whose referent must be guessed" (Abrahams & Dundes 1972:130). Although the question of whether the answer is guessed or whether it is known in advance is open to debate (see Chapter 7), there is some justification in the claim that true riddles are in a riddling situation ones to which the riddlee is expected to provide an answer. It is here a question of two roles and the performances and statuses accompanying them. If the riddler is far superior to all the others or refuses to accept the riddlee's answer as correct, the course of the riddling is disturbed. Taking the relationship between the image and the answer as our starting point, we could classify all elements that do not fit into the category of true riddles – such as wisdom questions and different joking questions – as forming a contrast to them. Such elements are in fact sometimes called "related forms of puzzle" (Bryant 1990:6) or "other verbal puzzles" (Green 1992:136). There is one thing which all other riddle types have in common; either the image does not contain the information necessary to supply the answer, or else the information as a whole is wrong.

The article "Riddles" (1972) by Roger D. Abrahams and Alan Dundes appears to take the relationship between the image and the answer as the basis for classification, even though this is not mentioned as an explicit criterion. Abrahams and Dundes divide riddles into five different categories, which are: 1. descriptive riddles, 2. joking questions, 3. wisdom questions, 4. puzzles, and 5. parody riddles. Categories 2 and 5, 3 and 4 are in fact very similar and could be combined. I shall, however, be using the clear basic classification proposed by Abrahams and Dundes here.

*True riddles*

The term "true riddles" is in widespread international use and the counterparts in various languages have similar contents. Other less frequently used names are "descriptive riddle" and "enigma" or "proper riddle". Archer Taylor (1951:1.) defines true riddles as "descriptions of objects in terms intended to suggest something entirely different". As an example Taylor mentions the riddle of Humpty Dumpty, which describes an egg as a man sitting on a wall.

As with all riddles, there are some very expansive models of expression or formulae in true riddles. These take the form of both statements and questions. Some of them are international, but each language and culture area also has formulae all of its own. The metaphors peculiar to true riddles are likewise partly international, partly highly culture-bound. I shall be dealing with the expressive devices peculiar to the true riddle category in Chapter 6.

## Joking questions

The heading joking questions covers many kinds of riddles the primary aim of which is to put the riddlee to shame. The shame is not, however, grave, since this subgenre never seriously puts the riddlee's wit to the test. Rather, the aim is to laugh at the joke while at the same time grasping the point, which often runs deeper than the mere play on words. Unlike true riddles, these riddles are almost never metaphorical. They are in most cases constructed on a formula in question form that begins with a seemingly serious question. Most of the joking questions in this book observe interrogative formulae beginning with "what?", "why?", "how?" or "what is the difference between?". The formula often sparks off a series of joking questions. I shall here be taking a closer look at those of elephant and Blondie type (for other joking questions see Chapter 1, The contemporary riddle). Both types have been popular for a very long time. The formulae of true riddles may in some riddling cultures be difficult (as is the case in Finnish riddles in Kalevala metre), but the formulae of joking questions are as a rule so simple that further questions can easily be improvised. The ease of invention may well explain certain crazes. A book of schoolchildren's humour from 1992 contains a sequence of 16 riddles in which the joke is achieved by placing a skunk in universal surroundings, such as on a skateboard, in an aquarium or a microwave oven. All the common joking question formulae are used (for example, "Mitä eroa on haisunäädällä ja pähkinävoileivällä? – Haisunäätä ei tartu kitalakeesi."/"What's the difference between a skunk and a peanut sandwich? – A skunk doesn't stick to your plate." Perttula 1992:10). Although the riddles in the book I have quoted may not be live tradition passed on from mouth to mouth (a skunk is not part of the fauna of oral tradition), the joking questions invented for commercial distribution are wholly traditional in their means of expression. The expressive model is easy and expansive.

The elephant – the first of a line of animals placed in absurd situations – is a good example of a lasting favourite in the joking question tradition. The elephant joke was presumably born among American college students and found its way to Europe in the early 1960s. In spring 1964 my fellow student Ulla Lipponen noted down elephant jokes in the student café at Helsinki University. These described the colour of an elephant, the clothes it was wearing or its adventures in an urban milieu, etc. (for example, Barrick 1964, conversation with Ulla Lipponen) (for example, "Miksi norsu on ryppyinen? – Koska kukaan ei silitä sitä."/"Why is an elephant wrinkly? – Because no one strokes it."). Although elephants later went out of fashion in the tradition of young adults, they were still a living part of children's lore in the mid-1980s, and "they can no longer be regarded as an endangered species". (Lipponen 1995:210.) But just who is the elephant? In the 1960s it was seen as a symbol for the movement for black equality, since "the elephant is a dark powerful character from the jungle in an alien setting" (Bronner 1988:125). The elephant was not, however, just a political threat; it epitomised the fear aroused in white society by the emergence of a black minority.

Some of this fear was of a sexual nature. For example, joking questions describing the elephant's colour ("Do you know why elephants are grey? – So you can tell them from blueberries."), its intrusion in what is felt to be the private region of the home, the bathroom ("How do you know if an elephant is in the bathtub with you? – By the faint smell of peanuts on his breath.") or its prodigious sexuality ("What's big and grey and comes in quarts? – An elephant.") have been regarded as indicating that it is the black man that stands hidden behind the image of the elephant. (Oring 1992:17–18 < Roger D. Abrahams & Alan Dundes 1969. "On Elephantasy and Elephanticide." The Psychoanalytic Review 56:228–237). One is tempted to ask whether the users of these joking questions were really aware of this latent aggression. As Elliott Oring quite rightly points out, "That jokes are meant to be funny is relatively certain. That they are also intended as assaults is far less certain." Folklore laughing at the expression of aggression would appear to have even more direct means at its disposal, but elephant jokes have given impetus to all manner of interpretations. Later, in the 1970s and 1980s, the elephant began to assume feminine features and could be interpreted as part of the emerging feminism. (Bronner 1988:125.)

In children's lore the elephant is an absurdly entertaining animal. The key to understanding elephant humour is to be found in the incongruence, as in the following riddle:

Why are elephants grey? – To distinguish them from blueberries.

Elliott Oring (1992:19) states in interpreting this riddle that the point of the humour "lies in the figures of the elephant or blueberry or the quality of greyness per se. Rather, the humour lies in the incongruous proposition that the greyness of the elephant is intended to distinguish it from a blueberry." Ultimately it is a question of "the perversion of logic and the violation of an established conceptual order" (Oring 1992:20). In children's lore it was gradually joined by a whole host of other crazy animals, such as hitchhiking hippos and mice in bathing trunks. But all these endearing animals live in a world that is modern, mechanised and motorised. (af Klintberg 1978, Lipponen 1995:210, Virtanen 1970:82–85.)

In autumn 1993 a boy in my daughter's class entertained the 14-year-old girls during their domestic science lesson with joking questions of the following type. This was my first contact with dumb blonde jokes.

> Miksi Jumala loi blondin?
> – Koska apina ei oppinut hakemaan olutta jääkaapista.
> Why did God create blondes?
> – Because apes never learnt to fetch beer from the fridge.
> Miksi Jumala loi tummaverikön?
> – Koska blondikaan ei oppinut hakemaan olutta jääkaapista.
> Why did God create brunettes?
> – Because the blondes didn't learn to fetch beer from the fridge either.
> Miten blondin aivot saa herneen kokoisiksi? – Puhaltamalla ne täyteen.
> How do you reduce a blonde's brains to the size of a pea?
> – By blowing them up.

Mitä se on kun toinen blondi puhaltaa toisen blondin korvaan? –
Tiedonvälitystä.
What do you call it when one blonde blows into another blonde's ear?
– Communication.
Minkä nimen blondi antoi lemmikkiseepralleen? – Täplä.
What did the blonde call her pet zebra? – Spot.
Miten blondi tappaa kalan? – Hukuttamalla.
How does a blonde kill a fish? – By drowning it.
Miksi blondi käyttää vihreää huulipunaa?
– Koska punainen tarkoittaa "stop".
Why does a blonde wear green lipstick? – Because red means "stop".

A certain theme may be wildly popular while this type of question is in fashion, but it is soon exhausted and the riddles no longer appeal. This rule does not, however, apply to dumb blonde jokes, the reason for whose popularity and viability can only be guessed at. There are long strings of dumb blonde jokes circulating on the Internet. In 1997 Ulla Lipponen was given 50 pages containing some 2,000 joking questions on this theme which a friend had printed from the Internet, at least some of them variations on the old models. In any case the dumb blonde is always a woman and there seems to be no limit to her stupidity. Naturally there is an exception to prove this rule, for Ulf Palmenfelt once sent me this joke about a blond boy:

Varför har blondiner blåmärken runt naveln?
– De blonda pojkarna är inte så smarta heller.
Why do blondes have bruises round their navel?
– Because blond boys are not very smart either.

When the Blondie film "Romy and Micheles's high school reunion" reached Finland in August 1997, it was immediately taken up in the advertisements for film pages. The advert bore the text "Even Blondie can find them" along with a picture of the film heroines and the Internet address for details of premieres, showing times, film presentations, Hollywood gossip, and so on.

Schoolchildren attending my lectures in 1987 were asked to write down any riddles they could think of. Among the results were the following joking questions about Ethiopians:

What does an Ethiopian say when he sees a drinking straw?
– That's a neat sleeping bag.
Why does half the famine aid to Ethiopia consist of soap?
– Because cleanliness is half way to a full stomach [a Finnish proverb].
Why do the Ethiopians keep their eyes shut?
– So that they won't see hunger. [In Finnish "to see hunger" = to starve]

These riddles on an international catastrophe theme have acquired a completely Finnish manifestation because they interpret a normal Finnish metaphorical saying in a literal manner.

The joking question is also culture-specific, and in order to get the point, the listener must be familiar with the people in the news in the country in question, be they politicians, sportsmen or pop artists. Some interesting examples of language- and culture-specific joking questions are given by Leela Prasad (1998:211–223). These are eagerly cultivated by young people educated in English medium-schools and colleges in urban India and used in multilingual communities where children at school are taught Hindi (the national language), the regional language and English. The language valued most highly is English, a fluent command of which is considered "more sophisticated" than speaking in the vernacular. The joking question either plays with homophones or with the fact that some word in either English or the vernacular calls to mind something that is ridiculous in the particular context, such as:

> What did one banana say to another?
> – Please marry me because I'm a *kela*.

Leela Prasad explains it as follows: "In an apparently simple way, the answer does something extraordinary. While *kela* in Hindi means 'banana', the article 'a' before the noun *kela* combines with it to produce the adjective *akela*, which means 'lonely' or 'alone' in Hindi. In short, we have a situation in which a banana proposes to another not only because they are kin – thus marrying within one's community, perhaps – but simply because it is seeking companionship." (Prasad 1998:216.) A joking question such as this mirrors the distinctive way in which English is often spoken in India, because individual words, phrases and even expressions from the vernaculars are readily incorporated into conversational English. – This is a phenomenon no doubt familiar in other bi- or multilingual communities; the Swedish-speaking Finns, for example, season their spoken language with expressions taken from Finnish that readily present themselves as being more appropriate or topical. Traditional forms in the border zones between languages could well do with more research!

Leela Prasad also demonstrates that although the joking question is in a way a form of in-group humour, the point of the joke is never directed specifically at "me", but always at the person tripping up over the correct pronunciation of English, or whatever the case may be.

> How do you describe a gujju prostitute turning to poetry?
> – Going from bed to verse.

We here need an expert to explain the point to us: Gujaratis, we are told, make certain mistakes of pronunciation, and "purportedly pronounce the idiom 'bad to worse' as 'bed to verse', and this mispronunciation becomes the humorous issue around which the joking-question revolves" (Prasad 1998:219).

These jokes cause most amusement to those who are close to the target yet nevertheless feel they are "safe" from ridicule. In the same way the Finns, some years ago, made jokes at the expense of their then Prime Minister. Because Finnish is not, unlike English, an Indo-European language, the English spoken by Finns is often clumsy. The PM in question had on his overseas tours visited zoos and had often seen the word "dangerous". Hence it gradually dawned on him, or so the story goes, that the word "dangerous" must mean "animal", but he mispronounced it as "tankero". (Note: Finnish is pronounced more or less as it is written. Some speakers have difficulty with the "soft" letters *d* and *g* because these do not occur in spoken Finnish.) This sparked off a host of "tankero" jokes all targeted at the mispronunciation of English and hence at a particular ethnic stereotype. Prasad (1998:213) does indeed point out that virtually no attention has so far been paid to the specific socio-political circumstances of the joking question.

Joking questions are the outcome of the riddlee's enticement to devise complex mental structures. The formula ostensibly reflects a true desire for knowledge and reasoning (Virtanen 1960:162), or even meditation on the origin and genesis of phenomena (" Minkätähe sorsalinnut uivat? – Ei ulotu jalat pohjaan."/"Why do ducks swim? – Because they can't touch the bottom with their feet."). As a rule joking questions nevertheless call for "a conditioned and virtually immediate capitulation" by the riddlee. For example,

> Riddler: Where does a 500-pound gorilla sit?
> Riddlee: I don't know.
> Riddler: Anywhere he wants. (Green 1992:137).

On the other hand one would imagine that if a formula is repeated from one riddle to another, the riddlee would be on his guard. Although there are possibly not quite so many joking question formulae as there are true riddle ones, new absurd question patterns seem to be emerging all the time. They are an easy way of jerking the rug from beneath the riddlee's feet. A comic or absolutely impossible image may at the same time act as a sign that it is futile to try even to hazard an answer unless the riddlee already knows it (elephant jokes). Most often the riddler will supply the answer to his question himself, thus indicating that the riddle is impossible to solve. The philosopher Socrates is said to have criticised sophistic questions because they were witticisms that made people look fools. Posing a question such as this is akin to pulling a chair from under someone (Ohlert 1912:14).

Parody and going beyond the borders of convention and 'good taste' are common in joking questions. The riddlee must be constantly on his guard, since he may get caught out having just learnt that the best thing is to admit immediately that he does not know the answer, as in the following "catch": "What do virgins eat for breakfast? – I don't know." (Green 1992:137.) This makes the listeners react in a way that embarrasses the innocent riddlee, as was indeed intended.

The joking questions and closely-related visual riddles include some surprisingly old riddles and jokes applying to the real-time world today. Their motifs range from historical figures to common items in everyday modern life, such as washing machines, floppy disks, TV, and winning the lottery. The influence of youth culture is also pronounced; rock concerts, hamburgers and coke are all to be found, as are the afternoon dances, wage agreements and air pollution associated more with the adult world. Television, radio and the press play an important part in the dissemination of topical motifs (Lipponen 1995:212).

## Visual riddles

In a category all of its own is the visual riddle presented by means of either a gesture or a drawing. The visual riddle is usually preceded by an opening formula in question form, "Do you know what this means?", or "Have you seen this one?", which provides the framework for the performance. The following are examples of riddles presented by means of a gesture:

> The riddler raises his thumb and asks, "Miksi kiinalaiset eivät käytä peukaloa? – Koska se on mun."/"Why don't the Chinese use the thumb?" and answers in the same breath, "Because it's mine." (Virtanen 1988:215)

The riddler holds his hand palm upwards with his fingers bent and asks "What's this?", replying, "It's dead" and at the same time turns his hand so the palm is facing downwards (Lipponen 1997:115).

Visual riddles were particularly popular in the 1950s, when in the US they acquired the name of "droodle" invented by Roger Price, who published his first book of visual riddles, *Droodles*, in 1953. The name droodle is a combination of the words "drawing" and "doodle" (= a meaningless pattern or figure) (information supplied by Bengt af Klintberg). The term spread to many languages, among them Swedish, Finnish and German, along with the new visual riddle tradition. In the 1970s Finnish children developed their own version, "toopeli". (Kaivola-Bregenhøj 1974a:123, Lipponen 1997:111.) But students today no longer know what "droodle" means and do not have any special name for this type of riddle. The following are perhaps among the most popular examples of this type of riddle:

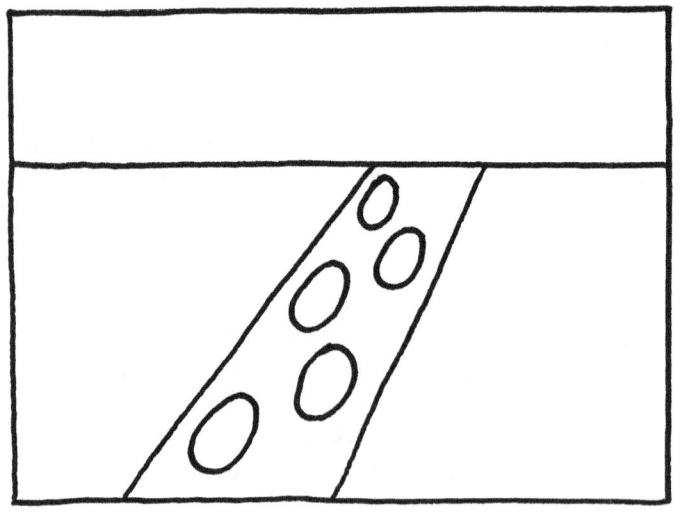

*Picture 3*
*A giraffe as seen through a half-open window.*
*(Abrahams & Dundes 1972:136)*

The giraffe riddle was one of the first to spread to both Finland and Sweden. In Finland it appeared in some children's magazines as early as the 1950s. (Lipponen 1997:113.)

There are various pictures denoting a Mexican, such as

*Picture 4*
*A Mexican riding a bike. (Roemer 1982:192)*

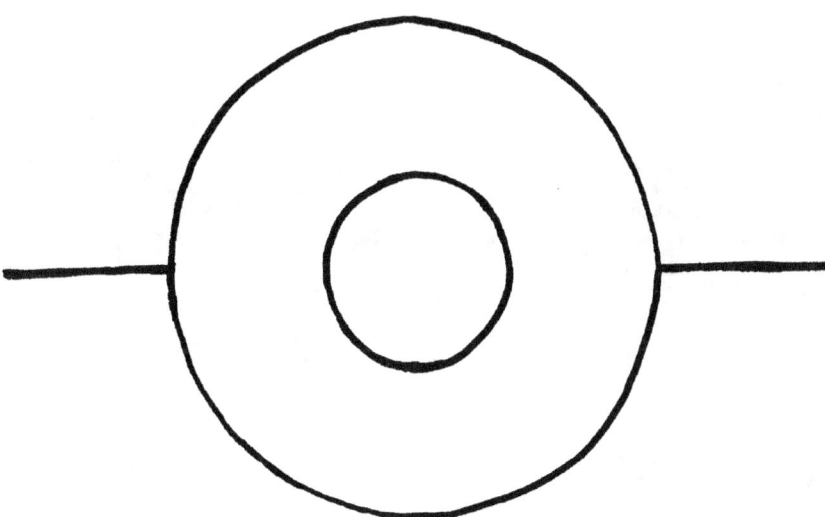

A droodle is not just any pictorial representation, since it always carries the potential for seeing something from an unusual angle. Grasping the right perspective is essential for an understanding of the image. It thus involves visual ambiguity, thereby making it a form of enigmatic expression. The riddler most often tries to mislead the riddlee by showing only part of the object in question (cf. the giraffe), or else the object is viewed from an unusual perspective. But the angle may also change so that the object is viewed from above (the Mexican). (Lipponen 1997:116.) Sometimes the answer can only be guessed if the riddlee knows the joking question attached to the same motif. But unlike many true riddles, the droodle is not tied to a specific language: whether the riddlee writes his language starting from the left or from the right makes no difference at all to its interpretation, for example. Like riddles, droodles are nevertheless culture-oriented, since it is impossible to interpret a totally alien picture, while understanding the picture calls for a culturally conventionalised system of rules, i.e. familiarity with the relevant code (Preston 1982:107–109, Roemer 1982:174, Hüemäe 1995). At the same time these riddles effectively spread stereotype visual information on, say, Mexicans to people the other side of the world. It seems odd that the Mexican, of all images, with its numerous variations should be by far the most common image and theme in the Finnish material (Lipponen 1997:118). Could the reason for this popularity be that the image is easy to vary again and again? Ulla Lipponen (1997:118) points out that the favourite themes are easily found in ever new contexts.

Droodles are by no means the only types of visual riddles, though they are at the moment extremely popular with schoolage children in Finland, and sometimes adults. Another is the rebus, which makes use of both images and letters:

*Picture 5*
*Can you see well? (Preston 1982:110)*

The language-oriented rebus, with its different variations, appears to be very popular in English-speaking cultures (for example, 'IOU' for 'I owe you'), and the earliest documents of its existence date right back to the 17th century. Examples of rebuses are also to be found in other languages, such as Finnish (Lipponen 1997:114).

A rebus has even appeared on a postage stamp in Denmark, where Torben Skov (1994) has sought to contribute to a water saving campaign:

*Picture 6*

The key to the rebus stamps lies in the card suit clubs, which in Danish comes out as the word "spar" meaning "save". The stamp on the left says "Save water", that on the right "Save $CO_2$".

The rebus is also a popular genre in contemporary children's lore. Young girls are clever at using them as a secret declaration of love. English declarations such as the following are common in Finnish girls' autograph books:

*Picture 7*
*(Lipponen 1992:86)*

I ♡ U 2 day
+ I ♡ U 2 morrow
―――――――――――
I ♡ U 4 ever

One well-known French rebus uses the letters G a, which when read out loud produce the sentence "G grand, a petit" meaning "J'ai grand appetit/I am very hungry." (Preston 1982:114.) This rebus is attributed to Voltaire, who is supposed to have written it in response to a dinner invitation by Frederick the Great which also contained a similar play on words (information supplied by Lee Haring).

Also belonging to the category of visual riddles are a number of tests of ingenuity, puzzles that have to be solved by, say, moving matches, adding something to a picture or solving its secret code. This tradition is not popular only with children, since many an adult will find himself being posed a puzzle such as this over a glass of beer. The following example begins with an arrangement such as this. The problem here is to move three matchsticks so as to produce two squares. The solution is:

*Picture 8*
*(Lipponen 1999:14, picture 38)*

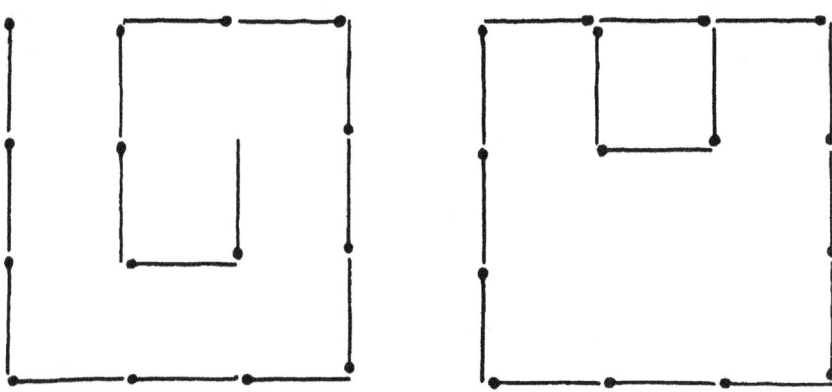

In order to solve the puzzle, it is necessary to divide the area into sections, numbers, etc., of equal size. In the following puzzle the clock face has to be divided up with five lines so that the sum of the numbers is 13 in each of the segments:

*Picture 9*
*(Lipponen 1999:134, picture 131)*

The image may also have some playful sums hidden in it. The question accompanying this picture of a man's head is: "How old is this man?" The correct answer is 39.

*Picture 10
(Lipponen 1999:40,
picture 164)*

Leea Virtanen and Ulla Lipponen were already presenting various tests of mental agility in their books *Ujo piimä* (1976) and *Kilon poliisi* (1988). The old-fashioned riddling tradition has now been taken over by joking questions, visual riddles, all sorts of tests of mental agility, puzzles and witty questions (see separate sections). The visual riddle tradition, for example, seems to be popular with both children and adults, and children report that their teachers may add a touch of light relief to a mathematics or psychology lesson by setting their pupils puzzles such as these. Maybe the popularity of games stimulated by computer games has laid the foundations for a new riddling tradition. (Correspondence with Ulla Lipponen 1997.)

TV shows are also posing visual riddles of a new type drawing on the popular tradition. The idea may, for example, be pinched from the rebus. Finnish television ran a highly popular quiz programme exploiting the contestants' ability to identify current events and people in the news. One of its favourite devices was to show a set of four pictures, the contestants' job being to say which of the four did not belong. Another was to get the contestants to recognise some highly topical event in the news by linking together the messages communicated by different pictures. One round in May 1998 presented a series of four pictures, the first of which showed people drinking beer, the second people drinking wine, the third people arm wrestling and the fourth a windmill. The quick-witted contestant came up with the answer: the election of Wim Duisenberg as President of the European Central Bank, the argument being: the first picture suggested Germany, the second France, the third a wrestling match, and the fourth was a visual metaphor for the country represented by the new ECB President: the land of windmills alias the Netherlands.

## *Wisdom questions*

Wisdom question riddles come closest of all to ordinary questions, because answering them calls for knowledge that cannot possibly be deduced from the image. The wit or cunning usually needed by the riddlee is no help in trying to find the answer. Nor is general cultural knowledge sufficient, because the riddlee will now need to have facts at his fingertips and special knowledge of, say, the Bible, arithmetic, or baseball. For example:

> What was the first operation in the Bible?
> – The removal of Adam's rib to create Eve. (Green 1992:137)
> How many outs in an inning of baseball?
> – Six. (Abrahams & Dundes 1972:137)

Wisdom questions are also known in the literature under the name of clever questions and shrewd questions; these terms would, in fact, be more appropriate. I shall nevertheless here be observing the terminology of Abrahams and Dundes.

Wisdom questions are very often a source of parody in which, for example, quiz questions of a serious nature originally requiring a knowledge of biblical history are turned into joking questions. For example:

> Mihin Jerusalemissa lyötiin ensimmäistä naulaa. – Päähän.
> Where was the first nail in Jerusalem hit? – On the head.
> Kuinka monta munaa Goljat söi tyhjään vatsaan? – Yhden.
> How many eggs did Goliath eat on an empty stomach? – One.
> (Virtanen 1960:163.)

The wisdom question that has come in for most study of all is the neck riddle. This riddle got its name from the fact that it is embedded within the tale of the prisoner who saves his life by posing a riddle which his executioner cannot answer. In another type of tale the man who can think up a question that is impossible to answer will win the hand of the princess. An example of a neck riddle could be the Samson riddle (cf. Chapter 1), the English version of which refers to a horse and a bird's nest instead of a lion and honeycomb (as mentioned in the Bible):

> There was a man convicted of having stolen a sheep; he was sentenced to death, but the magistrates said he could go free if he could ask a riddle they could not answer, and he was liberated for three days so that he might invent one. As he went out of prison, he saw a horse's skull in the roadside.

Returning to prison on the third day in despair, he noticed that within it was a bird's nest, with six young ones, and he thought of the following riddle:

As I walked out,
As I walked in,
From the dead I saw the living spring.
Blessed may Christ Jesus be
For the six have set the seventh free. (Abrahams 1980:8.)

The neck riddle is difficult to place indisputably in any one category, because the riddle itself is more akin to the metaphorical true riddles than to the wisdom questions devoid of fantasy. The styles and tones of neck riddles display wide variation, even though they resemble one another considerably in content. Every riddle of this type "has the power to reverse its own context, the context of death, to its inverse, the context of life..." (Stewart 1979:65). On the other hand it is a type of riddle based on the experience of a single individual, which he alone is equipped to answer. The important thing is in fact inventing a riddle, not solving it, because the riddlee will never be able to answer it. Both the status and the life of the riddler are at stake. In a narrative context the riddle is a functional equivalent of the task or test of skills. Roger D. Abrahams indeed points out in his study of the neck riddle entitled *Between the Living and the Dead* that the story answer in fact hardly "solves" anything. "The meaning and the solution are both too private, and too idiosyncratic to be really answerable. There is no way of answering these enigmas; the frame story may end successfully, but within the riddling the sense of confusion and mystery is maintained, even identified." (Abrahams 1980:19–23.)

The neck riddle is a highly cosmopolitan genre, and all but one of the riddles known in English are of international origin. A collection of riddles begun in Finland in 1966 proved that the genre was still known in the oral tradition, though it was becoming rare. One of the oldest sources including neck riddles is the *Hervararsaga* (cf. Chapter 1). This subgenre is always a combination of narrative and riddle that only functions as the sum of its parts. As a rule the riddle is embedded in the story, but there are also cases where the riddle is what tells the story. To take an example, the following riddle has a narrative solution, regardless of the fact that the story is almost reduced out of existence:

I killed no one and yet killed twelve. – There was a man, he injected poison in a chicken. He fed the chicken to twelve people and killed them.

Since the neck riddle falls somewhere in between the riddle and the folktale, it can also be analysed as the dialogue of genres. (Dorst 1983:416.)

Wisdom questions may also appear as part of a song. For example, in the ballad "Riddles Wisely Expounded" (Child 1) certain questions are posed in which the extreme value of some property is asked, using a comparative adjective for effect, by comparing the property to its own concrete symbol, such as "What is whiter than milk? – Snow." and "What is softer than silk?

– Down". These riddles are also known in Europe as questions in some folktales, and some are familiar in isolation (Haavio 1955:344–353) Although there are a number of suitable answers, only these approved answers are acceptable. Two questions are common in a riddling session: "What is blacker than a crow? – His feathers." and "What is not now and never shall be? – A mouse nesting in a cat's ear". (Abrahams & Dundes 1972:137.)

*Puzzles*

This riddle genre places the riddlee in the position of having to try to solve a task he is set. Again he needs special knowledge; this time not something he has learnt by heart but rather a performance and deduction. Arithmetic tasks or the solving of relationships are typical puzzles, such as:

> If a chicken and a half could lay an egg and a half in a day and a half, how long would it take five chickens to lay five eggs? – One day.

Solving all these questions calls for not only a basic command of arithmetic but also a smart mind:

> A man weighs 75 kg and his two sons 25 kg each. They want to cross a river in a boat that can only take 100 kg at a time. How do they do it? – First the father rows across with one of the sons. Then the son rows back and fetches his brother. (Lipponen 1988:57.)

Very similar to this in idea is the following puzzle, in presenting which the riddler also draws a picture:

*Picture 11 (Lipponen 1988:57)*

You've got to get a cabbage, a wolf and a sheep across to an island in a rowing boat so that the wolf cannot eat the sheep nor the sheep the cabbage. How do you do it? – First you take the sheep to the island. Then you fetch the wolf and leave it on the island, taking the sheep back to the shore. Leave the sheep on the shore and take the cabbage across and leave it with the wolf. Then you return for the sheep and row it across to the island. (Lipponen 1988:39.)

Arithmetic is only a minor point here, but the puzzle calls for just as much mental agility as the previous ones.

Questions presenting relationships in a complex way are also very popular:

Brothers and sisters have I none, but that man's father is my father's son. Who is he? – His son. (Abrahams & Dundes 1972:138.)

I was on a test flight with my friend, who is a test pilot, and the pilot's daughter. I had not seen the pilot for five years and was told the pilot had got married since we last met. When I asked the daughter's name, I was told it was the same as her mother's. I said, "Hi Susanna!" How did I know the girl's name even though I did not know the pilot had got married? – The test pilot was the girl's mother. (SKS. SV 129:2. 1992)

This puzzle and others like it was noted down from a 16-year-old schoolgirl, which just proves that roundabout word-play such as this may still amuse the teenager with access to all sorts of entertainment.

Puzzles may get drawn out into narratives that give the riddlee a ready solution but make him explain how the solution was reached:

A man wished to travel through a jungle inhabited by two tribes: the Full Bloods (who always speak the truth) and the Half Bloods (who always speak in opposites). Our man needed a truthful guide for his trip through the jungle, so when he saw three jungle inhabitants, he asked the first one, "Are you a Full Blood or a Half Blood?" The native answered, "Oogley comba." "He said he was a Half Blood," said the second native. "No, he didn't. He said he was a Full Blood," said the third native. From just this conversation the man was able to determine at least *one* Full Blood. Who and how?

The third one, at least, was a Full Blood and telling the truth; for the only answer the first one could have given, regardless of whether he was a Half Blood or a Full Blood, is "Full Blood". (Abrahams & Dundes 1972:139.)

Puzzles are very seldom used in riddling, because it takes longer to solve them than it does to answer other riddle types. They are nevertheless popular in children's lore. The following Finnish riddle narrative is one collected by Ulla Lipponen:

Matti and Maija lived in a little cottage on the edge of a forest. In the mornings Matti went off to work in the city and Maija stayed at home alone. One day, on arriving home, Matti found Maija dead on the floor, lying in a pool of water surrounded by broken glass. What had happened?

> – Maija was a goldfish living in a glass bowl on the top of a dresser by the window. A cat got in through the open window and tried to fish Maija out with its paw. The bowl fell on the floor and Maija the goldfish died. (Lipponen 1988:101.)

In form this narrative is such a simple puzzle that there is little left to think about once the answer is known, unlike the clearly more enigmatic story about the Full and Half Bloods.

A 16-year-old schoolboy from a little town in Eastern Finland said in 1992 that "once, a couple of years ago, we had a craze for telling detective stories. First we'd tell a little story, then the others would ask questions to which the teller answered yes or no." He also mentioned a television programme that may have served as a model for, or at least added impetus to this craze: "There's a programme on TV3 at the moment called Ariadne's Clue where they tell stories like this." His brief riddle narrative and long reply were as follows:

> A man is lying on his back, dead and naked in a field with a splint in his hand. What has happened? – Three men were up in an air balloon when it began to lose height. The men threw their clothes overboard. Because the balloon kept sinking, the men drew lots (by seeing who drew the long splint) to decide which of them should jump out. The man lying in the field had drawn the long splint and jumped.

This puzzle represents a completely new type of question that does not have a direct answer given by the riddlee or riddler but a solution that is reached by the listeners formulating questions bringing them closer to it, even though the riddler is only allowed to answer their questions with yes or no.

Puzzles also present themselves for parody, and all sorts of quasi-problems exist in schoolchildren's humour, such as:

> Once upon a time there were three men. They did one job in two hours. In how many hours will six men do the same job?
> – They won't do it, because the three men have already done it.
> (Virtanen 1976:25.)

## Parody riddles

Riddles are often asked during riddle sessions so that certain formulae, metaphors or content types are repeated. From the riddler's point of view these are a question of memorising, and from the riddlee's this is a factor making the answer easier to guess. For all the people taking part, such riddles involve a pattern of expectation (Abrahams & Dundes 1972:140) – a phenomenon that has been widely studied in relation to narrative, too. Parody riddles or witty questions make effective use of the fact that all conventions can be violated and no norm is insuperable. Causing the riddlee frustration is a form of entertainment typical of this riddle type, which is extremely popular in the present day.

Any type of riddle can be parodied. The bulk of schoolchildren's lore seeks its inspiration from the element of surprise afforded by parody. An American study (Sutton Smith 1976) revealed that riddle parodies were the second most common type of riddle used by schoolchildren. Example:

> Why did the chicken cross the road? – He wanted to get to the other side.

Questions of this type have always been popular. The catching wit may even lend itself to commercial use. Kentucky Fried Chicken has large street adverts saying: "Chicken worth crossing the road for" (communication by Fionnuala Carson Williams, 2000). Simple parody riddles are avidly cultivated by children and young people today. An example:

> Lentokone tippui Ruotsin ja Suomen rajalle. Kummalle puolelle haavoittuneet haudataan? – Ei haavoittuneita haudata.
> An aeroplane crashed on the border between Sweden and Finland. On which side should the wounded be buried?
> – You don't bury wounded people. (SKS. SV 369:2. 1992; Peterson 1985:46)
> Kukko muni vuorelle munan. Kummalle puolelle vuorta muna vierii?
> – Eivät kukot muni.
> A cock laid an egg on a mountain. Which side of the mountain did the egg roll down? – Cocks don't lay eggs. (SKS. SV 368:1. 1992.)

These two witty questions are taken from the repertoire of senior schoolgirls aged 17 and 18. The girls are friends, and the riddles they know are applications of the same formula. This is an easy formula that holds almost endless potential for playful invention.

The thing about parodies is that they upset the expectation that some sort of relationship must exist between the image and the answer. The listener feels he has had his leg pulled in trying to find an answer to the image according to the rules he has learnt and on hearing that he has been made to look a fool. For example:

> How much dirt in a hole 5 by 3 by 3 feet? – None.

> Three men walked into a restaurant. One man ordered an egg with a piece of bacon on either side. The second man ordered an egg on the right side and two pieces of bacon on the left side. The third man ordered an egg on the left side and two pieces of bacon on the right side. How could the waitress tell which one was a sailor? – She looked at his uniform (Bronner 1988:115.)

Pre-teenage children aged 10–12 seem to be greatly amused by the witty question in which there is no longer any sense to the question and answer, such as:

> A woman weighed 75 kg. She went to the shop and bought 3 kg of potatoes, a kilo of eggs, half a kilo of butter, 2 kg of carrots, a kilo of onions, 1,5 kilos of flour, a kilo of apples and 2 bananas. How many pancakes did she

have in her fridge?
– Four of course, because an aeroplane has three landing wheels! (Lipponen 1988:59.)

The last statement in this narrative already pulls the mat from under the listener's feet. The listener was probably expecting an arithmetical puzzle, or a trick question about slimming and the woman's weight. The question is impossible to answer, the listener debating the logic is made to look utterly stupid, and the sole aim of the narrative is to elicit a burst of spontaneous laughter. This may also be a device used by youngsters as a protest against the logical rules of adults, but it could no doubt be called a parody of the joking question.

The questions of riddle parodies or witties turn out to be "obvious" ones, in which case the riddle may be a pseudo-puzzle, the primary aim of which is to show that there is something wrong in the question. "Rather than showing the logic of the apparent illogicalness of the question, the answer exposes the illogic of the apparently logical question. What looks like a riddle turns out to be a 'stupid question'." (Sutton-Smith 1976:116.) For example:

> A banana, an apple, and an orange stood on a bridge. The apple jumped, the orange jumped. Why didn't the banana jump?
> – He was yellow. (Bronner 1988:116.)

The witty question has plenty of scope for variation. To begin with, a motif can be treated within the confines of a broadish narrative, a joke or a riddle. The following question, for example, is also known as a narrative:

> Three Finnish men were walking across a bridge. One had a spade and one had a hammer. What did the third man have?
> – Inflammation of the gums, because one Finn in three has inflammation of the gums. (SKS. SV 723:1. 1992.)

The key person in the question can also be changed to give the basic motif a suitable new look, as in:

> A stupid Swede, Superman and Batman were all in different corners of a football pitch, with a football in the centre of the pitch. Who reached the ball first?
> – The stupid Swede, of course, because the others are fantasy figures. (SKS. SV 777:1. 1992.)

The reply "the stupid Swede" places the story in the domain of neighbourly humour and ethnic joking. But the set-up can be changed so that the key figure is, say, a dumb blonde, or a stupid member of the Conservative Party. A popular, familiar formula provides an easy frame for an endless stream of questions and answers. The mood can shift from ethnic to sexist, political, etc.

There is on the borderlines of the puzzle, the parody riddle and the witty question a wealth of material designed to amuse and make both the listeners and the posers of the questions laugh. Some material defies categorisation, especially as the questions are constantly being varied and the same idea may be presented in the form of either a joke or of a riddle-like formula culminating in a question. And again it may be either short or long, almost assuming the proportions of a narrative. The most lively variations in the old riddling tradition are to be found in precisely the rich, varied, and constantly renewing territory alongside joking questions, visual riddles, puzzles, witty and parody questions.

## *Literary riddles*

The literary riddle constitutes a chapter all of its own in the history of the genre. The literary and popular or folk forms of the riddle differ clearly from one another in their means of expression and the way they are used. They have also spread in different ways. Studies of the literary riddle and its manifestations have been made by Archer Taylor (1948) and Mark Bryant (1983 and 1990), whose works provide a comprehensive cross-section of the contexts in which this type appears. The literary riddle tradition of the German-speaking area has been exhaustively investigated by Mathilde Hain (1966). The following distinguishing folk features by Don Hart inversely apply to the literary riddle and draw a line between oral and literary manifestations of the genre: "1) briefer statement, 2) lacks purposeful polish, 3) avoids conflicting details associated with two or more themes, 4) rarely deals with abstract themes, 5) general group familiarity of the subject matter, 6) widespread occurrence of analogous riddles in other societies, and 7) was not purposely composed for publication." (Hart 1964:24) The following example of a literary riddle is taken from the *Anglo-Saxon Riddles of the Exeter Book* (1963) believed to have been written in the 8th century. The answer to the riddle is a book-moth (book-worm).

> A moth ate a word! To me that seemed
> A strange thing to happen, when I heard that wonder,
> A worm that would swallow the speech of a man.
> Sayings of strength steal, in the dark,
> Thoughts of the mighty; yet the thieving sprite
> Was none the wiser for the words he had eaten!
> (Taylor 1948:94)

This riddle poem is an excellent illustration of the way the literary tradition differs from the oral examples quoted above.

Literary riddles may also be termed "learned" and "artistic", since they were invented by philosophers, clerics and famous writers. The earliest medieval literary riddles were in Latin or Greek; German Protestant academies were writing Latin riddles as late as the sixteenth century. But from the 16th century, large numbers began to be published in German, Spanish, Italian, and other vernacular languages. Many of the writers of riddles were famous and celebrated in the heyday of the genre. Of importance to the English riddle tradition was Symphosius, writing in Latin, who is thought to have lived at the end of the fifth century. He was a source of inspiration to Anglo-Latin writers in the 7th and 8th centuries, and through them the author of the *Old English Exeter Book* – the first book to be published in the vernacular. Many later writers, too, were to model their style on that of Symphosius in making up riddles. Some of Symphosius's creations spread in translation to other language areas, and some were even borrowed for the *Aenigmata et griphi veterum et recentium* appearing in 1604 and used in schools. (Taylor 1948:52–53, Bryant 1990:21,26.)

Another famous writer was Al Harîrî of Bassorah (1054–1122), representing a rich Arabic riddle culture, whose classic work *Maqamat* contains several chapters of enigmas of one kind or another. Many of the themes used by Al Harîrî are also well-known as folk riddle motifs, but he had his own inimitable way of handling them. A counterpart to, for example, the following riddle is known in European riddling, too:

> Take with thee the one of full-moon face and of pearly hue, of pure root and tormented body, who was pinched and stretched, imprisoned and released, made to drink and weaned, and pushed into the fire, after he had been slapped. – A loaf. (Taylor 1948:25–29, Bryant 1990:27.)

The popularity of the literary riddle varied over the centuries, but after 1500 it established a clear place for itself as part of literary culture. In Italy, for example, scholars devoted space in their handbooks of poetics to the history of riddling and riddles. Proof of their popularity is to be found in the collection *Le piacevoli notti* published by Straparola in Venice in 1550–1553. Each story in this anthology ends with a riddle in poetic form tying in with the plot. Here as an example is the riddle attached to "Le porco" appearing in an English translation by W.G. Waters in 1834:

> I prithee, sir, to give to me,
> What never did belong to thee,
> Or ever will, what though thy span
> Of life exceed the wont of man.
> Dream not this treasure to attain;
> Thy longing will be all in vain;
> But if you deem me such a prize,
> And pine for me with loving eyes,
> Give me this boon, my wish fulfil,
> For you can grant it if you will.

Further proof of the prestige enjoyed by the genre is the fact that scholars published riddle anthologies. Three such anthologies were published in Germany in 1602. The most celebrated of them was the *Aenigmatographia* compiled by Nicolaus Reusner, in which Reusner, himself a riddler of poetic disposition and Rector of Jena University, collected everything about riddles that was worth knowing. (Taylor 1948:72–88, Hain 1966:19–20, Bryant 1990:31.)

Riddles have been used in their works by such distinguished writers as

Cervantes, Shakespeare and Goethe. Either they invented them themselves, or they seasoned their language with riddles lifted from other sources. The plays of Shakespeare contain innumerable allusions to riddles and riddling, the most famous possibly being in the grave-diggers' scene of *Hamlet*:

> First Clown: What is he that builds stronger than either the mason, the shipwright or the carpenter?
> Second Clown: The gallows-maker, for that frame outlives a thousand tenants. (Bryant 1990:31–32.)

In *La Galatea*, published in 1585, Cervantes dealt enigmatically with wine, coal, letter and writing paper, jealousy, a man in chains, shears to snuff a candle. (Taylor 1948:106, Bryant 1990:42–43.)

The literary riddle has varied in popularity from one country to another. In Germany, for example, interest in this genre was suppressed in the 18th century by pietism and rationalism. In England it has never won widespread popularity and use, whereas in Italy it continued to flourish, and in France even enjoyed a rise in prestige in the 17th and 18th centuries. (Taylor 1948:110–111.)

The riddling magazines appearing in, say, France and England in the 17th and 18th centuries provided a special medium for the publication of literary riddles. The fashion was launched by the French *Mercure de France* (first published in 1672), which in time became the frontrunner of a flourishing industry in society riddling journals. In addition to poems, news and views the magazine published riddles, logogriphs and charades, the solutions to which were published in the next issue. In England the leading forum for enigmatic art was the *Universal Magazine of Knowledge and Pleasure* (first published in 1747). Both magazines continued to appear in the 19th century, but riddles gradually vanished from their pages. Little by little the genre lost its prestige. "From being at times the quintessential vehicle of high-society humour and literary drollery, it deteriorated at last into a children's amusement." (Bryant 1990:47–48, 51.)

Riddles were, however, published here and there, for example, in Turkey (Başgöz & Tietze 1973:3), in magazines for a long time to come, and some of them became rooted in the oral tradition (for example, FR 1977).

In Finland there were in the 19th century children's magazines in both Finnish and Swedish that published popular entertainment. The riddles found in these include both rebuses (cf. p. 64) and questions in poetic metre called charades such as those familiar in Central Europe (Bryant 1983:14–15). In a charade the reader has to guess certain syllables which, when combined, provide the answer to the riddle. For example, *Eos* (4/1863 in Swedish) and *Pääskynen* (4/1871 in Finnish) announced the correct answer in the following issue. Charades are by nature language-specific and thus impossible to translate.

An indication of the popularity of charades is a notebook dated 1820 into which Marie Marg. Hedman copied poetic riddles. Also referring to the same decade is the information given by Ester Margaret von Frenckell (1947:122, 259) that charades were sometimes acted out at Christmas or on other social occasions among the gentry. The characters in the charade acted out each syllable of the word constituting the answer in turn. The tradition continued at social evenings, school festivals, etc. Mark Bryant (1983:15) mentions that this form of acting is still "a very popular kind of parlour game".

A glance at children's magazines reveals that almost any kind of puzzle, from crosswords to plays on words and visual problems demanding simple logic, could serve as a riddle. Similar puzzle corners have also featured in newspapers, which proves that charades and other puzzles akin to riddles have not been a form of entertainment confined exclusively to children.

# 4 Sexual riddles

One riddle type that is still used by adults and is still very much alive is the sexual riddle. So far no comprehensive general treatises have been written on this subgenre, for the attitude to the sexual theme has long been negative and silent. Examples are difficult to find in riddle publications, even though the sexual riddle is well known in the oral tradition. I have nevertheless decided to treat sexual riddles in a chapter of their own, paying more attention to them than to the other subgenres. Sexual riddles are a content category that takes in metaphorical riddles of the true riddle type, joking questions, visual riddles, and the spoonerisms so popular in certain language areas.

Riddles are among the most outspoken expressions of folk eroticism. The use of sexual vocabulary is, however, rare in riddles, unlike in other forms of erotic folklore. Few sexual riddles have until recently been published; in most cases they have for reasons of propriety been forgotten (see nevertheless, for example, Fauset 1928 and Boggs 1934, which give examples of sexual riddles). One rare exception was the Finnish clergyman Christfrid Ganander, who published the first collection of Finnish riddles, *Aenigmata Fennica*, as early as 1783. Ganander appreciated the value of living tradition and did not censor his publication. There are numerous examples of puritanical publishers (see Hart 1964:138–141). The most renowned among them is Archer Taylor, who in the chapter headed Erotic Scenes in his work *English Riddles* (1951:687–688) mentions innocent answers given to sexual riddles but no images with a double meaning. The following riddle type 1425–1428, most obviously of a sexual nature, has, however, escaped Taylor's sieve:

> Something round, split in the middle
> Surrounded by hair, and water comes out. – An eye. (ER 1425)

It has quite rightly been pointed out that the bashful publishers are responsible for creating the highly proper yet misleading picture of folklore as something that is almost antiseptically devoid of sensuality (Launonen 1966:374). Yet this is a living tradition, and one still in use: sexual riddles and jokes are not merely a past form of entertainment, since they are continuously favoured by both adults and children (see Brown 1973 for examples).

Sexual riddles are in their forms of expression usually of two different types. Among the most common ones are images disguised as sexual and arousing erotic fantasies that do not actually mention a single improper word (for example, "Irvistä karvasta, pistä siihen paljasta."/"Spread open the fuzz, stick a bare thing in" or "What four-letter word begins with *f* and ends with *k*, and if it doesn't work you can use your fingers?"). But because the image inevitably sets the respondent's imagination seeking for a sexual answer, he is surprised when offered the innocent answer "hand in mitten" (FR 161) or "fork" (Dundes & Georges 1962:225). Far rarer are the riddles in which the answer is given quite frankly as either sexual intercourse or the male or female sexual organs, sometimes in a way that is coarse (for example, "Buried when alive; Pulled out when dead. – Penis". Hart 1964:149). In any case the answer is always unexpected, and this surprise element is in fact regarded as typical in obscene folklore and in 20th century jokelore in general (Dundes & Georges 1962:221).

The riddles offering an innocent answer use double-entendre to achieve their effect. This may extend to all levels of the language. The question, which may be a simile, a metaphor, or most commonly of all a list of distinguishing features, hovers between two conceptual worlds. The riddler must constantly retain both answers in his mind (Stewart 1983:40). The guesser, who does not know the "correct", i.e. the innocent answer observes the customary cognitive model and gives the wrong answer. This type of riddle is founded on the false expectation effect (Levin 1973). The majority of "innocent" riddles suggest copulation first of all:

> The old lady pitted it an' patted it; The old man down with his breeches an' at it.
> – She made up the bed, and he undressed and got into bed.
> (Boggs 1934:321)
>
> Hömötin, tömötin, johon paljas pistetään. – Kinnas.
> Crinkly, scratchy, you stick something bare in it. – A mitten. (FR 275)

The next riddle, however, hints at the male sexual organ:

> About six inches long, an' a mighty pretty size; Not a lady but will take it between her thighs. – The left-hand horn on a lady's side saddle.
> (Boggs 1934:323)

And the true referent of this riddle is the female sexual organ:

> An odd girl whose private parts are very soft. – A banana.
> (Blacking 1961:22)

Riddles very clearly make a big distinction between male and female actors. According to a study by Inger Lövkrona, the man represents sexual egocentrism, male assessments and concepts of women and women's sexual properties, reactions and behaviour. By contrast, the woman is as the main character of a riddle receptive and passive. (Lövkrona 1991:272–273.) The following riddle may be regarded as the ultimate in active and passive sexual relations:

> Father's was stiff when he came in, and he laid it on mother's hairy thing, but when mother awoke father's was slack and mother's hairy thing was wet? – Father came home when mother was sleeping and laid his stiff frozen gloves on mother's woolly cloth. When mother awoke the gloves had melted and the woolly cloth was wet.

As a rule sexual riddles are, however, dominated by the act, not its performers.

Many erotic riddles are international, though it is difficult to gain any precise picture of their distribution and frequencies in view of the small volume of material published so far. Suggestive riddles used to be regarded as age-old ritual questions (Schultz 1912:96), but also as relatively recent lore flourishing at the end of the Middle Ages and the beginning of the modern era. It is thought that they were invented by itinerant scholars in the 16th century (Peuckert 1938:107).

## *Erotic teasing*

The sexual riddle was, according to the Finnish descriptions, not only a means of charging the atmosphere but sometimes also a test used by the young men of the village to try the tolerance of a new serving girl. The girl had to be on her guard: it was a mistake to become angry, to show blatant astonishment or to take part in the jest:

> Then I went into service in the village of Kytösyrjä in Impilahti. It was an ancient custom for all the young men of the village to come and take a look at any new serving girl. They introduced themselves, under all sorts of names. One said he was Mr. Emptypants from Helsinki. When I refused to flirt with them, they began asking each other dirty riddles. In some of them the question was innocent but the answer was naughty. With others it was the other way round. Then it was best not to get caught up in their talk. Otherwise they would soon say you had a dirty mind. Their aim was to trip the girl up in her speech. The boldest one always asked the questions, the others answered and laughed. If the girl did not join in, she could not show she was offended. It would only have made things worse. If she joined in, she had to be sure she could hold her own. It was no use trying unless she really knew what she was about. If she pretended she had no idea what they were talking about, she was more likely to be left in peace, they lost interest in teasing her. But if she let them see she was angry, it went on and on. I saw it happen with a day worker from the farm.
> (SKS. Elsa Jaatinen AK 6:139. 1966.)

The above account describes the initiation of a new female member of the community involving a test of behaviour and teasing. It reflects the aggressive and domineering attitude to women of a predominantly male community in which a woman had no equal chance of defending herself. She just had to keep quiet and try to take the ribaldry as best she could, without showing that she was offended. The riddling situation may also be a clumsy attempt by the men to communicate their sexual interest. But again the woman at the receiving end was in a weaker position, because she had no way of combating the jests.

Erotic teasing is still part of the living workplace tradition, and the butt of the joke is often a younger member of the opposite sex. Embarrassment often goes hand in hand with teasing, and only the smart and lucky victim comes out with honour. Teasing is regarded as a form of male tradition and a means of amusing, embarrassing or insulting a woman (Simmons 1956:1). But women are also capable of it. The following quotation, though brief, from an answer given to a Finnish riddle collector is typical:

> The riddles are from the Rajala shoe factory at Kankaanpää, where a worker called Aili Kivelä put them to the young men working alongside her. (SKS. Olavi Mäkelä AK 12:64. 1966).

Sexual riddles have also been a means of testing the norms of the individual and community, of blurring and breaking them. These means are still in use, even though the riddling tradition has been transformed.

Erotic joking or the generation of an erotic charge is easy with the help of short joking questions. I quote two American sexual jokes analysed by Pertti J. Anttonen:

> What's the difference between a beer and a woman?
> – Beer is wet all the time.
>
> What's the difference between a Coke and a Man?
> – Coke comes in a can, but a man comes in your mouth.

Anttonen (2000:246–256) demonstrates by close analysis of jokes and their performance contexts that these two sexual jokes were, in an interactive situation observed by him, the last straw that caused the disintegration of a relationship. The words "beer", "wet", "Coke" and "your mouth" became fully charged with totally unforeseen meanings to which the man and the woman gave different interpretations in keeping with their own frame of mind. In telling the jokes, the man intended to be amusing, to provide some light relief and to demonstrate that he wanted the relationship to continue. By contrast, the woman found the key words offensive, and the man's feeble attempt at trying to make her laugh made her all the more determined to put an end to the affair.

This unusually close analysis of erotic jokes and their performance contexts proves that even an erotic riddle is tied to the context in which it is performed. We can never know, on reading archive material, whether the function of the riddle was to entertain, to tease, to woo or to offend.

## The use of sexual riddles today

Many true riddles exist only in archives and books. There is, however, always an exception to prove the rule. The following riddle, already included in the *Aenigmata Fennica* published in 1783, was recently sent in to the Folklore Archives:

> Pistä, kasta, menetä, vedätä, jollei mahdu, niin nuole pääst.
> – Neula ja lanka.
> Stick, wet, loose, pull, if it doesn't fit then lick the end.
> – Needle and thread. (FR 770)

The riddler was a 22-year-old woman student at a domestic science college who put the riddle to her fellow-students during one of their breaks. Although sexual riddles are indeed still part of the oral tradition, new riddle formulae are to be found more often than the traditional ones. The following riddle jokes were noted down in 1990 (background information in brackets; all examples from Ulla Lipponen):

> Miksi Saara nauroi? – Jumala koitteli häntä.
> Why did Sarah laugh? – God was trying her.
> (16-year-old girl; riddle known since the 1940s)
> Mitä tapahtui, kun seitsemän kääpiötä näki Lumikin suihkussa?
> – Seven up.
> What happened when the seven dwarfs saw Snow White in the shower?
> – Seven up. (13-year-old boy; riddle very popular; varies)
> Mitä yhteistä on miehillä ja tulitikuilla? – Molemmat syttyvät yhtä helposti.
> What do men and matches have in common?
> – They both heat up just as easily. (16-year-old girl)
> Mitä spitaalinen sanoi tullessaan ilotalosta? – Nyt se irtosi.
> What did the leper say on coming out of the brothel? – Now I've lost it!

The formulae of these riddles are familiar from joking questions and there is little new in their contents, either.

Sexual riddles are not told merely for fun or as a means of teasing someone; they are also a conscious means of making a protest and breaking fusty or outdated behavioural norms. America witnessed a fashionable wave of sexual riddles in the late 1960s (Bauman 1970) instigated by a mock secret society calling itself The Turtles. The society had its own mocking slogan and initiation rites, during which the following four riddles were as a rule posed:

> 1. What is it a man can do standing, a woman sitting down, and a dog on three legs? – Shake hands.
> 2. What is it that a cow has four of and a woman only two of? – Legs.
> 3. What is a four-letter word ending in 'k' that means the same as intercourse? – Talk.
> 4. What is it on a man that is round, hard, and sticks so far out of his pyjamas that you can hang his hat on it? – His head.

The most important thing was not for the respondent to find the right 'innocent' answer but to amuse the initiated (often opposite sex) by giving a sexual answer that was laughingly proven to be wrong. The aim of the lore was, among other things, to promote conviviality among drinkers in restaurants and pubs and to good-humouredly embarrass friends. It was common for men to ask women the riddles. By means of sexual riddles it was easy to break the conversational ice, and the erotic charge was very clear. Fundamentally this institution also parodied the initiation rites of various fraternal orders in America (Masons, fraternities, etc.), for their serious rites were likened to the mock rites of The Turtles.

The erotic riddle can even today still be an apt way of handling the taboos surrounding sexuality. In spring 1989 a 27-year-old Israeli student of folkloristics in Jerusalem (R.D.) wrote down the riddles put to her by a man living in the same mixed student hostel. There were 26 in all, and they were all sexual in theme. The material was provided by Galit Hasan-Rokem, Professor at the Hebrew University of Jerusalem. Why riddle jokes rather than, say, political jokes, R.D. wondered. She began to question her student friends and noticed that the sexual riddle can break the ice in situations where something is needed to get the atmosphere warmed up. But it is also a neutral way of speaking of something that is still considered delicate. One informant claimed that sexual riddles are also a means of expressing hidden feelings. A jest such as this amuses the listeners more than any other.

A sexual riddle may well incorporate some other joking point. The Israeli riddles were often spiced with ethnic humour:

What does a Georgian have that is long and hard?
– His name and the first class at school.

Why does a Polish woman close her eyes during the sexual act?
– Because she can't bear to see someone else enjoying something.

Why do Israeli men come quickly?
– Because they've got to run and tell the lads.

What do you call an English woman's nipple? – The tip of the iceberg.

These riddles are only fully revealed to the listener familiar with the stereotypes: the stupid Georgian with a long name, the sadistic Pole, the childish boasting of Israeli men and the frigidity of English women. Ethnic stereotypes are not, however, always international, so there is a limit even to joking. Many of the riddles popular among students were also culture-specific in that they tied in with contemporary Israeli politics, culture and everyday life.

Children and young people also test the limits of norms of one another or older people by means of sexual riddles. The border between the forbidden and the permissible is elastic and clearly shifts over the years. The following description, published in 1955, illustrates the boldness and desire to tease of a Philippine boy: "The riddle contest may proceed smoothly...until some naughty boy would pop up with a riddle having a double meaning such as the following Tagalog: 'The spearthrust has not yet been aimed, but the wound gapes widely open.' Of course, this would at once arouse a cry of objection.../and/ some bold girls would make a comeback... The arm of your father is surrounded with boils." (This is the answer.) (Manuel 1955:152)

In the early 1970s a group of junior schoolchildren wrote down the riddles they could remember for me during one school lesson (Kaivola-Bregenhøj 1974a:105–126). Among them were the following sexual riddles:

> Miksi paloauto on punainen? – Olisit säkin jos letkusta vedettäis.
> Why are fire engines red? – You would be, too, if you had your hose pulled.
> (Cf. the same riddle in Wolfenstein 1978:105–106.)
> Mikä on ihmeiden huippu?
> – Pultsari pökkii puhelintoppaa ja keskus saa kaksoset.
> What is the ultimate miracle?
> – A drunk knocks up a telephone pole and the operator has twins.

In children's lore the fire engine riddle appears in the following variation:

> Teacher: Why does a cow have a long face?
> Little Johnny: Well you would too if you had your tits pulled twice a day!

Ulf Palmenfelt (conversation 1998) recalls that this same riddle sometimes has an even bolder addition at the end: "and got fucked only once a year".

When the presenters of the riddles are children aged 8–10, the shift in sexual lore from a means of raising the erotic temperature to the level of childlike, daring entertainment is clear. These riddles are children's way of showing off to their friends just how much they know about the subject in question.

Far more daring are the sexual riddles contained in the anthology edited by Carsten Bregenhøj (1988), where the point of the joke may be aimed at, for example, homosexuals.

> Do you know why gays don't like space? – Because it's endless.

Whereas at one time it was the children's ears that had to be protected from sexual insinuations, those in need of protection today are more likely to be their parents, who are amazed at the vulgar language used by their children and the attitudes it reflects. The most astonishing thing as far as the adult is concerned is that the same riddle may amuse the child in early adolescence just testing his limits and the adult himself. In addition to providing entertainment the riddle is for the child often a way of transgressing the norms, of testing adults' tolerance and weighing up the various manifestations of sexuality.

Children's riddling tradition also contains examples of vogues that do not at first glance appear to be in any way sexual. One example are the moron joking riddles popular in the 1950s, such as:

> Why did the moron throw the clock out of the window?
> – Because he wanted to see time fly.
>
> Why did the moron take his cow to church?
> – Because he heard there was a new pastor.
>
> Why did the moron take a bowl and spoon to the movies?
> – Because he heard they had a new serial.
>
> Why did the moron take the bread and butter to the corner?
> – Because he heard there was a traffic jam.

Riddles such as these are analysed in *Children's Humour* by Martha Wolfenstein (1978), a psychologist specialised in children and child therapy but also interested in children's culture. She does not by any means regard riddles such as those just quoted as mere word-play aimed to achieve a crazy effect. Children's sense of humour varies with age, and joking riddles of the moron type are typical of "latency period children", i.e. children between the ages of six and eleven. Having tried to extort an answer from someone who possibly cannot provide it, the riddler answers himself to show how smart he is. Anyone who does not know the answer is plain dumb. The Freudian interpretation of riddles charges them with sexual meaning associated with the parents' nocturnal activities observed in early childhood. For example, on hearing the riddle

> Why did the moron throw the clock out of the window?
> – Because he wanted to see time fly.

my first reaction was that the image contains an amusing concretisation of the flight of time. Martha Wolfenstein (1978:116–118), however, links this moron riddle with the Freudian theory that throwing something out of the window may represent getting rid of unwanted siblings. This, she claims, explains why it is popular with so many children. Another link exists between the moron and children's desire to see something, i.e. the moron's wish to see something fly and the child's desire to see and interrupt his parents' intercourse. The explanation for this is that flying is a symbol for intercourse. The third interpretation concerns the clock in the image, which is a symbol for imposed routines, and in this case connects up with toilet training. Throwing out the clock thus represents a rebellion against the rules of cleanliness.

Wolfenstein's interpretations are so utterly Freudian that they arouse an immediate counter-reaction: it cannot simply be so. What is interesting and informative in her research is the idea that childhood and early youth clearly fall into different periods, in which different types of riddle appeal. (Cf. the idea of different ages proposed by Brian Sutton-Smith and mentioned in Chapter 3). Sexuality is an important field of life, and it may also be approached at the latent level of riddles. The comments and sense of humour revealed at interviews concerning riddles differ from those that occur to adults.

One explanation for risqué sexual lore in the present day is perhaps the general laxity in the way people speak. Sex is also fed to us, by the media for example, in a way that was once unheard of. We may on the other hand wonder how people living in the cramped living conditions in rural society, with large families all sleeping in the same room and even in the same bed, could possibly be ignorant of the facts of life. Sex has in any case ceased to be taboo. Limits do, however, still exist, for verbal exchange with sexual overtones is cultivated chiefly as the lore of peer groups.

*Sexual picture puzzles and spoonerisms*

From time to time there is a fashionable wave of picture puzzles (Preston 1982 and Roemer 1982). As with joking questions, only the person who sets the puzzle as a rule knows the answer, which always gives an amusing twist to a simple visual expression. Only a small proportion of picture puzzles are mildly sexual, such as this one – one of the oldest – which its presenter learnt while living in a student hostel in 1959.

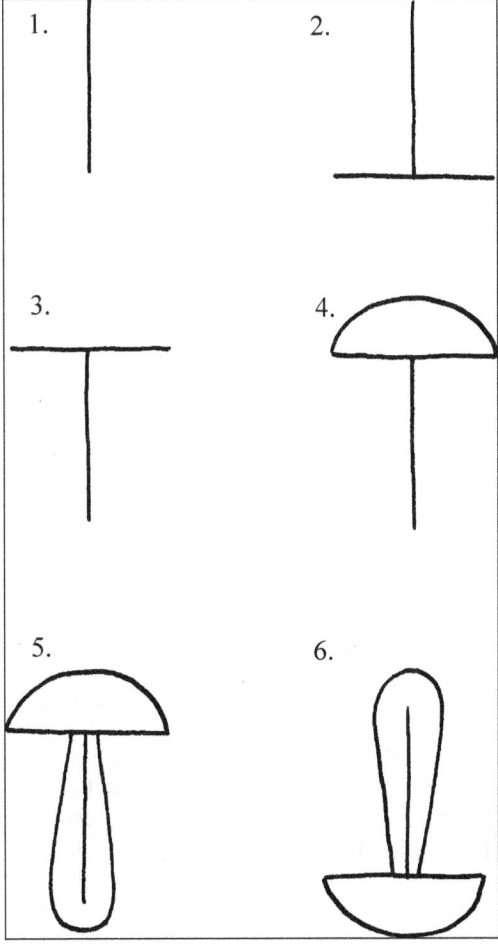

*Picture 12*
*"Big sister in the bath" is a series of drawings, each one accompanied by the question "What's this?" (from the collection by Ulla Lipponen).*

The picture proceeds in stages, and each stage is followed by the question "What's this?". No. 5 shows a mushroom, no. 6 big sister in the bath. Ulla Lipponen (in Virtanen 1970:73) recalls hearing this riddle cast as follows while playing in the yard as a child: "First someone says, 'Guess what I'm drawing now.' The picture has to be drawn hesitantly, as if the artist is only just envisaging the whole. First the cap of a 'mushroom' is drawn, then the stem and the crack from the cap to the stem. The picture is now ready and is given to the riddlee. The most common answer is that it is a mushroom. The drawer cannot, however, accept the answer and urges the riddlee to try again. The answer 'a lamp' is likewise rejected. Finally the jubilant drawer takes the paper, turns it upside down and explains that it depicts the riddlee's sister washing her feet in a bowl of water." The picture is a typical example of children's lore designed to make others look stupid (Virtanen 1970:70–92). In children's lore this final picture has been modified as

*Picture 13*

This popular picture is to be found in many variants. This time the explanation is "Sister pulling her tights on", but it could be viewed as a lamp, depending on the riddlee's imagination. Danielle M. Roemer (1982:194) presents a version of this picture in which the explanation is "A fat lady seen from behind pulling up her girdle".

The following pictures are taken from Finnish children's lore and depict Marilyn Monroe behind a tree.

*Picture 14*
*(Lipponen 1988:71)*

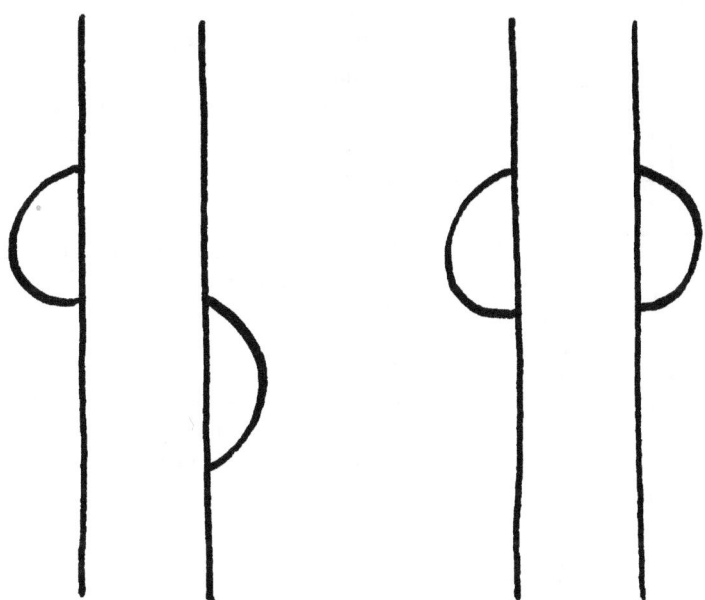

A person whose name occurs in connection with droodle imagery can consider him- or herself very flattered. These pictures are entitled "Marilyn Monroe behind a tree".

In American lore the curvaceous woman is sometimes Dolly Parton (Roemer 1982:193). Adults also amuse themselves by drawing picture puzzles. Again some lore is shared by children and adults alike, but the following series appeals more to adults who know at least something about the plays of William Shakespeare. It is called "Shakespeare's Plays" and it was drawn in 1987 by a woman of about 40 Ulla Lipponen met on a bus.

*Picture 13*

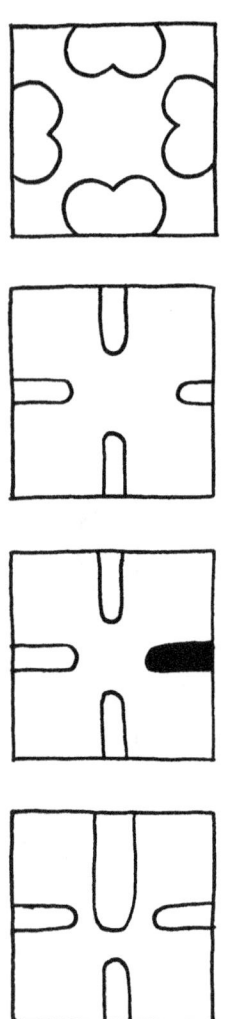

These pictures depict plays by Shakespeare: 1. The Merry Wives of Windsor, 2. Much Ado About Nothing, 3. Othello and 4. Midsummer Night's Dream.

The picture here says more than a thousand words. What makes them into a riddle is precisely the fact that the image conjures up two answers. The giver of the "right" interpretation is chastised on hearing the answer. The pictures are presented as a series, so that the clash between naughty pictures and world classics affords cumulative pleasure. This "Shakespeare" tradition is very much alive, since I saw an expanded version of it in 1997.

Also popular these days is a form of word play close to riddling known as the spoonerism, for example,

> What is the difference between a nun and a girl in a bathtub?
> –The nun has hope in her soul.
>
> What's the difference between a chorus girl during the day and a chorus girl at night?
> – A chorus girl during the day is fair and buxom. (Dundes & Georges 1962:222.)

The question part of the riddle always begins with the opening formula "What's the difference between". The answer is just as innocent, until the initial sounds have been reversed. A spoonerism is a transposition usually of the initial sounds of two or more words. The point lies in the answer, and the listener must know what to do in order to share in the joke.

Waln K. Brown distinguishes the two processes that have to be executed in order to discern the ultimate answer. He gives as examples the riddles:

> What's the difference between a well stacked broad in the day and the same chick in the nighttime? – In the daytime she's fair and buxom.
>
> What's the difference between a skinny broad and a counterfeit dollar bill?
> – A counterfeit dollar bill is a phoney buck.

"First, certain letters must be transferred from word to word, thus: *f*air and *b*uxom, *ph*oney *b*uck. Second, the whole answer must be put into place: "In the daytime she's fair and buxom; in the nighttime she's bair and fuxom" and "A counterfeit dollar bill is a phoney buck; a skinny broad is a bony phuck." (Brown 1973:96)

On hearing the question the riddlee cannot know it is a play on words and is thus at the mercy of the riddler. But on grasping the answer to the first riddle, the experienced riddlee will have grasped the cognitive model and will know how to solve the next spoonerism. The popularity of the spoonerism depends on the structure of the language. It is very common in Finnish because of the balance between vowels and consonants.

The material I have presented here covers a time span of almost a hundred years. Obviously both the sexual imagery and the use of riddles have during this time changed many times over. The examples take us from one country to another, from town to country and from an agrarian milieu to urban lore, and the users of the riddles have been heterogeneous in the extreme. Sex, which was, judging from the descriptions, once both secret and forbidden, is now open to all in numerous different manifestations. But we so far know virtually nothing at all about the use of sexual lore among, for example, different social classes.

On the subject of love, or the emotions in general, riddles remain silent. This is a genre that, as regards the scale of emotions, gives frank expression to pure sensuality and sexuality. Sexual enlightenment and the oversupply of sex have not robbed the subject of its charm. A masterly double-entendre still has the power to amuse even if it is vulgar, but at the same time it reflects the attitudes of the community and the figures of speech assimilated by people in different communities. The coarseness of the metaphors depends on, for example, the time and the situational context. Something that may today appear obscene may not have been in its time. It nevertheless appears to be clear that the people made to look stupid were the women who tried to prevent sexual riddles from being asked. The concept of obscenity and suitability may also vary from one social group to another. Sexual jokes are perhaps also a means of weighing up different sexual charges and tones.

Sexual riddles both ancient and modern constitute easily recognisable semantic chains testing the listener by playing with words, while examination of sexual referents from different angles is a constant source of new variations. One thing all sexual riddles have in common, however: the right answer is always in a sense the wrong one.

# 5 The contexts and functions of riddles

Riddles are a genre of folklore which, by their language alone, seldom merge imperceptibly with the discourse in which they are embedded and almost always require a specific use and performing context: "It is the riddling process and the riddling occasion and the presence of riddlers that produce riddles..." (Abrahams 1972:188–189). The situation may at its simplest be framed by one child saying to another, "Let's ask riddles", and does not always require a decision proper. As one informant put it, "The first riddle would sort of slip out in connection with something, and this would lead someone to ask another one. And thus the game was in full swing." (SKS. Aino Hanhisalo AK 2:2.1966.) At other times the almost ritual start to a riddling situation may be announced by the opening formulae that either precede each riddle or merely mark the beginning of a new situation (Harries 1971:383). These event signals indicating the transition to riddling discourse vary from one culture to another. In, for example, the African riddling tradition "the game is generally characterized by its sometimes quite complex formality, but the individual riddle tends to be starkly economical in design . In Europe a similar opposition appears to prevail: while the game tends to be less formalized, with the players coming straight to the point in putting the challenge the individual riddle tends to show a more elaborate design." (Raa 1972:107.)

Unlike genres such as proverbs easily slipped into the discourse, riddles demand a special performing situation, one reason being that they are "aggressive in design and purpose" (Abrahams 1968:150). But the use of riddles may indeed carry other emotional charges: tension, joy, shame, triumph. A performing situation is further needed because the passive bystander and receiver has to get in the mood to become an active participant. The performing situation also helps the participants to switch from normal discourse to the special language of riddles. But sometimes a contemporary riddle may be slipped into an everyday conversation in the following manner: "Ten-year-old Anne overheard her mother discussing 'spare tyres' with a friend and asked, 'What form of exercise is most slimming?'. At this point both adults fell for the ruse. None of their answers about works-out in the gym were accepted, since the right answer was: A shake of the head at the meal table." (Lipponen 1995:209.)

We generally use the term "context" in specifying the dimensions of a situation. The linguists often divide the concept into two parts, speaking of (1) the situational context, which refers to the oral and performing situation and the listeners, and (2) the cotext or linguistic context which, in the case of a narrative, refers to its position in the discourse. (Brown & Yule 1983:35–50.) I nevertheless wish to divide the concept of context into several subconcepts. In dealing with tradition we must also examine a third context, (3) the cultural context, referring on the one hand to factors belonging to the tradition bearer's background, for instance his occupation, his educational background and other social factors, and on the other hand to the culture in which he operates and the world of which he is speaking. The term is of long standing, for it was already used by Bronislaw Malinowski in 1935 in speaking of situational context and cultural context. In examining context we must also remember the cognitive structures at the speaker's and the listener's command – what Terry Winograd (1981:250) calls "things like a 'topic structure' representing what the discourse is about, a 'script' that is being applied, and a 'focus list' of things recently mentioned or thought about". This fourth, (4) cognitive context is obviously even more difficult to isolate than the others, for example, the reasons for thematic variation in the course of riddling or the participants' chains of associations when there are several rival replies to a given image. Finally I wish to present a fifth, much less frequently used context, (5) the generic context, by which I mean the conformities characteristic of the genre. Cognitive (4) and generic contexts (5) come close to one another.

The generic context has so far received little attention. It nevertheless helps both riddler and riddlee to make a detailed note of the conformities characteristic of a genre, such as the formula peculiar to it. In the case of riddles, for example, the generic context determines the extent and the way the images deviate from "normal language" and the type of irrealistic image solutions that may ensue. The differences in the images are likewise clear in the case of riddle subgenres, such as true riddles and trick questions. The generic context also incorporates cultural knowledge of, for example, the limits to the variation in performance permissible for riddles. This context acts as an aid to the riddle inventor and guesser by providing conventions and models for analogy (for example, structural models, images, metaphors and clichés).

Riddles were, like other folklore, for a long time collected and studied as isolated texts, in many cases even so that the interaction between the image and the answer – and their presenters – was overlooked. This approach stressed the status of riddles as oral literature while completely forgetting the part they played in the interaction manifest as a game between two groups. David Evans (1976:170) insists that riddle sessions should be examined as entities. "The riddles must be analyzed not only in respect to the social and behavioral context in which they are told but also in respect to all the other riddles that are told at the session. The total number of riddles told and the order in which they are told constitute part of the context of any single riddle."

Riddles have in most cases been published without any contextual information whatsoever. There are, however, some exceptions. John C. Messenger Jr., for example, who conducted fieldwork among the Anang of southeastern Nigeria in 1951–1952, presents 19 Anang proverb riddles in an article and equips each one with information on the way it is most commonly used. One of them is the following:

> The spear was driven into the trunk of the coconut palm.
> - Hope is placed in the younger brother.

The writer explains the culture-specific metaphor as follows: "If a coconut palm is not bearing well, a worker of magic may recommend to the owner that a spear be driven into its trunk. This spear is treated by the specialist so that it possesses supernatural power capable of rejuvenating the tree. Just as the owner employs magic to increase his coconut yield, an eldest son in trouble always seeks the aid of his younger brother, who can be relied upon to lend support. Male siblings in an Anang family have close affectional bonds, and the eldest is held in special regard by his brothers. He is usually named *apkan* 'first-born', and his siblings honour him in various ways and obey his commands. In war brothers fight side by side and make every effort to protect the eldest from injury." Messenger describes the function and use of the proverb riddle as follows: this riddle "advocates mutual aid and cooperative endeavour among kin, and is used by parents to inculcate these attitudes in their children. One might use either of the proverbs making up the riddle when asking advice or a favour from a distant relative or friend." (Messenger 1960:227.)

On the other hand even the best accounts of riddling fail to give any information on what riddles were actually posed. It is, however, clear that the social context imposes and provides divergent levels ignored in analysing riddles only as texts (Johnson 1975:142). Extensive folkloristic fieldwork among riddling communities has provided research with a wealth of information on the use of this genre.

## *Riddling situations*

The social or situational context of riddling can first of all be divided into organised riddling sessions, which often also act as competitions. The riddle occasion can within this framework be analysed more precisely. In his informative article "Riddling: Occasion to Act" Thomas A. Burns divides riddling situations into six broadly different occasions (1976:143–145). The first consists of riddles appearing as one component in various rituals. Many researchers have made observations on riddling appearing during a wake (for example, Bhagwat 1943:37–38, Hart 1964:47–49, Abrahams 1983:272–276). As this riddling situation, common in certain cultures, is alien and fascinating to the Protestant point of view, let me quote the description of a situation given by Roger D. Abrahams. The wake taped and published by him was held in April 1966 in St. Vincent, which belongs to the English-speaking West Indies. The situation was, according to Abrahams, typical: "It was noisy, boisterous, full of constant jokes and passing of bottles in and out the windows. In the yard, groups were playing guitars and singing popular songs; others were playing dominos, others drinking. Occasionally a verbal fight broke out because cursing (calling someone's name inappropriately) had occurred – according to my notes, an especially dramatic exchange occurred this night." (Abrahams 1983:275). During this wake 82 riddles were posed, including discussion.

As an example, let us take riddle 12, which sparked off considerable debate. A new line is used for each speaker, and the abbreviation RDA stands for Roger D. Abrahams. The account begins with a two-line riddle:

> *Whitie, black inside whitie*
> *Whitie' 'pon top blackie and whitie come out.*
> (Laughter)
> The person there (pointing to RDA).
> Blackie.
> OK, finish.
> Inside whitie.
> That's when you put tobacco in a pipe.
> And you crack a matches, put it on top the tobacco in the pipe, and smoke comes out. /ER 564/
> Right?
> Haay.
> RDA: What is that one again?
> (Mumbling) /bringing riddler closer to microphone/
> Man, a speak over again.
> Come in forward.
> Make it right.
> Make it closer.
> Riddle.
> Riddle. /three or four voices/
> Hard for you to guess this, perhaps not.
> *Whities, blackie inside whitie;*
> *Whitie 'pon top blackie;*
> *And whitie come out.* (baby crying)
> That is when a fix tobacco in a pipe in a white pipe.
> And then is strike the matches and put it in on top, on top the tobacco.
> And then smoke, you know.
> Unhuuh. Right?
> Right.
> Riddle.
> Riddle.

The discussion includes repetition of parts of the image, guessing, and the proposal of an answer, which the riddler does not immediately accept, and finally the demand from the participants to hear the riddle again and the new answer, which the riddler now accepts. The calls for a riddle at the end are a sign that it is time for a new riddle.

The light-hearted mood of the situation described by Abrahams comes as something of a surprise, but then riddling is not part of a serious death rite – it is a way of killing time during the night vigil. Abrahams notes that "by the end of the riddling, the level of inebriation was quite high".

The other – less frequently encountered – riddle occasions registered by Burns are riddling within courting, riddling as an educational encounter between teacher and student, riddling upon meeting someone, and riddling which occurs in embedded form in other expressive genres, particularly narratives and songs. The use of riddles in a courtship situation is made understandable by the fact that the riddle answer seeks a means of associating two unrelated terms. "...the answer (relationship) is concealed and secret. Once the answer has been given (or, figuratively, the marriage solemnizing act performed), the two unrelated terms are related and the relationship is no longer secret. In this sense, riddles could serve as miniature models of marriage." (Dundes 1963:220.) (For the performance of riddles at weddings see page 106.)

The sixth and most common occasion for riddling is leisure time, which is also the most common and best-known situational context. Sometimes riddles are used in such situations as a kind of warm-up, for example, before storytelling (Abrahams 1983:272). But there are also reports of entire long riddling sessions.

## Incidental riddling

Let us take four examples to illustrate incidental leisure-time riddling. The aim of these long descriptions is to turn the focus on the riddler, the riddlee, and the tone and progress of riddling situations. The first is given by David Evans in his article "Riddling and the structure of context" (1976). Evans describes the outward setting and the atmosphere as follows: "The session took place after dark on August 20, 1973, on the front porch of a house in an all-black rural area near Como, Mississippi. The participants, besides the collectors, were six males: an older man in his sixties, a middle-aged man, two young men in their twenties, and two boys under ten. The two oldest men and one of the boys were related by marriage, while the others were neighbours. The young boys did not pose any riddles and tried to answer them mainly near the beginning and end of the session. My wife Cheryl and I answered three of the riddles but did not pose any, and most of the time Cheryl remained resting in our car parked in front of the porch, as it turned out that she was coming down with a cold. The situation was what Goldstein called an 'induced natural context'. I had earlier observed the older men posing riddles to children, and since children were present at the time of the session (which incidentally had begun as an interview with the older man), I asked him to pose some riddles to them. The session quickly took on its own character as others began to participate, and I was able to recede largely into the background, only indicating my continuing interest occasionally by trying to answer a riddle. Thirty-four riddles were told altogether at a rate of about one riddle per minute. If the riddle was not answered readily, the poser gave the answer, and he or someone else went on to pose the next riddle. There was no leader of the session, although the older man tended to dominate because of his greater familiarity with the verbal traditions of the community. There was no atmosphere of competition, nor was riddling considered an intellectual exercise. Wrong answers were not ridiculed. Instead, there was an air of relaxation and fun. Entertainment seemed to be the main purpose, and most of the riddle answers drew laughter or smiles. Consequently the participation of my wife and myself in answering three of the riddles could not have disrupted or altered the session in any way and, in fact, may even have added to the feeling of relaxation. All of the riddles would have been answered anyhow whether we had participated actively or not." (Evans 1976:171–172.)

This researcher's account of a riddling session which he himself initiated clearly indicates the course of events, the presence and participation of the local people and the relaxed atmosphere, which did not appear to carry any element of competition or tension. Evans' account is, however, not complete without the verbatim transcription of all 34 riddles, which shows just how much verbal exchange, deliberation and comment accompanied the riddles and their answers. The riddle section runs to 10 pages and is most definitely worth reading. The ease and speed with which the riddles were posed are astonishing. The account does indeed prove that the tradition documented by the Evanses was still in the active repertoire of its users.

To supplement the researcher's view I now wish to take three descriptions by Finnish tradition bearers of a riddling situation as they remember them. In 1966 the Folklore Archives of the Finnish Literature Society held a competition inquiry about riddles in order to swell its already very extensive collections. This was published as a periodical inquiry. The competition yielded not only some 30,000 riddle variants but also about 500 pages of descriptions of riddling situations. By the early 1960s riddling was no longer a folklore genre in active use among adults. As a result it has not been possible to record a single riddling occasion in Finland; by the time researchers' interest was aroused in this form of performance, it was no longer in active use. The situations described by those answering the inquiry occurred between the turn of the century and the 1920s, some even later, up to the 1950s. They are already the tradition of yesteryear in the sense that young people today chiefly pose riddles in brief episodes overlapping with other discourse or socialising. Above all the accounts are interesting recollections, not live reports.

My first illustration tells about a spontaneous situation that could arise at any time: (the narrator was born in 1909 and reckoned this happened in 1920). "...but the riddles were always asked while we were working, during meals, and especially in the evenings as we went about our chores, and if there were any smutty-mouthed old men in the farm kitchen. Then you would hear some really coarse riddles, and how the old men would laugh if they managed to make us youngsters blush and stutter out some answer to their riddles. And if you didn't know the answer, they found it all the more amusing when you had to be told. For example, 'Karvainen alta kahtoo, nilkkopäätä nieleksii. – Lampaan vuona.'/'The hairy one looks from under, slurps up bare-headed. – A lamb.' and 'Päivät riippuu yöks reikään pannaan.– Oven ruoppi, haka.'/ 'Hangs in the daytime, put in a hole for the night. – A door hook.' These were sure to make us blush." (SKS. Alli Korhonen AK 8:162.1966.) This account brings out the social gathering in the evenings, when the people of the house got together to do the handwork and repairs necessary in a self-sufficient household and to pass the time together. These situations were important to the transmission of all oral tradition, for monotonous work was made lighter by entertainment in the form of oral folklore.

Riddles also carried novelty value, and a newly-learnt riddle might be asked in the course of conversation with friends or at the beginning of a school lesson. Some situation might also suggest a riddle image that did not, however, lead to any further riddling. One informant in fact mentions that the riddle was used much as if it were a proverb: "I was a young girl and spinning wool. Maija Tuomiaho dropped in and said, 'Loikares polvella makaa, odottaa koska reikään pääsee.'/'A hairy thing lies on a thigh, looking to see when it can get in the hole.' I found this offensive, because it was so vulgar. I didn't take it as a riddle. My mother realised and said, 'There it is on your lap.'" (SKS. Helmi Mäkelä AK 12:467.1966.)

The next example also reports on a spontaneous meeting, but one which, it appears, frequently occurred when the young people met for a riddle session in a house in the village (the narrator was born in 1911 and dates the event as taking place in 1929):

> Even in the 1920s people still remembered rather a lot of riddles here at Lakaniemi in Vimpeli. They were familiar to people of all ages, old and young alike. Whenever several youngsters happened to congregate for an evening, it often happened that they threw out a few riddles in between the chat. Sometimes they would spend a whole evening asking riddles and seeking the answers. This was the case one Sunday evening in January 1929, at Matti Lehtoranta's, in other words at our house. I had banked the fire up with resinous stumps, and little by little the young people congregated round it, coming together by chance to pass the evening. First of all there was my sister Lilja, who was born in 1905, and my sister Saima, born in 1914. Then there was Bertta Uusitupa from next door. She first saw the light of day in 1913, and then there was the daughter of a neighbour a bit further away, Helvi Uusipaikka, of 1906 vintage. Since they were gathered round my fire, I acted the host for the time being. I was assisted in this by the boys: Toivo Harju, a 1907 man, and his brother Urho Harju, a slightly younger model, 1909. Toivo Hokkala represented the year following the General Strike, which is why he once said the strike was not altogether complete. On this occasion he explained he was a bit of a witch because he was born with a tooth in his mouth. Then bringing up the rear was a little cobbler called Matti Takala, the same vintage as me, in other words 1911. It must have been around half past seven in the evening when the company as I have described it gathered around the cheerfully burning fire.

Youth work of different kinds was a major topic of conversation among young people at that time, and we again got talking on this theme. My father was a great man for books, and while we argued our own affairs he sat in his own room studying "The Philosopher's Stone". For some reason or another, he had begun to ponder over the size value of two words, because as he went out, he asked us: "Kumpi on suurempi sana, ei vai kyllä?"/ "Which word is bigger, no or yes?" Well now, that was quite a tricky question for us. We reckoned they were both as big as each other, because they are opposites and they can both cancel each other out. When father came back inside, he asked: "What conclusion have you come to?" Toivo Harju replied: "We decided they are of equal value." Father appeared to take it all with a touch of humour and explained with a contented smile: "If you ask me, an affirmation is always pleasanter than a negation, and because we should try to be as little edgy with one another as possible, I reckon yes is bigger than an abrupt no."

The initial impetus had thus been given for various deliberations, and the conversation turned to riddles and finding the answers to them. The first question was put by Urho Harju: "Mikä se on joka eläviä kantoi eläissään, kuolleita kantoi kuoltuaan ja elävien päällä kulki?"/"It carried the living while it was alive, it carried the dead after its death and it moved across the living. What is it?" The question was addressed to all those present, as always. Anyone could suggest an answer. If the answer was wrong, the whole group went on thinking, including the person who had already answered. The girls could not be bothered to think for long. If the right answer took too long in coming, they answered just anything, knowing it would be wrong. Bertta Uusitupa gave at least two wrong answers to the question posed by Harju. She was a girl who easily laughed, and she accompanied her wrong answers with a hearty laugh, and because the answer was so crazy, everyone invariably joined in. And it so happened that we couldn't find the right answer at all, so Harju had to answer himself. "It's a pine, used to make a boat. When it was dead it was made into a boat for carrying dead fish, and the boat was rowed over living fish." Joking and laughing, we criticised this riddle, and I for my part said: "What a long, complicated explanation! No wonder we didn't guess it." To which Hokkala added: "Oh we're good guessers alright, but even we have our limits." I tried to explain that riddles should be short and pithy, like "Ottaa niin enenee, pannaan niin vähenee. – Lakeistukko. Kun se otetaan räppänästä pois, niin valo saunassa enenee, kun se pannaan räppänään, valo vähenee."/"Take away, it increases, put back, it decreases." In reply I got the correct answer and explanation: "The cloth covering the smoke hole in the sauna. When you take it away, more light comes into the sauna, when you put it back, there is less light." I don't remember exactly whether anyone guessed this, or whether Toivo Harju knew it already.

Lots of questions were asked; here are a few examples. One of the riddles asked by Lilja Lehtoranta was: "Yksi leipä kaksi varrasta, muori vetää vaarin parrasta. – Se on rukki."/"One loaf, two drying poles, Grandma pulls Grandpa by the beard. – It's a spinning wheel." Helvi Uusipaikka asked: "Mikä se on semmoinen elukka, jolla on silmät korvissa ja kylkiluut nahan päällä."/ "What is an animal that has eyes in its ears and its ribs on top of its skin?" I remember Matti Takala asking: "Mies nurkassa, topelo kourassa, mikäs se on?"/"A man in the corner, a peg in his fist, what is it?".

At which Toivo Harju said, "I reckon it's Matti Takala". This caused a good deal of merriment. There was of course a right answer too: a barrel of ale with taps.

I think I asked more riddles than anyone else. Toivo Harju and Lilja Lehtoranta also asked lots, though towards the end of the session Lilja withdrew, began making the coffee and setting the table. My father even joined in for a minute, throwing out a couple of riddles, such as: "Elävä arkku, heiluva hauta, puolikuollut ruumis sisässä"/"A living coffin, a rocking grave, a halfdead body inside." And another: "On miehen nimi vakaa, pyöreä edestä ja takaa, keskellä kaksi hakaa."/"The man's name is steadfast, round in front and behind, two hooks in the centre." The answer to the former is "Jonah inside the whale" and to the latter "Otto". My father knew a lot of riddles, and he was one of the few who made them up himself. In this respect I have carried on his tradition a bit. The following will show you what I mean. "Tonkero pihassa seisoo, kelo nokassa makaa, ketkutin kelon nokassa."/"A post standing in the yard, a log lying on its nose, a dingdong on the log's nose." That's how I see a well winch. Another one: "Nostin reittä neljä kertaa, naputin kuputin joka kerta."/"Four times I raised my thigh, every time I tapped and rapped." That's a horse being shod, as I see it. No "improper" riddles were ever asked, and for two reasons. No one would have dared pose them in such a large company, with both men and women present. What is more, no one knew any riddles hinting at sex. This meant that children were usually asked the same riddles as adults. In those days no one could see anything wrong in riddles. "Which would you rather" riddles were, and still are, more or less unknown here. I've only ever heard a single one like that. On this riddling occasion not one like that was asked, they were just the ordinary old-fashioned riddles. We had learnt most of them at primary school under our teacher Oskari Harju, and the rest from older villagers and the day labourers who travelled from village to village.

At around half past nine Lilja served us coffee, and while we drank it the talk moved on to other subjects. We then sat on for a while by the glowing fire, joking and each boasting a bit about how clever we had been in solving the riddles.

We didn't actually keep any record of who guessed the answers and who didn't. No one was praised, to say nothing of a prize. But no one was criticised either along the usual lines, and we all joined in as best we could and as we saw fit, to counteract any bragging. In between the riddling there was lots of free, light-hearted ragging. This was not only the cause of laughter, you simply could not help laughing a lot. The guests departed in high spirits at around 10 p.m.--- (SKS. Eino Lehtoranta AK 10:407.1966.)

This account undoubtedly draws on memories of several riddling occasions. Although it cannot be a fully authentic analysis of a single situation, it admirably brings out the elements of group riddling. We learn how the riddling fitted into the rest of the discourse, the people present and what they were good at, the frequency of riddling in Finland in the 1920s, the way the session proceeded as people had fun untainted by rivalry and debated the answers, and an account of how some of the participants might think up their own riddles.

These accounts do throw some light on riddle occasions as a versatile form of interaction. They tell about not only the mood of the occasion and the people present, but also about the role games and status of the riddlers and riddlees. Various ways of finding the answer are revealed: deliberation, guessing, and knowing the answer in advance. We also get an insight into how a riddle should be, the process of learning and making riddles. The mood of the accounts differs greatly from that of the boisterous wake described by Abrahams, but as far as the game itself is concerned, the Finnish occasions have something in common with the St. Vincent riddling: "...in the riddling sessions riddles were propounded not only to be solved but also to be discussed, argued about, laughed over, and sometimes dismissed" (Abrahams 1983:276).

## *The traditional contexts and users of sexual riddles*

Although the archive records usually lack information on the contexts of folklore, we do know something about the contexts in which traditional sexual riddles were used in Finland. Among groups of young people this lore has always clearly served the function of raising the erotic temperature. In the farming community there were some jobs done by the young people of the village together, and these situations provided a setting for the transmission of oral tradition. V.E.V. Wessman (1949:VII) described the verbal merrymaking of a Finnish working community as follows:

> In the autumn the malt was sweetened in a malt sauna and spirits were brewed. Usually the work was done by the young girls from the farm. It was a laborious job, because it had to be watched over day and night. The time nevertheless passed quickly, because as soon as the boys caught a whiff of the malt, they sought out the girls and helped them pass the time by dreaming up all sorts of pranks. One popular entertainment was posing riddles for the girls to answer. And the boys were indeed sharp: for many riddles lead one's thoughts to something that would make a girl blush and giggle, whereas the object to be guessed might well be something as innocent as a tobacco pipe or a spoon, or such legitimate pursuits as weaving, spinning or father eating lingonberry porridge out of a bowl in mother's lap. Other riddles were less "risky".

The posing of sexual riddles was particularly popular among men. Often it was a way of cultivating the tradition of both the sex and the occupational group, as the following description illustrates:

> Nowadays riddling sessions are also held while the men take a break for a cigarette or at other free moments and in the living quarters. The riddles thrown out are seldom the old traditional ones of the Finnish people. Instead the popular ones are those criticised as being vulgar and obscene, such as "Mitä yhteistä on naisella ja kitaralla? – Molempia plimputetaan läven kohdalta."/"What do a woman and a guitar have in common? – Both are fingered at the hole". (SKS. Olavi Mäkelä AK 12:64.1966.)

It seems that the performing of sexual lore is often less inhibited among people of the same sex and it strengthens the group's cohesion (Virtanen 1988:215). It is also possible that men and women used riddles for different purposes. Transferring our thoughts from a Finnish milieu to the Spanish village of Monteros, we clearly see that riddles have a distribution that divides the populace by class as well as sex. "Riddles show themselves to be a popular form of spontaneous verbal entertainment among men and women of the working class and women of the elite. There is a definite tendency for working-class men to tell riddles more than any other single group and for male members of the upper class virtually to refrain from riddling at all. There is a moderate amount of riddling among women of all social ranks, though, as I have said, it is more common among elite women." (Brandes 1980:128)

Sexual riddles are the single most common riddle type that has come to be known in Monteros. Both men and women know and tell pretended obscene riddles. The content of the riddle nevertheless determines who tell them: men tend to tell riddles evoking male physical attributes, while women tell those concerning the female anatomy. Both genders may pose riddles suggesting copulation. Examples of riddles posed by men are:

> By day hung, by night pressed tight.
> – The crossbar of a door. (cf. ER 1744a, FR 843)
>
> I put it in red and I take it out red. – The pepper.

Examples of women's riddles are:

> I went down to the market, I bought a young girl, I raised her skirt, And I saw her thing. – A head of lettuce / compared here to a young girl; the outer leaves are the skirt/.
>
> A chap came: He put it in me, He removed it from me; Ask God that He do well by me. – A male nurse giving an injection. (Brandes 1980:133–135.)

The occasion on which women, too, may freely participate in the posing of such riddles is the olive harvest important to the village community. Otherwise women – and Brandes underlines "especially elite women – merely use this folkloristic device as a means of expressing otherwise taboo desires and concepts while safely keeping this slight degree of licentiousness within the secret confines of their homes". The handling of sexual motifs is normally to be avoided between unrelated men and women in Monteros. Pretended obscene riddles give men a chance "to expose their genitals verbally and to evoke images of the sexual act in the presence of women whom they covet but cannot otherwise take." (Brandes 1980:133-136.) Brandes refers to Sigmund Freud's analysis of "smut" (i.e. obscenity) in humour. Freud (1960:97) writes, among other things: "... smut is directed to a particular person, by whom one is sexually excited and who, on hearing it, is expected to become aware of the speaker's excitement and as a result to become sexually excited in turn..." Brandes sees in Freud's analysis an explanation for why men and women cultivate sexual riddles as "a subtle means of displaying their own sexual organs".

The performance of sexual riddles has been regarded as a means of wielding male power. But maybe women have power, too, at least power to tease men. Inger Lövkrona (1991:277) conjectures – though she does not have any descriptions of situations at her disposal – that women in a farming community, where there was strict demarcation between men's and women's jobs, might tease men encroaching on their territory. As a tool they might use sexual riddles with images in which the male organ acquires endearing, humorous and provocative names.

Some Finnish folklore collectors mention that women were in the habit of interrupting a game or changed the topic of conversation as soon as anyone began asking sexual riddles.

> ---I remember the women would not let some riddle be asked to the end but put a stop to it and interrupted so that it never got asked. (SKS. Aino Hanhisalo AK 2:2.1966.)

Women's chastity is also underlined:

> The farm hands and day labourers were bolder at asking more obscene ones, whereas the mothers and serving girls were more respectable. (SKS. Olga Hirvonen AK 3:369.1966.)

This information on the use of riddles dates from the extensive collection of Finnish riddles made in 1966 and throws light on the situation in the early decades of the 20th century. But are the details of women's attitudes necessarily as straightforward as this? Where was the limit to the presentation of sexual lore? Let us take a look at this question in the light of Finnish and Swedish folklore.

It comes as something of a surprise on examining the answers to sexual riddles (*Virtanen et al. 1977*) to find that a considerable proportion of them concentrate on the women's domain of life and work on the farm. 40 per cent of the answers to sexual riddles refer to the woman's domain on the farm, and only 15 per cent to the men's domain. 45 per cent are to do with the agrarian way of life in general and are sexually neutral. The corresponding figures for all Finnish riddles are, by way of comparison, 24, 23 and 53 per cent, respectively. Sexual riddles thus clearly point to women's work (cf. also Lövkrona 1991), but the same cannot be said of non-erotic ones. Could the reason for this be that women were considered the target for sexual riddles and sexual implications were hidden in the images familiar to them?

The invention of a riddle begins with the answer, for which an image is devised as a means of circumlocution (cf. also Aarne 1917:8). Does the fact that the answers to sexual riddles clearly tie in with the women's domain mean that the inventors and users of riddles were – contrary to what has been claimed above – for the most part women? To my mind we still have too little information to permit a conclusive answer.

But why do the descriptions of situations so often stress that the women objected to sexual riddles? This may be a case of a late change in attitude. V.E.V. Wessman notes in the foreword to his publication of riddles:

> Women are just as daring as men at asking "improper" riddles. Even young girls may, though sometimes giggling and blushing, pose riddles with a double meaning, or turn their faces away as they hand in a paper bearing a suggestive text. (Wessman 1949:VIII.)

This is also the impression created by the puritanical general view of the role of women given in the descriptions submitted for the collection project in 1966.

The sexual folk tradition is not confined to riddles alone and ranges from shanty-like songs sung by men to make their work easier to outspoken or erotic sexual sayings familiar to both genders, anecdotes and folktales, and the songs rattled off by young people to accompany dancing. Mixed groups of adults have from time immemorial cultivated open and risqué sexual humour, so why not sexual riddles too, which, being ambiguous, are far more exciting? We do, however, have very few descriptions and facts about what people talked about when they got together and the type of language permissible on a given occasion.

It is worth remembering in assessing the moral attitudes reflected in the descriptions produced in the early decades of last century that this was the period at which public enlightenment of all sorts – elementary schooling, the workers' movement, the youth association movement, the temperance movement, the farmers' associations, the country women's associations and many others – were, at least in the western countries, not only enlightening the people but also cleaning up their language and morals.

There were in many communities clear limits to the use of sexual lore that could not be exceeded. It seems to have been very common for sexual riddles to be banned when there were children present.

The limits to the use of sexual lore depend very much on the culture and are often influenced by, for example, religion, the position of women in the community, and on whether sex is regarded as a favourable resource or as a threat to beware of by imposing restrictions. Sexual insinuation may in some cultures be a natural part of everyday discourse. In for example, the Philippines such talk is not considered vulgar or obscene but as reflecting "an amiable attitude that puts normal sexual behaviour on the same level as other pleasant activities such as scratching and yawning" (Hart 1964:139). Riddle games can also be directly related to sexual socialisation, as among the Quechua-speakers of Peru. This reveals a direct correlation between the search for one's sexual identity and the creative manipulation of metaphors in riddles, insults, and songs. The young person skilled in the use of these traditional genres is considered more intelligent than the one who is not. Someone who is innovative with riddles, insults, and songs is also believed to be a good sexual partner. Unlike in western pre-industrial communities, the children there are also familiar with sexual metaphors even though they are too young to engage in sexual relations. (Isbell & Fernandez 1977:22–25.)

The performance of sexual riddles is, however, as a rule confined either to set situations or to groups of the same age or gender. For example, in the British West Indies sexual lore is an integral part of funeral rituals, the aim being to stress at a time of crisis that the living emerges from the dead. All can take part in the wake, so sexual lore is not restricted there to any particular group. (Abrahams 1968:155-156.) But among the Venda of Africa, for example, young people only asked sexual riddles among their friends, and never in the hearing of adults (Blacking 1961).

## *Riddle contests and organised games*

There are in both the oral and the literary traditions numerous accounts of riddling competitions and even strife (for example, Potter 1950:940-941). In some cultures, as in Hawaii, folktales transmit information on the old competition tradition (Beckwith 1992).

One of the most famous ones is the riddle of the Sphinx, which tells about a competition in which there were no spectators but the riddlee's life was at stake. This story about the Sphinx and Oedipus was already mentioned in an ancient Boeotian myth. (cf. Chapter 1)

The riddle of the Sphinx is one of a set of three thought originally to have belonged to the Oedipus story. The solving of a series of tasks such as this is most often placed in a narrative that culminates in the hero winning himself a bride. Both the Sphinx and the riddles are considered to be of secondary importance in the legend telling of the life of Oedipus, because the crucial point is not the winning of the bride but the tragic events that follow their union. But the riddle, representing man at different stages in his life, has spread all over the world. (Edmunds 1984:147-173.)

There are also reports of the losing contestant committing suicide or of death by way of punishment in the history of, for example, the Indian riddling tradition (Bhagwat 1943:10-11). Field experiences in different cultures have proved to scholars that competition is at times an element completely unknown in riddling, while in other cultures an image and anticipation of the right answer spur the riddling participants on to a natural battle for supremacy (for example, Başgöz 1965). The practices and rules of this competition are as varied as the contestants themselves. In his article Thomas A. Burns puts together the jigsaw puzzle of different practices. The initial impetus is provided by an event signal during which people are asked whether they wish to take part in the riddling according to the prescribed rules. The proposal then proceeds to the competition itself by organising the personnel and assigning the roles. The contestants are divided into teams, their status is confirmed and the roles of riddler, riddlee and audience are handed out. Strategic rules are applied to decide, for example, the riddles to be asked, the order in which they are to be presented, and the winner of the competition. The cultural differences are considerable on this score, since the competition may be won by the person or side that has the greatest stock of riddles to propose, or in another culture by the side able to supply the most answers, or then by the person or side able to answer the most difficult riddles.

Rules of interaction are called in to agree the sequencing of questions and answers. Cultural differences are also in evidence in, for example, whether any member of the team can propose or answer a riddle, or whether the riddle is put to a particular riddlee or the entire team. Burns distinguishes eight different sequencing patterns representing alternative forms of interaction between the riddlers and riddlees in his background material representing different cultures. The process of interaction may include retention of the answer until the riddlee guesses it, or "buying" the answer from the rival team. Buying may in some cases even be the only acceptable means of getting out of a tricky situation. When the rival team finds itself in a fix, the teams may either exchange answers, or the buying side may supply an answer to the riddle that previously stumped its opponents. The contest always ends with some degree of evaluation; this may be explicit or implicit, formal or informal. Formal closure seems to be virtually unknown. (Burns 1976:147–153.)

There are virtually no reports of organised competitions in the Western riddling tradition; this is endorsed by the source material used by Burns, which is predominantly African. Yet in Europe and America, too, riddling has sometimes acquired the nature of a competition, and the poor guesser has been derided and even punished, as in Finland (see below).

Competition may also be a natural part of a broader ritual entity, as at Turkish weddings, where riddling is an important part of the marriage celebration.

> In some places, a group of villagers visit the house or village of the bride on the last day of the marriage celebration in order to bring her to the groom's house. If the bride and the groom are from different villages, the traditional flag bearers participate in the visit. When the groom's party reaches the bride's village, they do not enter, but rather they stop and wait outside the village. Then a group of people representing the bride's side advance toward them with a flag bearer. When the two groups meet, the flag bearers of the two sides advance a little, raise their flags, and stand face-to-face in the middle of the two rows. After some traditional flag prayers, the flag bearer on the bride's side proposes a riddle to the other. It is customary that the bride's flag bearer propose the first riddle, with the other answering in turn. The flag bearers go on giving traditional questions and riddles to each other, in turn, until one of them fails. The loser offers his flag to the winner and takes his place on the winner's left side during the festival. Taking the left side and losing the flag is a shame not only for the flag bearer but also for the community. The villagers offer money or domestic animals in order to have their flag returned. If the flag is not taken back, the losing side has no right to suggest anything or object to any arrangement that the winners decree in the course of the festivities. (Başgöz 1965:136–137.)

Winning the competition adds to the elation at the wedding feast, while defeat casts a shadow over the loser and his supporters. One would assume that the contest began with riddles familiar to both in ritual manner, but that as it continued, the riddlee's skills were really put to the test.

The loser's lot is never a happy one. Often he has to swallow a ritual humiliation. In the Hindi tradition an unsuccessful riddlee is mockingly asked, "Done your best?" or "Had enough?", if he is forced to admit his ignorance. But the riddler who wants to enjoy his victory may continue the humiliation by asking, "Did you lie down in dog excrement?". Not until the riddlee answers in the affirmative is he told the answer to the riddle. (Dundes & Batuk 1974:91.)

One cannot help asking oneself on reading these accounts why people allowed themselves to be made to look foolish in this way. The reason has to do partly with ritual behaviour, as in the above account of the wedding, partly with the alternation of victory and defeat which presumably helped the riddlee to accept the situation, because he knew that next time he might be the winner.

It will remain for future research to decide whether the answers in the cultures favouring competition really were guessed, or whether they were already known. Kenneth Goldstein (1963:334) points out that the potential for competition simply runs out because the listeners know all the answers. "The contest can then continue in one or both of two possible ways: by changing the audience, or by the introduction of new riddles."

Thinking up new riddles is by no means an easy task, but the inventive riddler may solve the problem by drawing on his general knowledge of tradition. The following account from Turkey by İlhan Başgöz (1972:662–663) gives an excellent impression both of the multiple pressures in the competition situation and the clever way in which a riddler may gain mastery of the situation.

> In the summer of 1970, I witnessed such a riddling session in Mahmut Aga's tent, high in the Taurus Mountains, where a proverb was transformed into a riddle. When we, Mahmut Aga, his three daughters, aged 14, 16, and 19, and myself and a visitor, Cerrah Hüseyin, gathered in a tent one evening, I initiated a riddle contest. Cerrah Hüseyin is a very well known figure in the area. He is a good drum player, anecdote teller, singer, and accepted by the people as a real expert of folk literature. Cerrah Hüseyin and I, Mahmut Aga and his three young daughters formed two teams to tell riddles. I did not participate much, so it actually became a contest between the Mahmut Aga family and the foreign visitor, Cerrah Hüseyin. The girls were very good in giving and solving the riddles, and soon the riddling turned into a real challenge between Cerrah Hüseyin and the three young girls, male versus female, youth versus middle-age, family pride versus a foreigner. The girls, who defended not only the pride of their family but also their ability, gave a very difficult time to Cerràh Hüseyin, who also wanted to defend the superiority of his sex in a male dominated society and prove to me that his reputation was deserved. However, when he finally understood that he could not possibly beat these girls by asking traditional riddles – because they managed to solve all of them – he came out with an unheard one. It was, "It dresses badly, but it is seen beautifully. – Black tent."

The girls failed to guess it, and Cerrah Hüseyin saves his fame and his pride. The following day I questioned him about the riddle. He confessed that it was created on the spot by transforming a proverb. Otherwise, he said, "The people of the seven districts would have laughed at me as a loser to the girls."

The possible defeat and the fear of the shame it would bring on him culminates in this account in the riddler transgressing the borders between the genres of tradition (cf. Chapter 1). A riddler needs to be smart to win when he comes up against the borders of his own repertoire.

"Invented riddles" have presumably been used in the majority of communities to give riddling a touch of excitement. The smallness and permanence of communities nevertheless posed their own restrictions, since new listeners were rare. Despite this, riddling has continued to be popular because of its other functions.

Samson's riddle was an unsolved enigma to all but those initiated in its mysteries. According to the frame story the riddle of the Sphinx was, by contrast, a test of wits or mental agility. Whatever the relationship between the image and the answer in the culture in question, the competition was not from the researcher's point of view an intellectual exercise: "The person who does not know the riddle answer is neither expected nor encouraged to find it" (Haring 1974:202, cf. Blacking 1961:5).

Various tests of mental agility are highly popular on television today. Programme formats are even passed on from one country to another, and with figures in the public eye as their presenters or contestants, their success is guaranteed. One of the permanent favourites on Finnish television is a programme launched by the Finnish producer Spede Pasanen that has been running ever since the mid-1980s. Called Kymppitonni (Ten Grand, referring to the sum of money which the successful candidate stands to win), it exploits a riddling-like situation in which the presenter calls on each of the five contestants in turn to ask a question which the others must answer. The contestants sit in booths and cannot see the answer propped up by the person asking the question for the audience to see. Nor can they hear the other contestants' answers. A fictive sum is added to their account for a correct answer or deducted for a false one.

Seppo Knuuttila has analysed the way the programme works, the questions and answers. "I happened to watch it in the company of children, who joined whole-heartedly in the game. Once, when they got particularly carried away by the correct answers, it suddenly occurred to me that I was witnessing a Finnish riddling situation both modern and primitive, watching something on television that I thought was extinct." (Knuuttila 2000:261.) The folklorist in Knuuttila having been aroused, he taped a couple of dozen programmes and analysed the process involved.

In this particular programme, the contestants are, before the start of the game, given words or answers to which they have to make up questions. Having analysed some four-hundred questions, Knuuttila could pick out a recurring device of giving two clues in parallel (A is B but also C; for example, "You can eat it, but you can also go to work on it = an egg"); over the years this was to become an out-and-out mannerism (Knuuttila 2000:266). This is how formulae are generated in folklore, too, according to popular models. The questions also featured a high incidence of references to crystallised expressions (song lyrics, slogans, etc.) and proverbs, such as "It will out = the truth". Among the material there were ten "riddles" that had an obvious link with a proverb, such as "It praises its doer = work" (cf. the Finnish proverb "Työ tekijäänsä kiittää."/"The job praises its doer = work"/ English equivalent of "The workman is known by his work."), or "You cannot set this alight, however hard you try, it will not burn even in a fire = truth" (cf. the Finnish proverb "Totuus ei pala tulessakaan."/"The truth does not burn even in fire."). All the contestants guessed "work", but somewhat surprisingly, none of them guessed "truth". (Knuuttila 2000:267–268.) Some of the answers call for knowledge of some special field (cf. the wisdom question, Chapter 3), and as many researchers have pointed out, the riddler and riddlee must share the same culture for the game to be successful. Some of the questions in the TV programme would have been incomprehensible to anyone from outside the culture. This has also happened to the early true riddles tradition.

Seppo Knuuttila is right in stressing that the joy of spotting the clue to the answer and the humour inherent in the programme (which is, incidentally, completely free of smutty jokes with double meanings) are what have made it so popular for so long (Knuuttila 2000:269). Another factor contributing to the popularity of the programme is the opportunity it affords to criticise the well-known people chosen to take part (such as actors, sportsmen, politicians and stars from the world of entertainment) and laugh at their stupidity. And since the competition generally involves either honour or humiliation, the programme gives the best contestants a chance to win an extra bonus which they can donate to a charity of their choice. The bitterness of defeat is also evident, "because those who give the wrong answer seem quite genuine in groaning and sighing when they hear the right answer: 'Oh I should have guessed that!'" (Knuuttila 2000:263).

## *Riddles as part of their context*

Riddles appear from a text-oriented perspective to be a genre which, compared with, say, the narrative tradition, is little affected by the situational and linguistic context. But are things really so straightforward? We have only a few accounts by researchers of entire riddling sessions (Jones & Haves 1972, Roberts 1974, Evans 1976, Abrahams 1983), but their message is clear. In the context in which they are performed riddles fall into groups that either belong together thematically (Reeder 1981:231) or that resemble one another in structure. We know, for example, that in the Udmurt tradition riddles progressed from the familiar to the less familiar: in the first riddles the referent was a human being, then his limbs and actions; next came the house and the objects inside it, followed by the yard, the kitchen garden, the fields and forest (Gerd 1928:395). There are clear thematic links between riddle sections. Sometimes the session begins with neck riddles, arithmetic problems, or biblical questions, and the riddles that follow will usually be of the same kind (Goldstein 1963:332). The participants in the riddling might in Hawaii be expected to possess the ability "to compare a similar riddle which may parallel the first as exactly as possible and present an equally striking analogy" (Beckwith 1922:327). Roger D. Abrahams, drawing on material from St. Vincent, writes: "...one of the principles operating in the riddling session was that one riddle will sometimes suggest another; this suggestion can result from a framing element, from a method of description, from a technique of making the answer difficult --- or simply from the subject" (Abrahams 1983:275). Every riddle seems to have its own specific place: "The choice of riddles to be posed is not a random one, but instead each riddle ideally fulfils a function of helping to build a structural pattern for the session" (Evans 1976:181–184). This statement is supported by a description of the Finnish tradition milieu in which riddles are asked in thematic chains. The narrator was born in 1922 and dates the event at around the mid-1930s: "As a rule the riddlers began with some familiar theme, such as objects and people in the room, animals, vermin, utensils and things like that, and then gradually went on to more difficult, less familiar things like nature, the forests and lakes and the creatures in them. It would go so that one riddle would soon lead to another, and especially riddles designed to mislead that were reminiscent of some previous object mentioned but which actually meant something quite different." This account proves that the riddlees thought of the riddling as discourse that could continue for some time, not stopping at single riddles.

The schoolchildren of today still tell elephant jokes and modern crazy riddles in thematically connected series. John Holmes McDowell describes in his book *Children's Riddling* two riddling sessions to illustrate how a thematic chain may be continued once it has gained momentum. The following sequence is from a session in the course of which a trio of Chicano children aged six through eight elaborate a taxonomy of locomotion:

>What has eight wheels and rolls? – Roller skates.
>What has two wheels and pedals? – A bicycle.
>What has four wheels, no pedals, and a steering wheel? – A car.
>What has four legs and can run? – A mustang.
>What has three wheels and pedals? – A tricycle.
>What has four legs and can't walk? – A chair
>What has two legs, it can walk? – A monkey.
>What has long legs and it's hard to walk? – A seagull.
>What has two seats, four wheels, and they can roll? – A car.
>What has lots of windows and they can fly? – An airplane.
>What are those little clocks and it's in your car? – A dragger.
>(McDowell 1979:135–146.)

Riddling discourse may thus consist of thematic entities in the way familiar to us from oral narrative. The series of questions demonstrates the way children play with variation on a single image, such as "what has wheels" or "what has legs", until it has been exhausted. At the end of the series the riddlees try to set a new chain in motion, but the imagery of the last two riddles is presumably so different from what has gone before that for some reason or another in does not inspire them to continue.

The part played by cultural context is particularly significant in the cognitive process of riddles. The ambiguity inherent in riddles may be so empirical and culture-specific that it remains a closed book to the outsider. People who share the same culture perceive shapes, forms and actions in the same way. Whereas outsiders, who "do not partake in common experiences and do not form symbols from the same substance, would not be able to relate these riddles in any meaningful way" (Ben-Amos 1976:253–254). The following riddle from the Sandawe tribe of East Africa serves as a good example:

> Challenge: Degerata /hía ! 'war'kaka ts'exsu.
> Reply: Pháló.
> Challenge: In the *degera*-bush the dwarf-antelope has but one jaw.
> Reply: A woodcarving knife.

It is impossible to understand this riddle without Eric Ten Raa's (1972:98–99) explanation: "The Sandawe have two special carving knives, the *xorúts'ima* and the *phálo*. The blade of the former is bent around so that it forms a closed loop; this implement is used for carving out hollow shapes like wooden bowls. The latter is a knife with an elegantly curved blade which is not bent sideways but which looks straight when seen from above. The dwarf antelope or dikdik is a common animal which likes to seek refuge from its predators in thorny *degera* bushes, and most Sandawe children have seen its bleached lower jaws in areas covered with the bush; the two halves of the jaw are usually separated from each other. Such a single jawbone resembles the *phálo*: the U-shape of a complete jaw would bear a closer resemblance to the *xorúts'ima*."

Sometimes it is possible to show how a riddle can derive its entertainment value from local events, or from local geographical features. Local people's peculiarities are also potential material (Raa 1972:98). An image of this type may be incomprehensible both to the outsider and to other members of the riddling community. But the accounts covering an entire riddling situation indicate that each riddle and its answer is framed by lively debate of the metaphor and its possible solutions. The researcher investigating the relationship between image and answer has to seek the opinion of many tradition bearers in trying to decipher the code. For example, the article "Riddles from Ceylon" by Gwladys Hughes Simon (1955) based on a long period spent in the field proves just how much detailed information the researcher can if he or she wishes acquire with the help of a good local guide. When the answer to a riddle is, for example, a kitul palm, Hughes Simon reports in detail what stimulants can be obtained from this sugar palm, and how. The researcher cannot understand the relation of the image to the answer until he commands the cultural knowledge shared by those participating in the riddling.

Riddles may in the course of time also get blunted once their users no longer have any living contact with the culture producing them. This has been the case with many riddles containing mythological names. Appearing in the misleading image elements of Finnish riddles are mythical beings which lost their meaning among riddlers long ago. The two Finnish hidden images in the universal riddle about the sun and the moon serve as a good example:

> Kaks turjan lappalaista yhtä latuva hiihtää. – Kuu ja aurinko.
> Two Turja Lapps ski the same track. – The sun and moon.
> (FR 255, cf. ER 1001)
> Or:
> Kaksi maan haltiata hiihtelevät yhtä latua myöten.
> – Two earth spirits skiing along the same track. (Kuusi 1956:181–182)

The riddlee is effectively confused by having his attention called to the earth spirits and the Turja Lapps, which had, by this time, become unfamiliar figures. These riddles also demonstrate how the creation of a riddle can sometimes be stimulated by a metaphor or line for which a suitable answer is sought (cf. the section on the relationship between image and answer in Chapter 2).

Riddle scholars usually concentrate on certain characteristics of the genre and do not try to create an overall picture of riddles, their users, the meanings and life of the genre. Even more seldom do they analyse the nature of the community or culture using the riddles. An interesting theoretical experiment is the article by John M. Roberts and Michael L. Forman of 1971, in which they try to correlate riddles with types of society. As their starting point they used cross-cultural information from *Human Relations Area Files* and deepened their research with two closer analyses of riddling in Tagalog culture and among young American students. As a result, they discovered certain characteristics that were common to cultures favouring riddles: "--- riddling is associated with strong responsibility training, large domestic animals, rote learning, high political integration, more than one level of jurisdictional hierarchy beyond the local community, oaths, ordeals, and games of strategy" (Roberts & Forman 1971:516). It is not, unfortunately, clear from the article why precisely these characteristics correlate with the use of riddles. One of the significant factors seems to be responsibility training, by which a child is gradually initiated into tasks suitable to him and through this the maintenance of a complex society. Riddles are in turn related to this training. High responsibility training also contributes to an individual's caring about his performance in oral interrogation situations. Many of the questions raised call for further research, such as the information on the American material according to which "the conundrum, in contrast to other riddles, has appeal for respondents with high approach low avoidance attitudes toward oral interrogation and with a slight preference for games of physical skill ---" (Roberts & Forman 1971:526).

The weak point in Roberts' and Forman's research is the *HRAF* material, which is clearly of an arbitrary nature. For many riddle-using cultures are missing from the lists, and the longest list is that of cultures in which the presence of riddles is unreported. The hypotheses of the theoretical experiment are, however, interesting and deserve further study. New perspectives on the characteristics of riddle-using cultures could yield completely new information on the riddle genre.

## *The rules and restrictions governing the performance of riddles*

It seems that nowhere in the world has it been possible to pose riddles at just any time, since their use has been governed by various rules and restrictions. Sometimes riddles were used on occasions – such as weddings and funerals – important to both the individual and the community (for example, Virtanen 1960:182-183, Blacking 1961:2) while at others riddling has been restricted to specific seasons. The Finno-Ugric Udmurts, for example, only used riddles between about October 20 and January 6 (Gerd 1928:394–395). From Sweden come reports of riddling as one of the Christmas traditions (Ström 1937:50, Hellberg 1985:89). As a rule the restrictions derived from the fact that riddling ties in with the coming of the new year or the welfare of the cattle. According to Udmurt belief riddling at times other than the evenings of early winter might prevent the crops from growing (Gerd op.cit.).

Prohibitions and rules are common among the African peoples. The Venda ordered that riddles were not to be presented during the hoeing and planting season from October to January. The primary reason for this was perhaps that riddling was usually an evening entertainment, but during the farming season people needed to conserve their strength and go to bed early. There may, however, have been a link between riddling and the growth of the crop and the harvest (Blacking 1961:2). Among the Sandawe people riddles are identified with birds. Riddling might attract harvest-destroying flocks of birds, so during the growing season they could only be asked in secret (Raa 1972:101). A prohibition on the asking of riddles or other items of folklore during the daytime seems to be very common in Africa (for example, Messenger 1960:226). This may be because riddles were regarded as a form of entertainment, and were therefore indulged in in the evenings and during the less busy months of the year. The prohibitions might even assume the form of a threat, such as "anyone asking riddles during the daytime is threatened with becoming a fool", or "a dog will place a calabash of fat on your head and you will (have to) go about with it". (Cole-Beuchat 1957:134–135.) Threats such as this are also known in Turkish tradition: "the people who tell riddles in daytime will grow a tooth in the back of their neck" (Başgöz 1965:133). Ruth Finnegan (1970:441) in fact says of African tradition that riddles are, unlike proverbs, "regarded as a kind of marginal activity reserved for special times rather than a universal aspect of human activity and communication".

In speaking of rules and restrictions it would be easy to pick out examples that cancel each other out, since cultural practices differ considerably from one another in various parts of the world.

Riddles have as a rule been a genre accessible to all. Although there are no clear prohibitions, there are, generally speaking, clear norms for the presentation of sexual riddles. Western cultures have regarded these riddles as being unsuitable for children's ears. By contrast, among the Venda, for example, riddles with the genitals as the answer can only be posed among friends when there are no adults present. Groups of youngsters all of the same sex also amuse themselves with such riddles. The delicate nature of the subject has led to the imposition of rules. The use of riddles does, however, tie in with the cultural norms for the performance of other sexual tradition, too. Otherwise riddles have been performed in groups formed in very different ways (Burns 1976:146–147), in which the most varied of combinations are possible. There also appear to be unwritten laws governing the types of riddles deemed suitable for a given occasion. The riddles connected with ritual practices, such as initiation and death rites, might differ in nature from, say, leisure riddling. Initiation rites tend to prefer obscure questions to true riddles, whereas the riddles posed during wakes come closer to true riddles. Thomas A. Burns (1976:143) concludes that the reason for this possibly lies in the functional differences in riddling: "...whereas riddling or questioning during initiation is regarded as a serious test and an integral part of the ritual, the riddling during wakes seems to be more a means of passing the time during the night vigil and less immediately relevant to the serious business of the death rite itself."

## *The journey to Hymylä – the Finnish way of punishing the poor riddlee*

Success in riddling is universally followed by at least a momentary rise in status. Good guessers are often mentioned by name in Finnish accounts. Similarly, poor guessers may have to pay for their ignorance by enduring scorn and teasing or even concrete punishments.

There are some ballads and folktales telling of riddling battles in which the loser may even have to forfeit his life. Competitions between two teams are also known in some cultures (for example, Burns 1976, Haring 1974). It is, however, more common to frame a riddle with an opening and closing cliché challenging those present to a contest, with a promise of honour or a reward, or sometimes to the contrary – a threat of playful punishment:

> The fruit of England and the flower of Spain / Met together in a shower of rain, / Bound with a napkin, tied with a string / *Tell me this riddle, and I'll give you a ring.* (ER 349)

> Behind the king's kitchen there is a great vat, / And a great many workmen working at that, / Yellow is their toes, yellow is their clothes. / *Tell me this riddle and you can pull my nose.* (ER 450)

> In meines Vaters Garten / Seh ich sieben Kameraden, / Kein ein, kein Bein, / Kann niemand erreichen. / *Wer dieses kann raten, / dem will ich geben einen Dukaten. / Wer dieses kann denken, / Dem will ich einen Louisdor schenken.*
> (Petsch 1899:48, cf. p.39)

Such playful exhortations are not used in Finland as a frame for riddling, but riddling sometimes included a dramatic game unknown elsewhere called 'Hymylä' for punishing an unsuccessful riddlee. Hymylä comes from the Finnish word *hymy*, 'smile' and *lä*, a locative ending, approximately Smileland, but the place may also be called Hölmölä, Stupidland, varying even with Hämälä or Himola. The oldest known account of the game appears in the *Aenigmata Fennica* published by Christfrid Ganander in 1783, and many occasions were reported in rhyming Kalevala-metre poetry in the early decades of the 19th century. The most recent accounts of this folk-like farce are given in direct narrative and it was still recalled at the time of a riddle collection made in 1966. No researcher has had a chance to observe such a game, however, the reason being that riddles and riddling have only relatively recently begun to interest Finnish scholars.

There are three main episodes in the drama: 1. the departure for Hymylä, 2. the visit to Hymylä and, on the return, 3. the account of the journey. Before the game begins the participants agreed how many riddles could be answered wrongly before a riddlee was sent off to Hymylä. Usually the number was three. There were two opposing main roles in the drama: the incompetent riddlee and the group putting the sentence into practice. The departure for Hymylä might take place symbolically to the accompaniment of a jingle: "If you didn't know, you got sent to Hymylä. They said: 'Hyys, hyys to Hymylä, for not knowing that.' " (SKS. Taimi Pitkämäki AK 14:1.1966.) Sometimes the traveller was given more concrete advice: "If there were some people in the group who could not guess 3–4 riddles, they were sent to Hymylä with the words 'Hyys, hyys to Hymylä, you don't know anything'. This is a place of punishment to which the ignorant were sent. The people sent there had to dress up to look particularly stupid so the other people in the game could have some fun." (SKS. Aili Sivula AK 18:3.1966.) Hymylä was usually outside the room in which the riddling took place, so the traveller had to leave the other players and go out into the yard or the hall.

Sometimes other roles were added to the trip to Hymylä. Some of the people carrying out the sentence would pretend to be the people of Hymylä, who would talk to the luckless traveller and amuse the rest of the group by reporting on the reception and treatment afforded the traveller:

> Thus the girl was soon ready for Hölmölä. Now, she was dressed in the most odd, "billygoat" fashion and was sent out of the living room. Then began the guessing about how she would be received in Hölmölä. Someone tells that Hölmölä's dogs are barking, whereat the children go to see what they are barking at, and they bring back the news that a ragged old woman is coming who's drawn by a cat and the sleigh's upside-down. In addition,

she has horns on her head. Hölmölä's housewife takes fright just as she is salting her butter, and in her fright she throws ashes instead of salt in her butter, then overturns the milk pail into the hearth and lights the fire with her church silk. The daughter of the house turns a slops bucket over the stranger's eyes. When the latter asks to be allowed to wash, she is given a tar bucket and ordered to dry herself with bedding straw. Then she is asked about news from the world. When she doesn't know what else to say apart from those unsolved riddles, the poor creature, the likes of her, is pitied and given chaff mixed with buttermilk, the heads of last year's herrings and the holes of ring bread for her food. (Virtanen 1977:81.)

Obviously Hymylä is a topsy-turvy world in which all the customs and practices of our world are reversed. The accounts of the traveller's reception vary in their details, but it is always clear that he or she is made to look and feel ridiculous. The devices reported in the accounts to trigger laughter are partly clichés. Usually the visit is described by explaining that everything in Hymylä is different from the normal world. Deviation from the "right" way of doing things was a source of comedy. One popular device is pairs of elements turned upside down, such as "The porridge was stirred with an axe, the firewood chopped with a ladle". Changing role was a sure source of comedy: "The cows were baking, the women on a leash, the horses were making ale, the farmers were in the stalls. The boys were yapping at the manor, the dogs sat eating round the kitchen table. The daughters were grunting in the pigsty and the pigs were preening themselves in the parlour."

The visit to Hymylä might end with the "mistress of Hymylä" telling the disgraced traveller the answers to the riddles he or she did not know. The shameful journey was over, and the traveller was allowed to return. He or she was now expected to give a report of the journey. If he was able to improvise an amusing story, he had a chance to make good his loss and win the approval of his fellows. The following story of a "dumbbell's" journey was noted down in Lapland:

> Wonders I saw when I visited Häme: Pigs stirred, cows baked; sheep distilled and dogs litigated; snow buntings chopped wood, swallows cleft wood into shingles; a titmouse wove sticks, a squirrel carved beams. Cooking was done with an axe, chopping was done with pots; a wolf mixed, the tail slept; a hare ground flour, the head trembled. A log drew, an ox shook; the sleigh lasted, the road fell apart. (SKVR XII$_1$, 134a)

Some of the lines seemed to have been standard material in accounts of Hymylä, but the narrator had endless potential for using his or her imagination. The role-exchange is not as such a device of the Finnish Hymylä game alone, for it is known internationally as a form of popular jesting in, for example, Estonian and Scandinavian poetry. There is also an account of a topsy-turvy world in the fairytale Schlaraffenland published by the Brothers Grimm. In this upside-down world hot pancakes grow out of a linden tree, crows mow the hay, gnats build a bridge, frogs thresh the corn, a mouse ordains a bishop and babes in arms try to entertain their mothers (see Bolte & Polivka 1918, no. 158). The same scheme recurs in different parts of the world and the point of the story is always that things are different here. We do not do things in that strange, crazy way. (Haavio 1955:209–221.)

Although punishments are part of the final reckoning in riddling situations, the trip to Hymylä seems to be exclusively Finnish as a punishment game, though there is one report from South Estonia. In Finland some of the lines in the trip to Hymylä have counterparts in Kalevala epic poetry. Leea Virtanen points out that the jingle recalls an incantation scheme. "The guesser is treated like a bad disease; he is exorcised to go his way to the place where he belongs, and his conveyances are recited. However, whereas the conveyer in incantations is often the horse of Hiisi 'with iron reins along its flanks, an iron sleigh behind', the travelling equipment of the one being driven to Hymylä is parodically amusing and trifling." (Virtanen 1977:82.)

The trip to Hymylä sometimes also involved the paying of forfeits. The options were usually work, money or "bodily suffering". The work might, for example, be carrying water or chopping wood, but various jests were also possible. "The work often consisted of anything crazy. The person might, for example, be ordered to wash his or her face in a tar bucket and to wipe it on a chaff bin or the sooty beams of a Lapp tent. Others promised to pay their forfeit in money; this was the easiest way, because it only involved a trifling sum. The bodily suffering was usually tickling, which was far from playful as it was so thorough you still remembered it the following day." (SKS. Aili Sivula AK 18:3.1966.)

Although it was only a game, the trip to Hymylä was somewhat disgraceful and frightening. "The trip to Hymylä was so frightening that it was liable, even later at night, to disturb sleep if one had received that rebuking in the evening." (SKS. HAKS 769. 1927.) The reason for this fear was that the playful punishment in any case meant the sufferer became the centre of attention and was in fact proclaimed unfit as a member of the riddling community. The enforcement of the punishment also meant temporary expulsion from the community. The recollections of the course of the game are explicit in their admiration of a good guesser and the scorn and shame poured on a bad one: "Anyone who could not guess the answer therefore had to go and fetch wood or water and to shout at the door: 'It's stupid I am'." Or: "Those who guessed quickly were admired. People sometimes shouted: 'The rutabaga cuts! The head shines! The sawdust in his head has just been changed. There's no rag in his head.' The one who did not guess might be called: 'Dim attic, off to Hymylä (with you). Talks like a rotten sheep's head.' " (Virtanen 1977:83–84.)

The trip to Hymylä represents a form of popular ridicule at its most typical. The grotesque jesting gives rise to extreme hilarity in the group, which momentarily expels one of its members by traditional means and tests the limits of his or her tolerance. The game may produce a frightening experience accompanied by the tension and joy of surviving it. Hymylä was for the players something strange and different that was felt to be dangerous but that could be safely encountered in the company of familiar people. But meanwhile, exclusion from the in-group was frightening. Don Handelman (1996:45) argues that Hymylä "signifies the deconstruction of the social person, one who has failed at transformation by not penetrating the interior boundary of the riddle." It is thus a paradoxical world that "expands to entrap its victim".

Although the shameful visit to Hymylä and the cries of scorn that accompanied it were the fate of several riddlers in turn, the lot of the scorned was not an easy one. There is little mention of how the victim feels, but this is clearly indicated in passing. One might stress that "we did our best to remember, to make sure we didn't get sent to Himola, because that was a disgrace," or "people were loath to join in the riddling for fear of being disgraced". We also know that it was forbidden to get angry. In any case, the trip to Hymylä never ended in lasting disgrace. Once the traveller had suffered his punishment, he was taken back into the group. Bygones were bygones, though they might be difficult to forget. Sometimes the traveller would in turn become the riddler. In any case the game continued until it was time for the next person to set off for Hymylä.

## *The functions of riddles and riddling*

In the days of the text-oriented approach, attention was paid only in passing to the functions of riddles and riddling. Scholars to begin with focused on the distribution and form of the genre, and later on the analysis of its structure and style. The researcher making a close study of the sources will, however, also find mentions even in earlier publications indicating the significance of riddles to their users. In his book *Riddles in Filipino Folklore* (1964:42–66) Donn V. Hart, for example, quotes a wealth of older literature touching on the functions of the genre. Most writers were, however, content merely to mention the entertainment function and mild intellectual stimulus in speaking of riddles and riddling. It was, perhaps, not until William Bascom published his "Four Functions of Folklore" (1954) that scholars became more widely interested in attempting to discover why, how and in what contexts riddles were posed and solved.

With the increase in fieldwork in the 1960s scholars began to pay more noticeable attention to the uses and functions of riddles. It seemed only natural to inquire into the functional data while recording riddles. But this alone is not enough, since only some of the factors important to the users of riddles are revealed to the researcher as manifest functions. Some of the functions of riddling are latent, and even the users of riddles are not necessarily aware of them and are not therefore capable of offering an answer when asked. These functions are revealed only to the researcher who has become familiar with the overall social and cultural mechanisms of the community.

An example of the way fieldwork can broaden the researcher's perspective is the article by Thomas Rhys Williams entitled "The Form and Function of Tambunan Dusun Riddles" (1963). Williams bases his functional analysis on the assumption that "every act, every human relationship, every idea or artifact carries meaning only in relation to the local cultural resources and social behaviour of the group among whom such behaviour is observed". He attempts to provide empirical proof that riddling, which is part of cultural behaviour, cannot be classified simply as leisure time, or game activity. The individual folklore phenomenon is viewed as part of a broader context, and its dimensions are ultimately disclosed via the tradition as a whole. Context is not therefore understood in the narrow sense, only as a speech event – riddling – in the course of which riddles are communicated, but as the whole cultural and social framework for a folklore product. John Blacking (1961:2), for example, stresses that African Venda riddles can only be understood in relation to the patterns of Venda society.

It must be borne in mind in analysing riddles that there are several different functions at work simultaneously in a riddling situation, only some of which are perhaps immediately evident. Riddling provides a form of entertainment, but at the same time the communication fosters a sense of affinity among those taking part, brings out cultural metaphors and terminology, expresses the values and norms of the community, and so on. The functions of individual riddles may in turn vary from one performance to another. David Evans (1976:184) claims that the metaphor "Big at the bottom, smaller at the top. Something in there goes flippety flop. – A wooden churn." regarded as being sexual was not considered sexual at all in the riddling sessions which he studied. But the sexual riddle may serve to charge the atmosphere, as a means of stimulation or even offence, or to teach young people the practices and norms approved by the community. And even within the same culture, riddling may differ in function, for example, when transferred from an urban to a rural milieu (Başgöz 1965:132). On the other hand, there are differences between the riddle subgenres. For example, the Anang from Nigeria use true riddles to amuse but proverb-riddles both to amuse and to instruct – to teach children proper behaviour (Messenger 1960:225). Any interpretation made by the researcher must in the final analysis be examined within the cultural, situational and even linguistic context of the riddle.

Let us now take a look at the views expressed most frequently in the literature on the functions of riddles and riddling. Every performance involves entertainment, a pleasant and at the same time exciting way of passing the time, even though this is not specifically mentioned. The function most often mentioned alongside entertainment is education. The didactic function of riddles is an ancient one, since the oldest documented riddles are Babylonian school texts (Potter 1950:939). Riddles are often thought to sharpen the wits of the participants, and this is expected to apply especially to children. It has, however, quite rightly been pointed out that this claim has seldom been conclusively documented (Hart 1964:61). William Bascom (1949:7) nevertheless sees a clear educational function in the Yoruba tradition: "Like proverbs, riddles are an important element in the education of young children, among whom they are especially popular." To illustrate this Bascom quotes numerous riddles connected with the king informing people how they should behave in the king's presence. Many different areas of behaviour are mentioned in research, such as growing up (Blacking 1961:2), the rules for working social relations (Williams 1963:104), and the gender differences and roles accepted by the community. Children can, for example, be taught the deference necessary in speaking to adults by means of riddles. But the telling of riddles may also involve far more comprehensive levels of learning. Thus riddles, like other childlore, may provide a model for assimilating the complexity of the language: "By learning the formulaic dimensions of dialogue, the child acquires competence in verbal reiteration, in asking and answering formal questions, and in varying codes of behaviour." (Haring 1985:184.) This observation is of universal relevance. It has further been stressed that the disorientation inextricably woven into riddling ultimately leads to the re-examination of the culture's cognitive orders, language, and tropes (Green 1992:138).

The observations made by researchers do, however, differ from one culture to another and prove that riddling does not have any universal functions recognisable the world over. For example, the riddles of the Christian Filipinos do not have any educational goals. But even though these riddles are not used as a medium for teaching the Filipinos values or customs, they would nevertheless appear to carry an implicit educational meaning. The reason for this is that riddles enhance the participants' powers of observation and their ability to spot analogies while training their memories and mental agility. (Hart 1964:60.) In the Venda community, by contrast, the only educational value inherent in riddles lies in the fact that they may be an asset to fuller participation in Venda social life. Having made a study of 300 Venda riddles, John Blacking came to the conclusion that only five of the riddles taught children something practical, such as the prohibitions concerning incest, how to cook, or how to build a house. Yet not even these riddles can be regarded as an educational medium comparable to proverbs. "The prime function [of Venda riddles] is social, and in this sense they might be regarded as 'education for life rather than for living'." (Blacking 1961:1–5.)

Kenneth Goldstein is one of the few scholars to have made observations on the functions of Western-European riddling practices. Before the First World War riddle sessions used to be very popular in Scotland. But parents also asked riddles as a means of teaching similarities and dissimilarities and ways of expressing them. The work conducted by Goldstein in the field nevertheless demonstrated that riddling had by the end of the 1950s lost its educational function, and that riddles were used only as a form of entertainment. The same narrowing of the function of riddling applies to the contemporary U.S. and other Western societies. Entertainment ranks highest, even though some scholars do stress that riddles are important to the cognitive development of the child (Green 1992:136). It is indeed worth debating whether, in analysing the educational function of riddling, scholars have been so concerned with the contents of the riddle and the meanings it conveys that they have overlooked riddling as a form of interaction. The need to reassess functions becomes evident in a study by John McDowell (1979:223–226), in which he points out the socialising and enculturing effects of riddling. For the child, riddling entails, among other things, a command of the conversational roles of riddler, riddlee and audience – all part of the game –

and skill at handling interactive situations. In order to acquire this, he must observe others' behaviour and adapt his own role to the needs of the situation. Participating in riddling teaches fundamental conversational etiquette, which involves taking turns, the avoidance of simultaneous talk, and the art of following the tone and content of the discourse. Riddling is also an opportunity to practise the legitimate assertion of the self, for in occupying the role of riddler, the child assumes temporary authority which the others must obey. On the other hand, producing the right answer marks the riddlee out as a riddling hero and gives him a chance to shine in the eyes of his peers. Succeeding in this calls for a command of an arsenal of interactional skills.

Communal values, crises and conflicts, and attempts to solve them may be involved in the asking of riddles in certain cultures. We may speak of 'the participative energies of the group', which has to be coaxed out by shocking the participants with a riddle (Abrahams 1972:187). This proves just how charged and active true riddling situations are. The riddle is then no longer a conventional question and answer but a means of establishing and oiling relations within the group. "In Africa riddling should be seen as both a model of social reality and a device whereby children learn skills the society values" (Haring 1974:200). Tradition is the key to the awareness of group membership. Riddles help Venda children to discover their identity both as individuals and as members of the community (Blacking 1961:7). A fact such as this clearly shows that riddles and other genres are more than mere texts: they are forms of cultural communication.

Viewing riddles in this way affords a completely new perspective on their use. Riddling can indeed be regarded as a game – as of course it is – but it can at the same time be seen as a medium for asking questions important to either the riddling group or the entire community. One of the functions of Dusun riddles is magical. In a world tinged with fear of both personal and community crises – such as birth and death, sickness, flood and famine – riddles act as a safety valve for reducing the pressure of fear. Crises can be discussed in riddles with no fear of the consequences brought by direct verbalisation. Dusun riddles have a mimetic, or automatic prayer function. (Williams 1963:105.)

Riddles may also act as a means of channelling aggression into acceptable behaviour. There are many practices of aggression and violent behaviour in Dusun culture. Aggression has fixed forms and names ranging from annoyance to anger and attack. Outbursts of aggression are, however, channelled if possible into the forms of defamation or dispute proffered by tradition, and an argument may, for example, be settled by resorting to rumours or riddles. In the course of riddling the opposing parties can abuse one another by presenting suitable riddles. The tone of voice, the speaker's stance, and the difficulty of the riddle are effective means of showing contempt for the other. If the causer of the argument is not able to rise to the riddle challenge, the riddler goes off with his nose in the air, proclaiming his opinion on the stupid riddlee for all to hear. Through riddling, aggression and the resulting tension and possible conflict seek a socially acceptable outlet. (Williams 1963:101–103.) Communities that value the arts of rhetoric, debate, argument and conciliation may use riddling as a means of practising and maintaining these verbal strategies. Riddles help people to see sometimes surprising links between both things and the words describing them. (Glazier & Glazier 1976:209.)

The patience of those participating in riddling is often sorely tried if the discourse is long drawn out. Disorientation is all part of the game, since not even the "right" answer is always the correct and accepted one. Some subgenres of riddle also rely on the false expectation effect. Examples here are many of the sexual riddles (cf. Chapter 4) and the fashionable waves of contemporary riddles as joking questions (cf. Chapter 3). The riddling tradition may also parody itself and thus once again try its listeners in a new way, such as this:

> A batter in a baseball game is at the plate.
> No one is on base.
> The pitcher throws a football, and the batter hits it over the left field fence. He carefully lays the bat down, runs to first and touches the base, runs to second and touches the base, runs to third and touches the base, runs home and touches the base.
> The catcher asks the umpire for another ball, and the umpire calls him out. Why?

The riddlee, being unable to answer the riddle, gives up. He is then told the answer, which is "He didn't touch second base". At that point he will exclaim "But you said he did!", to which the riddler will reply "I lied". (Abrahams & Dundes 1972:141.) The people to ask about the functions of this riddle parody, or some topical version of it, would be the youngsters who used it. To the scholar analysing it at his desk it may appear as a test of the listener's tolerance and sense of humour which he must pass in order to be accepted as a member of the group.

Riddles have also been regarded as regulating a culturally approved statement of order. Elli Köngäs Maranda (1976:131) calls this function a cognitive one and regards it as fundamental and possibly even universal. It is a means of either supporting the basic values of the community or of questioning and reassessing them. This may be actually just two sides of the same coin. Riddles can be seen as devices which are used to demonstrate control over words, objects and ideas that are central to the life of the riddling group. At the same time the question-and-answer pattern reactivates our ability to bring together all manner of elements in the world. "Riddles are like any creative or recreative form in rehearsing playfully the deep sense of order shared by the community." This function proves to be extremely important in time of crisis, such as death or initiation, when the culturally accepted order and the continuity it affords are threatened. (Abrahams 1972:182, 196.)

Riddles are an easy means of questioning and protesting against the values and hierarchy which society takes for granted. Charles Francis Potter (1950:943) gives as an example of this the folk riddle of the Reformation and Renaissance, which makes a protest against social inequality. Class-consciousness and resentment of the fortunate members of society could be freely expressed through the medium of riddles, whereas an open statement of one's views might well bring recriminations. To illustrate his point Potter picks out certain folklore motifs, such as "motif H551, where a princess is offered to any man, commoner or not, who can outriddle her, or motif H561, where the solvers of riddles are clever peasants, even girl peasants, who, though doubly handicapped socially, gain advantage, perhaps wealth and position, through their intelligence". The modern riddle lends itself as a tool for not only joking but also for criticising and even expressing a point of view. When, in spring 1993, the police raided the headquarters of the notorious Hell's Angels in Helsinki, I received the following report from one of my students: "I heard this riddle when five people aged 18–25 were chatting about the police, and especially stupid policemen, at which a 25-year-old boy asked, 'What happens when Hell's Angels clash with the Beagle Boys /nickname for riot police/? – An innocent dog dies.' "

Riddling may also act as a forum for discussing new things of current importance to the community. At their riddle sessions the Lau of Malaita made up new riddles expressing their views on the new Western technology just making its appearance in the community. Riddles and myths constituted a pair of opposites in Lau tradition: "Functionally, myths seem to reinforce the established order, whereas the primary function of riddles is to question at least certain kinds of established order. Where myths prove the validity of land claims, the authority of social and cultural rules, or the fitness of native conceptual classification, riddles make a point of playing with conceptual borderlines and crossing them for the pleasure of showing that things are not quite as stable as they appear." (Köngäs Maranda 1971b:53.) Riddles provide a traditional channel for expressing an opinion but in a way that is softer than a direct comment, sometimes disguised by humour. The riddlee seldom has to stand alone behind the criticism, leaving it instead for the community to accept and pass on.

## *A contemporary case in Northern Ireland*

Folklore can, in time of political conflict, provide an acceptable means of venting pent up emotion. The following examples are from Northern Ireland, which has long been featuring in the news. A few background facts are, however, necessary in order to understand both the situation and, especially, the joking questions. Since 1969 instability in the state of Northern Ireland (established in 1921) has increased, resulting in violence which has caused over 3,600 deaths. The current population is 1,577,836 (Census: April 1991) and largely practising Christian, of which a little under two-thirds would be of Protestant background and a little over one third Roman Catholic. Small numbers of other major religions are also represented, but only the Protestants and Catholics are, as a rule, mentioned in speaking of the conflict.

Here, first, are the joking questions, followed by some comments on their form, content and use:

1. What's the fastest game on earth? – Pass the parcel in a Belfast pub./ Parcel refers to parcel bombs which were common at one time (but not recently). "Pass the parcel" is a popular game at children's parties./
2. What's the longest road in Ireland? – The Garvaghy Road because it took the Orangemen two weeks to go down it.
3. What's the difference between an apple and an orange? – You can't get an apple bastard.
4. What's the difference between a banana and an orange? – You can't say "Banana bastard".
5. What's the difference between a Sinn Féin member and a rottweiler? – The rottweiler can be interviewed on the radio./The voices of Sinn Féin members were not, until 1994, allowed to be broadcast./
6. What's the difference between youghurt and Loyalists? – Youghurt has a culture.
7. Have you heard about the new lemon order? – It's like the Orange Order only more bitter.
8. Why do you bury Protestants 12 feet deep? – Because deep down they're not bad bastards./twice the normal depth/
9. Why do seagulls from Northern Ireland fly upside down over England? – Because it's not worth shitting on the bastards below.
10. Why are Diana and Orangemen like each other? – Neither got through the Tunnel./"The Tunnel" is a district in the town of Portadown now mainly inhabited by Roman Catholics./
11. What do you do when a Loyalist throws a pin at you? – Run – sure he's a grenade in his mouth!
12. What do you do when a Loyalist throws a grenade at you? – Take the pin out and throw it back!
13. When does a Catholic become a Fenian? – Whenever he leaves the room.

These examples are quite at home in the company of others of their kind, since questions beginning with "what", "why" and "when" are common in this subgenre of the riddle. Superlative formulae (1–2) and questions on the pattern "what's the difference between" 3–6) and "what do x do when" (11–12) are also popular models for forming new joking questions. As is commonly the case with riddles, these, too, play with words that can be understood in more than one way (for example, "culture" in no. 6 and "bitter" as the epithet for both the fruit and the Orange Order no. 7). There are only two riddles among those quoted here in which the question part does not directly refer to the answer (1–2). They are not examples of a true riddle metaphor providing both misleading and leading hints to the answer, or of traditional joking questions (see Chapter 3); rather, they are outspoken political comments inserted in the discourse. It is immediately evident that they refer either to the Orange Order (3, 4, 10 and also 7 if it is part of the series of "fruit" riddles), or to the Loyalists (6, 11 and 12) or to the supporters of Sinn Féin (5). The religious factions are mentioned outright by name in riddles 8 and 13. It is surprising to see that the majority of the joking questions are targeted at the Protestants (who do, admittedly, constitute the majority of the population of Northern Ireland) and riddle 13 is the only one to cast a critical glance at the Catholics. One cannot therefore help wondering whether the extreme Catholics are more immune from the criticism through folklore, or whether the one-sided nature of the material is due to the time or way in which it was collected. The riddles were, according to Fionnuala Carson Williams, collected "from those on the side lines; moderates not members of particular groups."

These joking questions are taken from a collection made in different ways since the mid-1990s. They are all part of the collection of folklore on the Northern Ireland conflict undertaken by Fionnuala Carson Williams, who is a fellow of the Cultural Diversity Group of the Community Relations Council of Northern Ireland, which body I wish to acknowledge for permission to publish the texts. Items 4, 5, 9, 11 and 12 were noted and kindly submitted to the collection by Kathleen Quinn, while item 8 was noted and kindly submitted by Bernard MacCaughey. To all of them I express my gratitude for the opportunity to use this interesting lore. I am also particularly indebted to my colleague Fionnuala Williams for her numerous explanations, which helped me to understand the background and vocabulary of the riddles. In organising the collections Williams has made use of e-mail and the telephone. In appealing to persons working at her own university she explained: "Part of my research is to collect stories, more precisely folklore, about the current Troubles. – Such lore has important functions, such as to lower tension, air subjects which are otherwise taboo and express needs, and thus give an extremely valuable insight into the period."

Some of the respondents spontaneously reported on the use of the riddle they recalled and voiced their opinions on the functions of this type of lore. Karen McKinty, who is project coordinator at the Queen's University of Belfast, remembers that she heard riddle 1 when she was a child: "I can't remember when I heard the joke but I must have been pretty young, primary school age anyway." She then describes the way she learnt it and its meaning as follows: "I was of the generation whose school education included things like 'Never pick up things on the street, not cassette boxes, not pens, nothing (the paramilitary used to put anti-handling devices in them). Never walk past unattended cars, Never look in a bag found lying around to see who it might belong to', etc., etc. These became normal – like 'Never cross the main road without an adult.' Considering I lived in Bangor (a peaceable place at the start of the Troubles – which has only been bombed three times over the years), this says a lot for the concerns of the teachers. Most of the problems were in rougher areas, but the warnings were NI-wide."

On expressing my interest in publishing Karen MacKinty's riddle and its explanations, I received the following assessment: "the creation of jokes to deal with crisis is something that I have always been aware of. On several occasions over the years colleagues, friends and I have commented that the extremity of shock caused by a situation can be judged by the lack of jokes on the subject. We will comment that 'you can tell how much of an effect this has had – I haven't heard a single joke!' " Like the folklorist dealing with various kinds of catastrophe, she had been left wondering what disasters are such that they give rise to a host of jokes that may in some people's opinion be manifestations of bad taste but that nevertheless act as an outlet of pressures (cf. the Estonia and Challenger disasters) to the poeple closely involved.

Sometimes an item of folklore is explained on presentation. The narrator of riddle 10 felt the joke was sick. Another said of his father that he "plays golf with a (religious, i.e. Christian denominationally) mixed bunch of guys who tease each other mercilessly". A third concludes her description with "we laugh at the absurdities together". Spontaneous statements such as these are the best indication of the power of folklore to relieve some of the pressure caused by conflict. Jokes may also be told to complete strangers. Fionnuala Carson Williams heard riddle 6 at a New Year's Eve party at the Belfast Boat Club in 1997. She had never before met the male barrister of about 45 who told the joke. Some jokes may be presented as series of questions (obviously 11 and 12, but undoubtedly also the "fruit" riddles, 3–4 and 7), thereby giving them greater impact.

Can an outsider ever fully understand all the functions of joking questions? I doubt it. But in order to obtain a closer feel for the jokes presently circulating in Northern Ireland, let me add a few explanations. The Orange Order named in the riddles was founded in 1785 and is a brotherhood which currently draws its membership, claimed to be in excess of 80,000, from all the main Protestant denominations. Its main commitments are to Protestantism and the maintenance of Northern Ireland within the United Kingdom (of Great Britain and Northern Ireland). The Loyalists, again often mentioned, are extreme unionists who support the political union with the United Kingdom, sometimes to the extent of supporting violence to that end. The Loyalists are also Protestants. Sinn Féin, mentioned in riddle 5, is the political wing of the Irish Republican Army, the IRA. The word "Fenian" in riddle 13 is a derogatory term used by some, mainly in Northern Ireland, to describe any Roman Catholic, with the implication of disloyalty to the United Kingdom. – Naturally there are many shades of meaning attached to these facts which the outsider cannot understand even when they are explained.

Bilingualism is another device available to the people of Northern Ireland:

    14. What does the IRA man say to the policeman?
    – Go n'éirí an bothar leat.

Fionnuala Williams explains this as follows: "Literally 'may the road rise with you', an old blessing given to one setting out on a journey. In this case, of course, the presumed sense is 'may the road rise with you because it is exploding'." The joke can only be understood by someone who speaks the language, appreciates the re-application of the old saying and the relationship between the IRA man and the policeman. It thus involves many layers of in-group humour.

Joking questions make wide use of place-names that provide the local people with a signpost to the political point of the joke. The place-names are familiar from such news items as the attempt by Orangemen to march through a mainly Catholic-inhabited district of town. In order to understand no 2, for example, the outsider has to know that it "refers to July 1997, when an Orange parade was banned from marching down that road but eventually let through by the authorities. The road is in the town of Portadown – currently in the news now again. I recorded the joke in January 1998." The following riddle also refers to the same town and the defiant Protestant marchers.

    15. Did you hear about the dyslexic Orangeman?
    – He stood in Duncrue Street for two weeks.

Duncrue Street is a little street in central Belfast. And I quote Fionnuala Williams, who again provides the key: "After the first controversy about the parades at Drumcree a commemorative medal was struck for Orangemen who had remained at Drumcree and eventually got marching along the proscribed route. The medal had the spelling 'Seige of Drumcree' instead of 'siege' and was given a lot of press coverage – so the joke builds on the image of the dyslexic Orangeman but obviously in an unkind way, perhaps equating the disability with lack of intellect." This example well demonstrates how a whole group can be stigmatised by a slight and, in itself, innocent slip. The derogatory function of the joke is blatantly obvious, but the teller cannot be accused of defamation.

# 6 The expressive devices of riddles

Riddles are made up of two parts: an image and an answer. In some cultures the image takes the form of a question, while in others – such as the Finnish riddle tradition – it is mostly a statement. There are examples of the former to be found in the Anglo-Saxon tradition (for example, Archer Taylor:1951), while the latter is represented by many African traditions (for example, Finnegan 1970:427, Blacking 1961, Ten Raa 1972:107). The image is, however, always an implicit question which, when presented in a riddling situation, requires the right answer.

The language of riddles is in some cultures, even in its simplest form, usually so marked that the riddle stands out from any surrounding discourse. Finnish riddles, for example, favour the Kalevala metre and even more frequently alliteration, whereas rhymes are less common. One consequence of the Kalevala metre are parallel images, likewise that the riddle statements tend to be divided up into lines of a certain length. These features of poetic language are also characteristic of other genres, such as proverbs. The most usual metrical patterns of Vietnamese riddles are likewise among the stylistic devices cultivated by proverbs and lullabies, and in some cases even art poetry uses the same patterns. Riddles thus differ at the level of style from other poetry only in that in a performing situation the lines are framed by opening and closing formulae. (Cong-Huyen-Ton-Nu 1971.) It must in fact be stressed that "metrical patterns are part of a folk poetic system in a particular language rather than peculiar to a single genre of folk poetry" (Dundes & Vatuk 1974:153).

Other special features of the language of riddles are, for example, euphony ("Heikki veikki venterikki, vääräsääri vänterikki, istui pellon pientarel---"/ "Henry mandy dandy, bandylegs galandy, sat at the side of the field ---" FR 78), in some language areas rhyme, and above all paradoxical images.

The language of riddles is not, however, marked in all languages. Scholars have made observations on the other devices by which a riddle can be made to stand out as a genre from the surrounding discourse. Elli Köngäs Maranda

(1971b:58) points out in speaking of the use of opening formulae that "a formulaic opening serves artistically the same function as does a special well organised style; it announces the occasion, it directs the expectations of the audience." When the riddle is verbalised as a simple statement that does not easily stand out from the surrounding discourse, it can also be underlined by placing it within the framework of a game with complex rules (Raa 1972:107).

The special features of the language of riddles vary according to language and cultural region. In northeast Scotland, for example, a good riddle must rhyme, or it must employ a formulaic opening or ending (Goldstein 1963:332). Old Swedish riddles belonging to the same Indo-European language group indicate that there was once a common poetic tradition. In the following example (given here only in Swedish), rich alliteration is combined with assonance and rhyme:

> Oket å boket / å barkatt o bett.
> I skogen ä dä hogget / i smijja ä dä smett,
> på fårakätten tar dä si föa. (Ström 1937:20.)

One popular effect in Russian riddles is the anagram, i.e. the image and answer sound alike (Toporov 1987:181–190). In the Finno-Ugrian Cheremis language one of the characteristics of the riddle is its widespread use of onomatopoeic devices and more succinct language than normal. On the other hand the vocabulary of the riddle is richer than that of narrative text (Saarinen 1991:171–175). The succinctness of the language typical of riddles is also pointed out by Eric Ten Raa, who notes that the riddles of the African Sandawe people are "seemingly less elaborate than many European riddle sentences" (Raa 1972:109).

Chinese is monosyllabic, and in the standard Mandarin dialect there are, due to the paucity of sounds, only 420 different syllables. Homophones are thus common and are highly serviceable for riddle making by punning on sound. The meanings of Chinese characters are, furthermore, often many and varied. This provides good potential for speech play. For example, the picture riddle showing a number of goldfish in a pond suggests the phrase *chin yü man t'ang*, which means, literally, "gold fish fill pond". "But in the spoken language *yü* means 'jade' as well as 'pond'; so by substitution of these other meanings, the picture conveys the felicitous wish, 'may gold and jade fill your home'." (Rudolph 1942:68.)

Many Chinese riddles are based on the shapes of Chinese characters so that the image incorporates two to four components, each of which has its own meaning. The character riddle, as it is called, may consist of either the separate parts of a particular character, or of their arrangement to form the complete character, or else the entire character itself is the character riddle. But an image may also be created by using the technique of character dissection. This type of riddle is used among both the folk and the literati, and many of the riddles are in poetic metre. (Rudolph 1942:69–79.)

The majority of the riddling traditions known to us are oral, but the point of this Chinese type of riddle is to be found in the ambiguity inherent in the written character. The use of these riddles must have called for a good command of the read and written symbols. Naturally we cannot ever fully appreciate the Chinese character riddles in translation. There are, however, publications that help to give us an insight into Chinese culture (cf. Mau-Tsai 1986, Plaks 1996).

As a form of text the language of riddles differs in most cases from everyday speech. To some extent form governs content. At content level the riddle as a linguistic form also imposes certain restrictions limiting the potential open to the riddle inventor (Kaivola-Bregenhøj 1978:7–8). On the other hand poetic language provides many models for expression to support the riddler's creativity and memory.

The person skilled in the riddling tradition has in his competence a vocabulary characteristic of the genre, a stock of metaphors and, in connection with these metaphors, the ability to construct contrasting, antithetical and paradoxical images, a familiarity with morphological-syntactic structures, and above all the art of combining these elements of riddling language according to the semantic codes peculiar to the genre (Kaivola-Bregenhøj 1978). Only someone with a thorough command of the language and socio-cultural frame of reference of the community in which the riddles are performed can possess such competence.

In speaking of their own experiences in the field, researchers are aware of their own lack of competence and seldom venture to ask riddles themselves, even though they may try to answer them. The reason is often that they are afraid of altering the course of the riddling session ("...the participation of my wife and myself in answering three of the riddles could not have disrupted or altered the session in any way..." Evans 1976:172) or of influencing the local tradition ("I was wary of posing riddles...for fear of influencing Lau riddling in some way." Köngäs Maranda 1971b:55). Elli Köngäs Maranda does, it is true, admit to regretting this, for on giving the right answer to riddles addressed to her "I receive warm praise from other participants in the session". In debating the reasons for her wariness – one of the basic fieldwork teachings she had received – she wisely says, "...the collector's ethics need not force him to play dummy when he lives among the group he is studying" (Köngäs Maranda 1971b:55–56). The researcher spending longer periods in the field is "exposed" to the tradition, and it would be very strange if he did not at some stage become competent in its production. Ultimately he is, however, a researcher observing the life and use of tradition out in the field.

*Ambiguity*

Marked riddle style sometimes even goes against the linguistic norms – something that would not be acceptable in ordinary speech. Riddling is a form of verbal exchange in which those taking part consciously place themselves open to the risk of being taken in. They have, in agreeing to take part, accepted the fact that they will be confronted with statements that do not observe the principles of cooperation normally applied to communication. The aim is then linguistic ambiguity, by means of which the riddlee is misled into focusing on the wrong detail. As has been pointed out, everyone likes the unusual linking of subtle images (Barley 1974:149). Giving the right answer has been regarded as indicating that the riddlee realises the language is ambiguous. He has learnt the cultural art of how to manipulate ambiguity (Haring 1985:166). The term used to apply to such contradiction varies to some extent from one researcher to another. Robert Georges and Alan Dundes (1963), for example, speak of contradictions or oppositions in analysing the technique of confusion, and Roger D. Abrahams (1968) points out that opposition is the most salient of the techniques by which the image is impaired.

Ambiguity is encountered at the phonological, morphological and syntactical level of language (Pepicello & Green 1984:21–36). A good example of morphological ambiguity is the trick question "What's black and white and red all over? – A newspaper.", in which there is a play of homophony between a simple lexical item (the adjective red) and a verb plus its past participle morpheme (read). This is obviously oral tradition, in which the different spelling of the words escapes the riddlee (Green & Pepicello 1978:8). The answer to a popular riddle may, however, sometimes become familiar to the user of folklore. In this case he no longer exults in the ambiguity of language (Barley 1974:151) unless the image is given a new interpretation. The trick question quoted here by way of example was so popular in America in the 1970s that people began to "seek out ways which introduce humour and which would enable them to claim credit for wit. They do so by transforming the phonetic puzzle into a literal description of an object or being, then replacing the ambiguity of the riddle with an oddity in the solution, as the following answers demonstrate:

   – A chocolate sundae with ketchup on it.
   – A sunburned zebra.
   – A blushing zebra.
   – A skunk with diaper rash."
   (Ben-Amos 1976:251–252)

When riddles are in active use, new interpretations such as these add to their entertainment and use value. The riddles quoted border on the crazy humour cultivated by young people and children. All the joking questions popular in contemporary tradition make use of crazy humour such as this and rely for effect on the clever use of ambiguity. The right answer (known only to the riddler) culminates in laughter shared by all.

Ambiguity is also to be found in the answer to a riddle if the words in the answer form a homophonous pair. In the following examples the homophonous pair is given in brackets.

   Why is a man clearing a hedge in a single bound like a man snoring?
   – He does it in his sleep (his leap).

When is it hard to get your watch out of your pocket?
– When it keeps sticking (keeps ticking) there.

This observation was made by W.J. Pepicello and Thomas A. Green (1984:33–35), who indeed stress that "to understand the wit involved in riddling, it is necessary to scrutinize the entire structure of the riddle act to determine at what point the element of wit (through ambiguity) is introduced." Not even in riddles of this type is the ambiguity ever the result of chance, since it is sought as an effect characteristic of the riddle.

Ambiguity is founded above all on exploitation of the potential of language and points to the situation that prevails when two or more different underlying semantic structures are presented by a single surface structure. The phonological form of an ambiguous structure is identical in all its semantic interpretations, but this correspondence may have several sources (Green & Pepicello 1978:5). Riddles conceal and reveal their referent simultaneously. The ambiguities occurring in them may act "as operators that permit the transformation of categories and also their construction" (Hamnett 1976:387). Linguistic ambiguity can be supplemented by the riddlers' knowledge of the socio-psychological world (Barley 1974:151), and apart from being purely linguistic, it may be empirical, or it may be founded on social and cultural presuppositions. Thus, for example, the riddle "What belongs to yourself, yet is used by everybody more than yourself? – Your name." is possible only in a culture in which private ownership is taken as a matter of course and is the only form of ownership (Ben-Amos 1976:251).

True riddles are a genre displaying little improvisation or individual variation. The focal point of the riddle is the object, thing or concept given in the answer, and the statement constituting the image observes models of analogy peculiar to the genre. These models operate on the various linguistic planes. For example, in the riddles of the Finns (Kaivola-Bregenhøj 1974:169–184) and the Cheremis (Saarinen 1991:37–39) the majority of the fixed models of expression are based on some kind of paradox, antithesis (the linking of opposites), or, on a milder scale, contrast (the likening of different things). The basic form of the riddles of the African Yoruba people has been reduced to an entity consisting of two conflicting, disproportionate or impossible claims (Bascom 1949:4).

The following four schemes of the unexpected are to be found in Finnish riddles:

1. The negation of the prerequisite for the action or its expected and natural outcome, for example:

   Mikä jalatonna juoksee? – Pilvi.
   What runs without legs? – A cloud. (FR 194, ER 260–265)
   Ei heinissä hajoo, eikä vedessä vajoo. – Päivänpaiste.
   Doesn't break up in the hay nor sink in water. – Daylight. (FR 79)

2. A biological or logical aberration arising from one of the following: the illogical relationship between a concept and its location; an epithet attached to a concept contrary to expectation; the interchanging of the characteristics

of two antithetic concepts; or the illogical functioning of a concept, for example:

> Ori tallissa, häntä katolla. – Tuli ja savu.
> A stallion in the stable, its tail on the roof. – The kitchen stove. (FR 707, ER 413)
> Yksi hiiri, kaksi häntää. – Kenkä.
> One mouse, two tails. – A shoe. (FR 1174)
> Mahtuu pieneen peltoon, vaan ei suureen metsään. – Astuva.
> Fits in a small field but not in a large forest. – A twig harrow. (FR 533)
> Yöksi pukee, päiväksi riisuu. – Akkunan lauta.
> Dresses for the night, undresses for the day. – A window sill. (FR 1217)

3. Negation of the simile, for example:

> Musta kun pappi, eik ou pappi, kiiltää kun nappi, eik ou nappi,
> lentää kuin lintu, eik ou lintu, möyryvää kuin härkä, eik ou härkä,
> männöö muan ala kun mato, eik ou mato. – Sitsontijainen.
> Black as a parson but isn't a parson, shines like a button but isn't a button,
> flies like a bird but isn't a bird, bellows like a bull but isn't a bull,
> goes underground like a worm but isn't a worm. – Dung beetle. (FR 613)

4. Bypassing of the extreme value or symbol of a property, for example:

> Mikä on korppia mustempi? – Synti.
> What is blacker than a raven? – Sin.
> Korkeamp kun hevoin, matalamp kun sika. – Satula.
> Higher than a horse, lower than a pig. – A saddle. (FR 374)
> (Kaivola-Bregenhøj 1974:181.)

These schemes of expectation apply to the image. Including the answer in the investigation, we see that the image plays with an impossibility that proves, once the answer is known, to be self-evident and expedient. The unexpectedness springs either from the mutual relationship of the elements in the statement (single-statement riddles such as "Mikä on härän silmä pirtissä? – Oksa seinässä."/"What is the ox's eye on the wall? – A knot." FR 154) or from conflict between the states expressed by the statements (riddles with two or more statements, such as "Paita alla, liha päällä. – Kynttilä."/ "Shirt underneath, meat on top.– A candle." (FR 720, ER 588), (Saarinen 1991:149). Sometimes the image is completely realistic in itself, but it always comes as a surprise in its relation to the answer.

The point at which the irreality occurs in the image varies. It is, however, by means of close analysis of a sizeable volume of material, possible to chart the regularities. Irreality is not created solely by the combination of metaphorical and non-metaphorical elements, even completely metaphorical elements can be equally contradictory. (Saarinen 1991:154–160.)

The unexpectedness of the relationship between image and answer in most cases relies on metaphorical expressions. The riddle is most often linguistically anomalous, so that the listener notices it. Quechua riddles lack "the obligatory markers of common discourse which relate them to the realm of ambiguity. This absence of obligatory markers linguistically signals to the participants that semantic categories are ambiguous in riddles" (Isbell & Fernandez 1977:40). The very shift in the discourse in the direction of riddles is in fact a sufficient indication to the experienced person that the language is subject to genre-specific rules. "The riddle about a 'black bird' that 'gets in its nest and sings' can only mean a priest up in the pulpit"; once the allegorical hidden image has been solved, it is empty and of no importance (Kuusi 1954:135). And indeed, the impossible image of the riddle is always bound to the special nature of the genre. The unexpected element is always resolved in the answer. Once the images have been discovered, they are more or less disposable. But the next time the question is asked, the relationship between the metaphorical image and the answer is once again open.

One subgenre of the riddle relying entirely on linguistic ambiguity is the joking question (see Chapters 1 and 3). Just at the moment joking questions are very popular in the Western world at least, and they have numerous contexts and functions. Although they are international, the puns typical of the genre only work in a given language. The following riddle, for example, is restricted to the German-speaking area: "Welches ist das längste Wort in der Hl. Schrift/What is the longest word in the Holy Book? – Das Halleluja, das ist drei Ellen (drei l.) lang/ – Halleluja, it's three ells long." (Peuckert 1938:204). Perhaps the best-known joking question in the English-speaking area is: "What is black and white and red (read) all over? – A newspaper.", which relies on the fact that the verb "read" and the adjective "red" are pronounced in the same way.

A Finnish anthology of joking questions (Lipponen 1995) contains some 1,500 texts selected from children's lore collections submitted to the Folklore Archives of the Finnish Literature Society between 1986 and 1995. The bulk of the material was collected from schoolchildren aged 10–15. The majority of the questions in the anthology operate with ambiguities at various linguistic levels and cannot therefore be translated. They are only amusing to Finns.

The expressive devices of the joking question are impossible to define in general terms since the genre is inevitably tied to language. Analyses have been made by, for example, Thomas A. Green and W.J. Pepicello (1984) in the English-speaking area and Klaus Laalo (1998) in the Finnish. One thing that variants in different languages have in common is that "the means and possibilities of language are proven and the boundaries of normal usage tested in language play" (Laalo 1998:270).

Joking questions are particularly popular with children and teenagers, possibly because "when children's awareness of language increases, they develop an interest in language games involving recognition of the language they have recently achieved" (Laalo 1998:270). But the joking question can also be part of adult tradition if the content and message are fitting for the occasion. Illustrating this are the contemporary Irish joking questions quoted in Chapter 5.

*Riddle metaphors*

Riddles are a genre in which ambiguity is acceptable at all levels of language. They favour metaphors the purpose of which is both to mislead the listener and to bring to light a new aspect of a thing, an object or an action that is as a rule highly familiar to all. They demonstrate that two linguistic categories that are from one perspective different are in fact similar when viewed in another light. Riddles explore the established order in play. (Lieber 1976:262.)

Riddle metaphors cannot be forced into a single scheme by comparing them unequivocally to the metaphors of, say, spoken or poetic language. The scale of expression in riddles is a wide one, ranging from creative invention often improvised on the spot via extremely worn or commonplace metaphors to images the meaning of which has become completely obscure.

The majority of riddles are built either wholly or in part on a metaphorical image. Alongside these metaphors there are some simple lists of symbols and literal statements (cf. Georges & Dundes 1963:112–114). In a riddling situation it is, however, often impossible for the tradition-bred to spot the difference between the two. Sirkka Saarinen, who has made a detailed analysis of the grammar of Cheremis riddles, divides metaphorical riddles into non-realistic and realistic. These categories are also to be found – though under slightly different names – in the article by Robert A. Georges and Alan Dundes written in 1963. Cheremis riddles reveal four phenomena, namely metaphor vs. authenticity, and non-reality vs. reality, that intermix in many ways. (Saarinen 1991:137-150.) Any part of speech or of a sentence can in a riddle be metaphorical. Elli Köngäs Maranda (1971a:205, 207–208) regards the reversal mechanism as a characteristic feature of the riddle metaphor and mentions the following two-way metaphors in Finnish riddles: needle = bird, sausage = serpent, sword = serpent, scissors = crab, scissors = swallow, container = human being, mill = man, hen = woman, sheep = bishop, hair = hay.

Metaphors vary in riddles in both degree and quantity. Some riddles are realistic in the sense that the relationship between the image elements is neither conflicting nor contrary to expectation. The respondent nevertheless always knows that the image is not a statement in normal language and that "literal interpretation of the riddle is not right even if the image contains no illogical details" (Kaivola-Bregenhøj 1978:105–106). It is, however, difficult to identify the metaphorical elements in the actual riddling situation, especially if there is nothing contradictory about the image. Some of the riddles in the Cheremis material were true-to-life in that their imagery was true as regards the answer. Furthermore, some of even the metaphorical riddles contain negative expressions which point to the lack of a certain quality and thus lead the riddlee to the right answer. (For example, a negative verb or word or a caritive-adjective, such as "Is black but is not a crow, has horns but is not a cow. – A beetle.") In some riddles, on the other hand, there is some completely arbitrary word (such as a proper name) standing for the referent. (Saarinen 1991:139–151, 164–165.)

The only factor linking the various metaphorical expressions of riddles is their relationship with the solution: there must be some factor linking the metaphor with the answer. The answer is the criterion for determining whether or not a metaphor is apt. Due to the relationship between the image and the answer, the riddle metaphor does not merge unnoticed with the discourse in the way a metaphor used in everyday speech does. On the other hand the answer checks the chains of association set in motion by a fresh and interesting metaphor. Nevertheless, the relationship between the metaphor in the riddle image and the answer is a highly complex one. To the listener the answer may be either disappointing or stimulating, but at its best it gives him the pleasure of discovering a new perspective. (Cf. Chapter 7)

The metaphors occurring in true riddles can roughly be classified as "living" or "faded", i.e. those that are used in riddle language and those that have either become so familiar that they no longer attract attention or that have passed out of use. The border between these two categories is a nebulous one and varies from one culture area to another. The metaphors are backed by a set of analogy models that is exploited by the riddle language and the formula system regulating its use. These models have yielded a host of clichés that recur in numerous riddle metaphors.

Let us take as examples of Finnish riddles types beginning with the word "akka" (an old word for a married woman which nowadays has a derogatory connotation), its synonym "ämmä" or the same words equipped with an attribute, such as "musta akka" (a black woman) or "lyhyt akka/ämmä" (a short woman). Of the 1,248 riddle types presented in *Finnish Riddles*, 30 have the "akka" metaphor. These riddle metaphors do not rely solely on this cliché-like name for a woman and are often supplemented by a word for part of the woman's body or clothing and an adverb of place, likewise a cliché, which is not a metaphor. For example:

> Akka loukos, sata silmää pääs. – Seula.
> An old woman's in her nook with a hundred eyes in her head.
> – A sieve. (FR 17)
> Äm istu loukkas sata hamet yl. – Luuta.
> An old woman is sitting in the corner wearing a hundred skirts.
> – A broom. (FR 1234)

The metaphorical "akka" is given a precise meaning in the linguistic context of the riddle, but because it is the opening word in the riddle it acquires a very clear and clichéd role in the image. "Akka", which has the basic semantic features +animate and +human, gives the competent riddlee a dependable hint that the referent proposed as an answer must have the feature –human (in all 30 cases) and in most cases also the feature –animate (in 28 cases; in only 2 cases is the answer an animal). Elli Köngäs Maranda also pointed out that the metaphor and its referent belong to opposing categories, for example, the categories animate and inanimate. "By establishing an identity between these classes, riddles remind the speakers of the language that these classifications are not unassailable." (Köngäs Maranda 1971b:54.) The word "akka", used of a married woman, also communicates that the answer will most probably be something connected with the life of the mistress of the household. Among the 30 riddle types in the example material there are 25 in which the object in the answer belongs to the woman's everyday world, such as a stove, broom or churn. (Kaivola-Bregenhøj 1978:81–89.) This is as far as the expressiveness of the words "akka/ämmä" goes; semantically they are, in other words, sufficiently vague to be used alongside other metaphorical words to describe numerous objects or structures in the country home or yard.

"Akka/ämmä" serves as an example of a productive metaphor for describing all sorts of referents (Köngäs Maranda 1971a:209–211). As part of the network of metaphors even words as common as this can give more information about the referent than may be deduced from their semantics alone (Saarinen 1991:15). To the experienced riddlee such words act as hints to the answer. Roger D. Abrahams aptly speaks of "conventionalizing" which operates on nearly every riddle that emerges. "Whenever a riddle begins 'My father', the audience assumes that an object (or related objects) is being described. The same is true when traits or actions begin the description." (Abrahams 1972:195, cf. also Cole-Beuchat 1957:143–144.) Some objects have, furthermore, been found to apply more strongly to one sex than to the other (Gustafsson 1980:15).

The degree of metaphor varies in riddles (see also the examples in Haring 1985:165–166). If the riddle image consists only of a simple metaphor, it causes a considerable amount of trouble. The respondent can never know which of the riddle elements are metaphorical and which should be taken literally. The situation is made all the more difficult by the fact that the same expressions are true in some riddles but metaphorical in others (Saarinen 1991:151). Almost every element of a riddle may be metaphorical, for example,

>An old man with grey hair on his stomach.
>– A pumpkin. (Blacking 1961:9)

or consist of an extended metaphor, in which case each line of the metaphor constitutes a new metaphor with a counterpart in the answer part of the riddle:

>Metsän viisas viepi ajan tiedon pellon parantajalta.
>– Kettu vie kukon tunkiolta.
>The wise one of the woods takes the telling of time from the improver of the field. – A fox takes the cock from his dungheap. (FR 548)

In very many cases the answer to a riddle is surprisingly short compared with the metaphor.

The person skilled in the riddle tradition has the competence both to solve riddles and to invent new ones. The potential for varying most metaphors is almost endless. For example, the 126 variants of FR type 341 fall into the following five categories:

> A1  Kirjava karja ja musta paimen. – Seurakunta ja pappi.
> Spotted cattle and a black herder. – A congregation and parson.
> A2  Musta härkä mulleroinen kirjavassa karjassa. – Pappi kirkossa.
> Beefy, black bull in spotted cattle. – A parson in church.
> A3  Kirjava karja, musta paimen, valakee parta paimenella.
> – Pappi ja seurakunta.
> Spotted cattle, black herder, herder has a white beard.
> – A parson and congregation.
> B1  Musta härkä mylvii kirjavaan karjaan. – Pappi saarnaamassa.
> A black bull bellowing at spotted cattle. – A parson preaching.
> B2  Punanen navetta kirjavaa karjaa täynnä ja musta sonni mylvii keskellä.
> – Pappi kirkossa.
> A red cowshed full of spotted cattle and a black bull bellowing in the middle. – A parson in church.

Variant groups A1 and B1 are the ones with the greatest frequencies. This type, chosen completely at random, demonstrates that the metaphors of riddle questions always provide some scope for variation: a black herder, black bull, black bull bellowing. There is, however, always one fixed element – the adjective "black" referring to the pastor. The "spotted cattle", which also appears in Kalevala-metric poetry, meaning the congregation is stable in a type like this, but the riddle image can further be supplemented by a verb, an extension or an adverb of place. The picture of variation would undoubtedly by diversified further if all 126 variants were subjected to closer inspection.

The field of application of an individual metaphor is not often limited to one riddle only but provides a basis for several images. For example, "spotted cattle" may, apart from a congregation, refer to beans, as in FR riddle 340:

> Kirjavaa karjaa ajetaan niinistä siltaa myöden malmiseen linnaan.
> – Papuja vieritetään pataan.
> Spotted cattle are driven along a bast bridge into a metal castle.
> – Beans being dumped into a pot.

A black bull is in turn a common metaphor for a sauna stove, while the two riddle variants belonging to category B2 were improvised by exploiting a metaphor referring to a mouth and teeth (cf. for example, ER types 499–501). Variation on the basic metaphors and the wide potential for combining them tempt the riddler to invent new riddles. Often different variants have their own regional frequency.

## *The culture-bound riddle metaphor*

Some riddle metaphors are common international property known in direct translation and looser counterparts in different language and culture areas. For example, of the 1,248 riddle types in *Finnish Riddles*, 117 (9 per cent) have counterparts in the type index *English Riddles from Oral Tradition* by Archer Taylor (1951) analysing international counterparts. ER type 367–369, the widely-known White Bird Featherless Flies Without Wings, is one of the international riddle metaphors that have interested countless researchers (cf. the bibliography in Taylor 1951:120–121). Antti Aarne (1920:159) and Archer Taylor (1951:115–122) are among the scholars who have investigated the earliest manifestations of the metaphor, its fixed elements and variation, distribution, borrowing, and the various answers attached to it.

Study of the national applications of international metaphors nevertheless reveals that the popular metaphors in widespread circulation have cultural variants of their own. The link with context is particularly clear on examination of the riddles known in only one language or culture area. For example, of the 1,248 riddles in *Finnish Riddles*, 683 (55 per cent) have no known counterpart in the riddling traditions in the other closely-related Finno-Ugrian languages, in Swedish, Russian, the Baltic languages or English. Similar geographically restricted riddles are of course to be found in the folklore of all language and culture areas. (For example, Cole-Beuchat 1957:136, Haring 1974:204, Reeder 1981:239, 256–257.) African Venda riddles display a marked absence of any reference to European language or culture (Blacking 1961:10). On the other hand the researcher will sometimes come across some astonishing cultural loans. For example, European technology and customs are imported goods, and this is also reflected in riddles (Cole-Beuchat 1957:147, Köngäs Maranda 1971b:59–60). Riddles are, however, primarily bound to their users' own cultural, social and economic contexts in that the objects to be guessed are chosen from their own living environment. Nor does tradition ever rely purely on loans; it is created and varied where it is used. Riddle metaphors thus embrace certain cultural references that are never revealed to the representative of an alien culture.

The way we view the world is also bound to the language we speak. In the English language, for example, the term "eyes" is applied metaphorically to plants and objects (Ben-Amos 1976:252). This image is not necessarily familiar in all languages. But riddle metaphors also contain references to oral literature and material culture or customs (Cole-Beuchat 1957:145) the meaning of which is only clear to those with the same cultural competence, or maybe even some special field of it. This is the case when, for example, a line from a charm or poem is used as a metaphor, such as:

> Mytty mättähän takainen, kiekura kiven alainen, kieko kannon juurinen.
> – Kärme.
> A bundle behind a tussock, a coil beneath a stone, a circle like the root of a tree runk. – A snake. (FR 638)

This Finnish riddle ties in with the clichéd metaphors of the snake charm (cf. SKVR VII$_3$, 1067) but its successful image is undoubtedly also clear to the listener not familiar with the most common context of the metaphor.

139

The borders between genres are not always rigid, and images may be common property with a variety of uses.

The researcher analysing the riddle metaphors of alien cultures finds himself faced with certain problems. He cannot hope to understand the riddles of the new culture area before he has learnt the fields of imagination of the group he is studying. An explanation may often be necessary, but even then the meaning of the riddle is not always revealed, because we do not recognise the similarity linking the two ideas (Harries 1976:324). Riddles at least to some extent draw on the basic cultural metaphors that are conventional, generally accepted and that combine culturally perceived similarities. Admittedly the uniformity of cultures should not be overestimated, since they split up into numerous subcultures. In using a metaphor riddles bring with them "a temporary threat of discontinuity" (Abrahams 1972:182), or they disrupt the systems of conceptualising reality prevailing in the community instead of creating new ones (Saarinen 1991:20–21). It is precisely here that we find the element of surprise characteristic of a riddle metaphor and the play on conventions.

The analysis by Eric Ten Raa (1972:100) of the riddle tradition of the Sandawe people of Africa is highly revealing. He demonstrates by means of examples just how much special knowledge the listener must have before he can grasp all the allusions inherent in the metaphors of an alien culture area. For example, the riddle

A hornless cow finishes up the country. – A hyena.

refers to young initiates pacing about the camp while waiting for their initiation period to end. Only a person entirely familiar with the cultural references in the metaphor can understand the image. Ten Raa writes: "A hornless cow is an incomplete animal, an anomaly. Of young girls it is said that 'they have no horns yet', meaning that they haven't developed their breasts for which reason they are still incomplete. Initiates in circumcision camps (in particular boys) are called 'hyenas' (tékele) as long as they have not yet become complete people, i.e., been reintegrated into society as young men. Hyenas are witches' familiars and therefore anomalous animals symbolising outcasts and socially incomplete beings; they are hornless cows. The expression 'to finish up the country' is a Sandawe idiom for carelessly pacing up and down like hyenas while waiting for lions to finish gorging themselves on their kill." – In this case the answer to the riddle is thus also metaphorical.

Tradition bearers may also offer different explanations for their choice of riddle images and answers, and the researcher attempting to test the explanation given by one with a second tradition bearer will find that the latter cannot see any sense in the explanation given by the former: "It is most unlikely that *all* the finer points of a complicated riddle pun are recognized by a single riddle player" (Raa 1972:104–105). Familiarity with a culture is not therefore always a key to the full understanding of a metaphor. Riddles may, furthermore, demand the special knowledge of many subcultures. And they always involve the surprising fact that the ambiguous element of a metaphor is subject to more than one conventional interpretation (Pepicello & Green 1984:81). Maybe this is one reason why the same riddle can be asked again and again. A riddle metaphor is not always exhausted on a single occasion even if the right answer is given. Riddling is a social situation in which such elements as entertainment value, speed, making a fool of others, and being right weigh far more than the analysis of a metaphor.

In the case of the image the analysis has covered not only the metaphor and the simile, but allegories, too. The Russian scholar V.P. Anikin sees a strong link between riddles and allegoric speech that stems from the fact that people began to use conventional substitute names for, for example, concepts of a delicate nature in farming and hunting, since it was not considered wise to mention them by name. A secret hunters' language, for example, thus evolved. The raven, the snake, and the cat were not spoken of by their proper names but rather as "the upper one", "the lean one", and "the one behind the stove". Sometimes the roots of the substitute words stretch a long way back in time, such as 'the gay one', 'the handrail' and 'the yoke' for a rainbow among the Belorussians. One of these names also appears in a riddle: "The painted yoke overhangs the river." Some splendid euphemisms have been invented for the beasts of the forest such as the bear, like the "king of the rocks", "the terrifying one" and "the respected, the venerable one" among the Altaic peoples.

The connection between allegoric speech and the riddle is in Anikin's opinion genetic, and it is also manifest in the choice of themes taken up by the riddle. The riddle was born out of concepts that could not be mentioned by name and for which a euphemism had to be devised. For example, among the peasants who lived on Lake Pskov, the word "priest" was prohibited while fishing. The same prohibition applied to the words "bear", "hare" and "fox". These words, to be avoided while hunting and fishing, thus gave rise to a riddle. Yet the words "judge", "landowner", "prince" and "tsar" did not, contrary to expectation, engender riddles. (Anikin 1975:25–37.)

Although Anikin does give a long list of words subject to verbal prohibition, his theory of the genetic link between the themes of prohibitions and the themes of riddles is not convincing. This explanation does not solve the question of the origin of riddles. Rather, Anikin's material illustrates the way the same metaphors and euphemisms are used in different genres in incantations, beliefs and riddles.

## Riddle formulae

Proceeding from an idea to its verbalisation, the riddle tradition bearer has at his disposal a number of expressive models, clichés, patterns, fixed forms or linguistic designs. Different terms have been used in speaking of the structural models of small-scale folklore (for example, Scott 1965, Kuusi 1967, Kaivola-Bregenhøj 1974b). The term "formula" refers to the basic scheme or common mould of minor genres, such as proverbs and riddles, into which new folklore products can be cast (Kuusi 1967). This term, adopted from the classical study of proverbs by Archer Taylor (*The Proverb*, 1931), has not, however, acquired a meaning in folkloristic literature restricted exclusively to the structural scheme of minor genres. It has also been applied to, for example, the clichés with which riddles begin and end (Taylor 1951, Scott 1965, Bascom 1949), and it has further been used in research into the rune (Parry 1971) and the prose tradition (for example, "formula tale"). Roger D. Abrahams and Alan Dundes (1972:140) speak of the conventions of expression and say these are important because they provide the framework by which riddles are recognised and remembered. "Each riddle announces itself as being of a certain type by its conventional phrasing. This conventional frame creates a pattern of expectation on the part of hearers, allowing them to hazard a guess at the answer, since the range of possible answers is limited by the riddle's conventional mode of proposition."

The term "formula" is, however, a serviceable one for the analysis of minor genres, one reason being that it has not so far been enlisted into the service of any particular research aspect. At the same time it does not rule out any of the potential approaches: "formula" can be interpreted as a morphological-syntactic, stylistic or semantic model. It should not, however, be viewed as a cliché-like, stereotype phrase repeated verbatim time after time. The concept of formula embraces a number of ideas at various levels of expression. Matti Kuusi claims that the analysis of these linguistic and idea models must of necessity be condensed since the formula-like features are so numerous. He also stresses that the apparent distance of syntactic structures does not prevent them from being used as functional alternatives for one another, and that seeming proximity, or identicalness, does not guarantee functional affinity (Kuusi 1967:72–87).

Archer Taylor set the trend for the formula analysis of minor genres in 1934, in writing of the problems encountered in the study of proverbs: "Characteristic of the invention of many proverbs is the use of older, already existing models. Instead of studying the history of a single proverb, one can therefore endeavour to learn how, when, and where a proverbial formula came to enjoy currency or passed from one culture to another." (Taylor 1934:13)

Taylor has a number of hints to offer the researcher in speaking of fashionable formulae, the free application of a given formula, the relationships between a formula and literature and its influence on tradition, the varying cultural background of a formula, and the part played by linguistic changes in generating new proverb types (Taylor 1934:14). He did not take these ideas up again at a later date. Other research into the structure of riddles (for example, Cole-Beuchat 1957:138–140; Reeder 1981:237, 247) has been closely committed to the idea of formulae or patterns and their variations (Bascom 1949) as models regulating the expression of riddles. Only the terminology varies. Isbell and Fernandez, for example (1977:34–38), use the term "structural transformations" in describing a situation in which a very creative twelve-year-old girl invented a new riddle by utilising one she had just posed. ("A red stone that is impossible to grab, grasp or lift.

– Fire." and "A widow who is impossible to grab or grasp. – A shadow.")The material collected by them in Peru contains a number of examples of spontaneously created riddles. "Home-made" riddles are acceptable, but to be successful, they must observe the norms of riddle language.

On examining true Finnish riddles it is possible to discern 17 formulae that cover 50–55 per cent of all riddles. Their criteria vary, and each model is as a rule governed by several criteria simultaneously. The analysis of formulae relies on identification of the means of expression peculiar to the language in question – in this case Finnish – and of the way they are used as models in the riddling genre. Morphological-syntactic and stylistic criteria are among the most common ones, but allowance must also be made for the number of structural elements and their position in the riddle statement. (Kaivola-Bregenhøj 1978:10–16.)

## *The international riddle model*

One international formula that transcends many linguistic frontiers is the two-member antithetical formula as illustrated by the following Finnish riddles:

1. Kesät makaa, talvet liikkuu. – Reki.
   Lies idle in summer, moves in winter.– A sledge. (FR 314)
2. Maalla kaatuu, vedessä seisoo. – Verkko.
   Stands in water, falls on land. – A net (FR 520)
3. Kahdesti syntyy, kerran kuolee. – Lintu.
   Born twice, dies once. – A bird. (FR 223)
4. Kesällä mahassa, talvella selässä. – Turkki.
   In the "belly" in summer, on your back in winter.
   – A fur coat. (FR 303)
5. Eespäin iltasella, takaperin aamusella. – Uunin pelti.
   Frontwise in the evening, backwise in the morning.
   – An oven vent. (FR 57)

The basis of the formula classification is the regularly recurring structural elements of the traditional genre and their manner of linkage. It is necessary to define the basic unit of the analysis so that we can name the criteria of the ground plan or model of the formula. I term this unit the formula member, and it is also the smallest independent structural unit of the analysis, though it, in turn, is made up of member components. The degree to which individual riddles are bound to the formula is determined by formula criteria. By examining the structure and number of the members as well as the regularities prevailing between them, we can elucidate the criteria of the formula. The antithetical formula comprises a group of structurally fixed, two-part riddles. The formula members are an unspecified adverbial such as one of time, place, manner or other and a predicate verb (riddles 1–3), or an adverbial and either a nominal or an adverb (riddles 4–5). The formula itself is a combination of two antithetical members. It is not always a direct antithesis but an unusual relationship between states expressed by the members (cf. Saarinen 1991:154–155).

This formula is popular with riddlers and my comparative examples clearly exhibit its creative variety. A formula element alone is not a sufficient criterion for conformity; it must be supplemented by an opposition between the components of two elements. The applications of the formula in different languages indicate that this antithetical structure is international at least within European limits. Let us take a few examples of English, German and Turkish riddles:

> Goes up unready (with difficulty), Comes down ready. – Wall paper. (ER 1458)

> Something goes down laughin' an' coming up cryin'. – A bucket. (ER 768a)

> Hard on the edge, And soft in the middle. – A bed. (ER 1249b)

> Sweet when it is unripened, bitter when it is ripened. – An infant. (Ba göz 1972:657)

> My father has a thing, it's green outside and white inside. – A coconut. (ER 1500b)

> Wächst im winter, dorret im sommer. – Eisapfen. (Wossidlo 1897:339a)
> Grows in winter, dries in summer. – An icicle.

> Hinten frisst's und vorne kommt's. – Dreschmaschine. (Hanika-Otto 1930:85a)
> Eats behind and comes in front. – A threshing machine.

> Des Tages hohl, und des Nachts voll. – Mausefalle. (Hanika-Otto 1930:116)
> Empty by day, full by night. – A mousetrap.

> Oben spitz und unten breit, durch und durch voll süssigkeit. – Zuckerhut. (Wossidlo 1897:247a)

> Pointed at the top and broad at the bottom, sweet throughout.
> – A sugar cone.

Some of the riddles demonstrate how lines that supplement or continue the riddle can be appended to the two-member antithetical formula. At its simplest this formula provides an easy-to-use model, applications of which are to be found in almost any riddle anthology (cf. Köngäs Maranda 1971b:52). Among the simple riddles are, for example, those based on the relationship of inside and outside. The riddle tradition of Peru provides applications such as these:

> Outside it is disagreeable
> Inside it is agreeable. – A cactus fruit.
> Outside it is agreeable
> Inside it is disagreeable.
> – A hot pepper. (Isbell & Fernandez 1977:33, see also Blacking 1961:1013)

In evaluating how formulae span cultures, more extensive study should be made of the verbal traditions germane to different languages and cultural areas.

Among the applications of the antithetical formula of 2+2 construction are riddles combining the expressive devices of several formulae. Often the syntactic-stylistic model does in fact provide a medium for ideas that vary somewhat in content. Every model is surrounded by a band of "borderline cases" (Kaivola-Bregenhøj 1978:76–80) – riddles that are structurally similar but that differ from one another in their semantic realisation. This also demonstrates that a formula can suggest ideas for expression, but that it does not act as a straitjacket, nor is it a pattern that is turned out mechanically.

The starting point for the classification was a corpus of Finnish riddles in which the applications of this antithetical formula are simultaneously regulated by four criteria, namely, 1) the structure of the formula members, 2) the minimum number of members, 3) the stylistic criterion and 4) the syntactic criterion. The riddles I have compared indicate that criteria 1-3 are adaptable as such to the classification, by means of the formula, of the riddle tradition in different languages. With reference to this formula the stylistic criterion of antithesis is all-pervasive and extends to the expression of both components of the members ("kesät makaa/lies in summer", "talvet liikkuu/moves in winter"). The two-member antithetical formula is an example of a riddle pattern in which the degree of crystallisation varies somewhat in the applications of the formula in different languages. Examples of this are English-language riddles in which the verbal component varies from a single verb to a verb plus modifiers ("lives-dies", cf. "shineth bright – is raked up in its own dirt"). These divergences do not, however, change the overall picture of the crystallisation of the formula. All the generalisations concerning formula are based on the frequencies in the material.

Michael L. Chyet (1988) exploits and develops structuralist methods in studying the riddles of the large Arabic-speaking area. He proves convincingly that both the topic-comment concepts (Georges & Dundes 1963) and formula analysis (Kaivola-Bregenhøj 1974b) can be used to identify the structural features in the genre which occur from Morocco to Iraq. Numerous examples "should prove beyond doubt that we can indeed speak of the Arabic riddle as a discrete phenomenon." Not only is the Arabic-speaking area extremely large; it is somewhat heterogeneous at the level of both language and culture. The result is an interesting demonstration that the riddle is at the level of deep structure more closely tied to language than to cultural context.

Some formulae operate at linguistic level. According to the classification of Alan Dundes (1964:36) this represents the level that is completely dependent on the language in which the riddle is presented. This level covers, for example, rhyme, assonance, alliteration, onomatopoeic and other stylistic devices. It is also known as the textural level, in contrast to the structural level. An expressive model manifest at textural level may be characteristic of the entire genre, but still not suffice alone as the criterion for, say, defining a riddle. Maung Than Sein and Alan Dundes (1964) made a survey of the stylistic and textural characteristics of Burmese riddles. Whereas strict syllabic rhyme patterning proved to be a stylistic device favoured by riddles, it was also a feature of Burmese poetry as a whole. Their final conclusion was thus that "a genre *qua* genre must be defined independently of textural characteristics."

A riddle whose central idea operates at linguistic level cannot be translated into another language. A good example of this are the Cheremis riddles using onomatopoeia, i.e. the sound of the words, as their expressive device. Often the meaning of such onomatopoeic words is only apparent from the context. Their semantics may nevertheless become established, so that, for example, the words "Cip cip, kup kup, apšat plak δ l δal" (totally onomatopoeic) in a riddle referring to a wedding are repeated in other riddles referring to weddings. Descriptive words thus in a way acquire fixed meanings and they cannot be used completely at random. (Saarinen 1991:118, see also Haring 1974:205–206.) A similar observation has been made by Andrius Valotka (1992:26), who stresses that "riddles including onomatopoeic words nearly in all cases have only one answer." Contrary to expectation, the freedom to imitate words of the inventor of a riddle is thus very limited.

Another example of language-bound models of expression is the spoonerism. This phenomenon would appear to be familiar in many languages, but its popularity and devices vary (cf. page 87), for example,

> What is the difference between an angry rabbit and a counterfeit 10 $ bill?
> – One's a mad bunny and the other's bad money.
> (Stupid Jokes for Kids 1991:13)

In England and Ireland, for instance, Christmas crackers often contain spoonerisms (communication by Fionnuala Carson Williams).

## *The semantic formula*

In analysing formulae it is not sufficient to operate merely at the level of verbalisation; allowance must also be made for the semantic expressive scheme concealed in the linguistic model. The perspective must then be broadened from the image to the conformities governing the linking of the image with the answer.

Let us take a closer look at one Finnish riddle formula (Kaivola-Bregenhøj 1978) to show that the semantic structure of the formula is far more heterogeneous than the syntactic structure. At syntactic level the riddle, which adheres to the "nominative absolute" scheme, has five components: (A) "A man (B) in the earth, (C) his hair (D) in the wind. – (Answer) A turnip." Classification of the applications of this formula according to the main semantic binary features appearing in the material yields the following oppositions: ± animate, ± human, ± inside, ± nature, ± part of A, ± correlates with A and ± part of the body. Analysis of the research material reveals that the majority of the feature combinations theoretically possible are in fact never used in applications of the nominative absolute formula. Some of the combinations have not been used because of a logical inconsistency in the scheme, while others belong to a register of the expressive potential of the genre that has not yet been exploited but that could be used to create new riddles. The feature combinations manifest in the material form a group of content schemes with which it is possible to verify the semantic choices and limitations that must be familiar to the inventor of the riddle.

52 contentual schemes are needed to classify the 106 nominative absolute riddles in my material according to the criteria presented. The most popular is:

(A) ++ (B varies) C --- D +++ Answer --
or Answer +-

This should be read as follows:

A +animate and +human
B (varies)
C -animate, -part of A, and -part of body
D +animate, +part of body, and +correlates with A
Answer -animate and -human, or +animate and -human.

Let me take a few examples of this pair of schemes:

Akka pankolla, kaksi piirainta hampaissa. – Uuni ja patsaslaudat.
An old woman at the oven with two pies between her teeth.
– An oven and two shelf beams. (FR 21)

Mies mäellä seisoo, rautahousut jalassa. – Heinähanko.
A man standing on the hill, iron trousers on his legs.
– A pitchfork. (FR 434)

Pieni mies metsässä, sadehattu hartioilla. – Sieni.
A little man in the woods, a rain hat on his shoulders.
– A mushroom. (FR 746)

Ukko uunilta putosi pesinpytty persiessä. – Pappi saarnaa kirkossa.
An old man fell off the oven, a washbowl in his arse.
– A cockroach. (FR 1092)

This scheme applies to 37 per cent of my research material (Kaivola-Bregenhøj 1978:74). As we can see from the examples, adjectives and verbs may further be added to the basic components of riddles. The contrast between the riddle image and the answer is in agreement with an observation by Elli Köngäs Maranda (1971a:214) according to which the primary contrast springs from a combination of animate and inanimate, and "the most common juxtaposition is between human and cultural object". There is also clear contrast between human beings and wild plants.

There are in addition a number of borderline cases that reinforce the concept that one syntactic expression model covers many semantic schemes.

The riddler is, however, also regulated by the clear and clichéd rules at the level of content. For example, the applications of the nominative absolute formula in my material do not include any answers referring to a human. Breaking this rule is against the norms and the riddle may fail to win popularity. Variations at semantic level nevertheless appear to be far more common than those at syntactic and/or stylistic level.

The semantic analysis of a riddle may also begin by examining the types of question which receive an answer in the image. This is the approach chosen by Zoja Michajlovna Volockaja (1987:225–245) in analysing Slav riddles in which the referents are natural phenomena. In order to arrive at the right answer, the riddlee must find in the image an answer to the questions "who?", what?", "what does X do?", "what can be done using X?", "where is X?" and "when does X appear?". Riddles are constructed from elementary semantic components, the combination of which produces different riddle structures. The components are by nature either nominative (who/what?), predicative (descriptions of functions and states), attributive (what sort?), possessive (what has X got/not got?), subjective (who can influence X?), locative (the place where X occurs) or temporal (the time at which X appears). The main types of riddle constructed from these components are nominative, predicative and attributive; the numerous subcategories reveal the variety of ways in which semantic components can be combined in riddles.

Before arriving at a synthesis – sought by scholars though its very existence has sometimes been doubted (for example, Georges & Dundes 1963, Scott 1976) – applying to the riddle genre as a whole, it is necessary to study bit by bit the rules for making riddles, and thus to chart the "generic grammar" observed by those inventing and using riddles. The scholar with large riddle collections at his disposal soon notices that material-oriented classification can almost never hope to be exhaustive. Having identified an expressive model, the scholar immediately comes across more liberal applications of the model and deviations. It is obvious that he must chart not only the rules but their exceptions, too. This clearly proves that riddles are created not out of the mechanical combination of structural elements but by a series of options whose conformity also allows creative improvisation.

It is easy to observe that many riddle formulae are made up of certain basic elements that can be combined in different ways. Let us take as an example a group of Finnish riddles containing similes:

> Seisoo ku saksa, istuu ku isäntä, rätäjää ku rakkikoira. – Vokki.
> Stands like a travelling shopkeeper, sits like a master, barks like a cur.
> – A spinning wheel.
> Päästä kuin osa, keskeltä kuin kerä ja takaa kuin petkelen terä. – Kana.
> Like a prong at the end, like a ball of yarn in the middle and its backside is like the blade of a barking tool. – A chicken. (FR 34)
> Lattian laajuinen, lehden kevyinen. – Savu.
> Broad as the floor, light as a leaf. – Smoke. (FR 457)
> Puun pituinen, punalangan paksuinen. – Puun sydän.
> Length of a tree, thickness like a red thread. – The pith of a tree. (FR 820)
> Musta kun pappi, eik ou pappi,

lentää kuin lintu, eik ou lintu,
möyryvää kuin härkä, eik ou härkä,
männöö muan ala kun mato, eik ou mato. – Sitsontijainen.
Black as a parson but isn't a parson,
flies like a bird but isn't a bird,
bellows like a bull but isn't a bull,
goes underground like a worm but isn't a worm. – A dung beetle. (FR 613)
Mikä on hanhea valkoisempi. – Enkeli.
What is whiter than a goose? – An angel.
Mikä on mustaa mustempi. – Murhe.
What is blacker than black? – Grief.
Korkeamp kuin hevoin, matalamp kun sika. – Satula.
Higher than a horse, lower than a pig. – A saddle. (FR 374)
Julmempi kuin susi, nöyrempi kuin lapsi. – Tuli.
Crueller than a wolf, more humble than a child. – Fire.
Pienempi Jumalaa, suurempi kuningasta. – Surma, kuolema.
Smaller than God, greater than a king. – Death. (FR 736)
Enemmän muas reikii, kuin taivaas tähtii. – Sänki.
More holes in the ground than stars in the sky. – Stubble. (FR 43)

One thing shared by all these riddles is their comparative element. However, if we compare the morphological structure of an individual comparative element, the coherence or composition of comparative elements and the number of elements in the riddle statement, we begin to see some differences. Approaching the examination via the stylistic characteristics, we may see the following differences in the riddle sentences: a property is compared to a concrete symbol of it (whiter than a goose); the metaphor and the object referred to are expressed using the same word (blacker than black); the second element refutes the first, because the vital attribute of X does not refer to X (black as a parson but isn't a parson); there is direct opposition between the elements (higher – lower), or the opposition is indirect (crueller – humbler), but despite the direct opposition of the adjectives in the riddle image the elements are not necessarily opposed to one another (smaller than God – greater than a king). The analysis can then be modified by estimating the importance of Kalevala metre and alliteration in the verbalisation of the riddle image (i.e. the Finnish version of the riddle is "*s*eisoo ku *s*aksa, *i*stuu ku *i*säntä). It would also be necessary to examine the semantic relationship between the image and the answer. Looking at the above group of examples, we immediately spot the abstract answers 'angel', 'grief' and 'death', which deviate from the object, animal and concept referents familiar in an agrarian milieu.

The above examples clearly prove that the closer the properties of some expressive model are defined, the larger the number of criteria required becomes. Since the formula analysis method begins by examining the crystallisation and variation of a folklore item, it can also be developed case by case according to the approach required by the material. Formulae are no more commensurable at the level of linguistic expression than they are at the level of content. There is no universally valid method of distinguishing formulae and their characteristic features; formula analysis involves the application of different research aspects.

In a community in which riddling is a live tradition in regular use, improvisation may play a considerable role. The following 19 riddles form a thematic entity which John McDowell calls "probable and improbable conversants":

1. What did the big chimney say to the little chimney?
2. What did the Aggie say to the other Aggie?
3. What did the three Aggies say to the other four Aggies?
4. What did the rug say to the floor?
5. What did the dead penguin say to the live penguin?
6. What did the rug say to the floor?
7. What did the ten Aggies say to the one Aggie?
8. What did the one Aggie say to the zero Aggie?
9. What did the blue whale say to the duck?
10. What did the whale shark say to the great white?
11. What did the live duck say to the other live duck?
12. What did the baby say to the cradle?
13. What did the blue whale say to the great white?
14. What did the (burping noise) say to the great white?
15. What did the uhhhh say to the great white?
16. What did the burp say to the great white?
17. What did Spiderman say to Ironman?
18. What did the Martian say to the human?
19. What did the man say to the store?

The riddling session consisted of four Anglo, middle-class children, two boys and two girls. The situation was recorded on video in a studio in 1979, and the strange situation, the cameras and the presence of adults made the children hyperactive. There are two traditional items in this sequence, numbers 1 and 6, and they were asked by the girls. The remaining items were improvised spontaneously by the boys. The children were concentrating so hard on inventing amusing questions that they could not be bothered to answer them. Each question is regulated by the formula "What did the X say to the Y?" The following rules further apply to elements X and Y: "1. The question specifies two entities allegedly in conversation. 2. Neither of these entities is normally included in the category of speech participants ('the man' in 19 is an exception). 3. A motivation for dialogue must exist, either in the form of shared identity (little chimney, big chimney) or habitual proximity (rug and floor)." (McDowell 1979:146-156 and 1985:204–206.)

These seemingly simple, casually improvised questions are thus subject to a clear set of rules based on logical analysis of the components. Although the children are not aware of the existence of the criteria, they can in principle go on improvising "proper" questions until all the acceptable entities have been used. McDowell does not report why the question sequence ended and what happened next. The children probably got bored with the subject (for example, "the Aggie", a numskull figure in Texan popular culture, was milked dry in four questions) and began to look around for some other theme.

The crystallised means of expression – the formulae – used by the riddling tradition provide the riddler with a way of supplementing his repertoire and inventing new items for the riddling community. We might even speak of the reclaiming and recycling of riddles. The language of riddles is, however, difficult to command in the case of traditional true riddles. Proof of this are the hundreds of riddles of which there is only a single variant in the sizeable Folklore Archives of the Finnish Literature Society. Often these riddles clearly offend some rule of riddling grammar, and they have for this reason never passed the test of the riddling community. They have remained one-off products used by a small circle, but at the same time they reflect an ability to improvise on tradition and to exploit the potential of language. Correspondingly, some popular riddles may run to several hundred variants.

# 7 From image to answer

All riddling situations involve some form of competition – a test of knowledge or wit. They may, however, vary from specially arranged contests between two teams and the audience to free-form questioning inserted in the discourse. Even if competition is not known in some cultures, in every case there are nevertheless two opposing parties, one of which is in possession of knowledge with which it tests the other.

Researchers who have conducted fieldwork among communities that still have an active riddling tradition stress the importance of the riddle poser. "A riddler is given status because he has been willing to let himself be a channel of energy by which the community may be entertained, reinvigorated, and brought together" (Abrahams 1972:194). At the start of riddling the riddle poser clearly holds a higher status than the riddlee. If, however, the riddlee passes the test, the statuses are temporarily equalised. He may even be compared to the initiate who, in the course of a *rite de passage*, accedes to a status equal to the initiated who initiates him (Glazier & Glazier 1976:203–204). The poser holds both intellectual and social power: "Intellectually the poser has the knowledge required to answer the riddle; socially, the power to determine whether an answer offered is acceptable" (Haring 1985:178). In some communities his power robs the riddlee of all chances of success. At Monteros in Andalusia, for example: "The riddler, we may say, is accorded dictatorial authority to determine precisely what the answer should be" (Brandes 1980:129). The role of the riddle poser cannot, however, be generalised any more than that of the riddlee, since it varies from one culture to another. For example, the accounts of Finnish riddling clearly stress the status of the riddlee. Yet there is always power involved, for a person who gives a wrong answer could be symbolically or playfully banished by the group posing the riddles (cf. Chapter 5).

## The relationship between the riddle metaphor and the answer

The "right" answer to a riddle metaphor is always found in the end – this is one of the rules of the game. But whether the answer always provides the key to the metaphor is quite another matter.

Many definitions of riddles stress that true riddles "give the hearer enough information to guess the answer --- Descriptive riddles or riddles in the strict sense can usually be solved without great difficulty" (Taylor 1949:3). Taylor's views are akin to the riddle research published by Antti Aarne in 1918–1920. Aarne claimed that one feature of true riddles was that solving them called for invention and sharp wit (Aarne 1917:3). Guessing is also mentioned as one way of solving a riddle in the definition of the genre given by Robert A. Georges and Alan Dundes in their article published in 1963. The focal point of this definition does in fact lie elsewhere, in the structural definition of the genre, and the mention of guessing may be due to the literature.

How are riddles in fact solved? There are many possible answers to this question, and they vary greatly from one culture and riddle subgenre to another. In a riddling situation the experienced riddlee recognises the frequently used, cliché-like metaphors and arrives at the correct answer either by using his knowledge of the genre and his wits or because he is familiar with the most common images and knows the answer in advance. We could, however, shift the perspective and ask: does the competence of a folklore adept imply an ability to derive from a riddle image precisely that correct answer which the poser and the riddling community expect of him?

## One image, many answers

I will first try to determine the relationship between the riddle metaphor and the answer by examining riddle anthologies. It is easy to pick out examples of Finnish riddles demonstrating that one riddle image may have many different answers. Here is an example included by Christfrid Ganander in his anthology of riddles in 1783:

> Tuonelassa tuoppi tehty, täällä vantehet valettu. – Kaivo.
> A stoup was made in Tuonela, the hoops (were) cast (up) here. – A well.
> (Tuonela is the underworld in ancient Finnish mythology)

There are numerous alternative answers among the variants to this particular riddle, but four that feature more than any other: a cow's horns (37 variants), a well (32), a ring (16), and answers on the theme of a new-born baby (27). The answers to different variants often fall into groups in which the same referent is varied slightly. The "well" answer thus takes in a further 3 variants the answer to which is a well bucket, while the following variations appear on the cow's horn answer: a calf with horns growing (4), a calf (2), and a calf and cow (2). The theme of the new-born child stimulates the following

153

alternative answers: having a baby, the birth of a baby, giving birth to and clothing a child, a child, a babe-in-arms, a baby's christening. "The moon" is the answer to eight variants. The following answers appearing in 1–4 variants might also be given to this riddle: birth and engagement, a bride, church bells, a coffin, an egg, a finger, a glove, a hole in the ice, a human, a hymn book, money, a pot, a pot and handle, the sea and shores, snow, a spinning wheel, a still, the sun, a well and spring, and a window. Often the second line of the image is altered to better suit the answer, as in,

>"täällä kullat kaunistettu" (morsian)
>"here the gold is beautified" (a bride)
>"täällä kimmit kiinnitetty" (kirkonkello)
>"here the blocks are attached" (a church bell)
>"tällä maalla täytetähän" (pata, saapas, sormus, vatsa ja kuu)
>"this with soil is filled" (a pot, boot, ring, stomach and the moon)
>(Kuusi 1960:120).

Six riddles have been noted down without an answer. There are 155 known variants of this riddle accumulated over the years in the collections of the Folklore Archives of the Finnish Literature Society. This riddle nevertheless displays the rarer extreme on the variation scale compared with the numerous riddles to which hundreds of users have decided on one and the same answer.

The variation in the answers is an indication that the relationship between the image and the referent is on the one hand well thought out (cow's horns, well, ring, new-born baby and moon – 114 items) yet on the other hand undoubtedly the result of pure conjecture (all other 41 variants). The fact that many true riddles can have several answers proves that new cultural classes are invented in using riddles (Lieber 1976:262). The images are semantically often so vague that there are several suitable answers. We may also, in the manner of Lee Haring (1974:199), speak of the greater applicability and fertility of certain metaphors. In some variants of our example riddle the Kalevala-metre "Tuoppi tehty Tuonelassa / A stoup was made in Tuonela" is replaced by the line "Tuolla maalla tuoppi tehty / In that land a mug was made", which in Finnish sounds much the same. In both cases the riddle applies the near/far formula, possibly emphasising not so much the Tuonela concept as the misleading contrast between near and far widely familiar in the riddle tradition. Many concepts that may at first sight appear strange thus present themselves as answers.

The different answers attached to the same riddle image may also have their origins in different riddling communities. In our example riddle the distribution of the main answers – cow's horns, a well, a ring and a baby – would appear to support this assumption. There is some overlapping in the regional distribution of the answers, but the main regions clearly avoid one another. The "well" answer centres on Western Finland, the "ring" answer on North Ostrobothnia and neighbouring Kainuu. "Cow's horns" is the answer given partly in the same regions as "ring", but it tends more towards Eastern Finland. The baby theme and its variations also centre on the same easterly regions. The other answers do not have such a clear regional distribution. –

The material demonstrates that some answers are mutually exclusive, and also that 2–3 different answers may be known in the same tradition areas.

The wide range of answers does not, however, do full justice to the life of the tradition. In order to complete the picture we need more information about the people using the tradition and their choices. For example, the Finnish Literature Society's archives contain hundreds of variants on riddles once used by different groups and they prove that each riddle image – even the ones that seem most senseless – in most cases has only one acceptable answer in its performing context. The people supplying riddles appear only in exceptional cases to have told the collector that a particular riddle image had several answers. Of the 155 variants in my material there are only three for which the riddle collector has noted down two different answers.

Once again it is, morover, possible to find cultural differences. For example, it is quite common in many African communities for riddles to have parallel answers in the oral tradition even though only one is given in publications (Hamnett 1967 and Haring 1974). Choosing a suitable answer is not, however, a random affair, and in most cases the riddle poser decides which answer is acceptable.

It is, however, quite possible to imagine some situations in which people were not unanimous about the answer. When the riddle was presented for the first time and no one but the poser knew the right answer, the riddlees might be stimulated to try out various alternatives. The following account presents a typical riddle situation:

> The mail came from Kristiina by horse carriage, and it always arrived in Vanhakylä in the evening, sometimes terribly late because of blizzardous road conditions. Then, while waiting for it, the time would've dragged if we hadn't invented something.
> – Well then, while sitting there, some riddle pops into somebody's mind. Väinö Alanko was clever in exactly those, and so he throws out a question:
> – Akka maas, ukko puus, ukon munat akan suus. – Sanokaa mikä se on./ The old woman's on the ground, the old man's in a tree with his "eggs" in her mouth. Say what it is.
> – It's a well with a sweep, comes at the same time from the mouths of many, for this riddle's number one among riddles because it puts one to thinking about obscenity.
> Väinö picks at his nose, this was a confirmed habit of his, and he was also the village's spitting champion.
> – No, mikä on karvainen juuresta ja punainen päästä…?/Well, what's hairy at the root and red at the end..?
> –It's a strawberry, breaks in Aune Jaakkola, who already started to blush. She was the village's most sensible lass, a quarter of a year older than me, and went to the upper grade of elementary school.
> Väinö frets 'cause he didn't get to tell the riddle to the end. He snaps at Aune:
> – Why did you break in, there would've been somebody who didn't know.
> –We sure knew it, comes from everybody's mouth.
> Väinö, cross at the interruption, says to Aune:
> –Aune, now you tell us some sort of riddle that nobody knows, since you're so smart.

Aune thinks. Everybody waits, and Väinö starts to cackle, and at once Aune delivers:

– Mitä varten jänis juoksee tien yli?/Why does a hare run across a road?

– Cause it can't go under it. This comes from everybody's mouth. Väinö laughs:

– Tell the sort of one that nobody knows. That one's even in the ABC book.

Again Aune thinks, strains, and tries. Nothing comes to mind. Should she invent the very sort that nobody's heard of? Oh, oh, how did that potato riddle go?

[Aune next poses a question "Missä maassa on noita?" in which the hind part of the word for "potatoes," *perunoita,* is detached and employed alone. *Noita* ("tatoes") is, among other things, a noun denoting "witch." The word *maa* is also used in two senses: as "land" and as "field". The correct answer to the play on words is: "in a potato field".]

– In what land (/field) do you find a witch (/tatoes)? is asked all of a sudden.

– There's one in every land.

– There's no such thing as witches.

– Witches, witches (/tatoes, tatoes) grumbles Väinö, and Aune smiles

She's invented a riddle that nobody knows. Everybody's thoughts seek out the solution to the riddle. Väinö growls suspiciously:

– You invented it yourself – there isn't any answer to it.

– Yes, there is.

– Well, say it!

– No, I won't say, try to guess!

– God darn it, I know it, says Onni Mikkola, the smallest in our group.

– Well, say... no, no, don't say it yet. Whisper it in my ear.

This is Aune's request, and Onni goes over to her and whispers something in her ear.

Aune laughs.

– No it's not in Parkano. There are witches elsewhere too. There's a whole lot of them too. But say in what land (/field).

– That's not a riddle.

– Yes it is, and now I'll say it: in a potato field.

– Didn't I say that it was invented, sneers Väinö. There aren't any witches in a potato field.

– There's craft behind it, says Aune. Doesn't a potato field have po-tatoes? Everybody laughs. Väinö feels embarrassed. He, too, tries to invent something of the sort that's never been heard before. The others wait, and so the game continues. Now this perhaps isn't to the T how it happened. But in many of those riddle situations I attended, it happened thus that no riddle that was unknown would turn up any more. The young people of that time had good memories, because they didn't have to store so many things in their minds as people do nowadays. Everybody remembered what they had heard just once. Now when an empty spell came upon the crowd, the game had to be changed, or then one had to invent some new riddle oneself. We also tried to work up some old, worn riddle so it'd be different. I think that it's just by that way of Aune's that these riddles of the Finnish people have been born. While a little boy and even as a grown-up man I've tried to invent new riddles. That calls for intelligence, and one's got to admit that there have been some mighty wise shavers among those forefathers of ours. (From Isojoki. Kaivola-Bregenhøj 1977:72–73.)

The riddling community involved here consisted of children who daily arrived to await the coming of the mail, and it is easy to imagine that the composition of this group from the small village remained more or less constant. From this follows the situation presented in the depiction where everyone knows the riddles asked and their solutions, and the answers come as "from one mouth".

We know from Finnish tradition that these attempts usually ended in either communal laughter or criticism of the answer. On the other hand the refusal to accept any alternative answers was the subject of later debate, and the name of any riddlee who made too many mistakes stuck in the mind of the others. Teasing opponents by changing the answer was not always permissible, for the group control generally regulated the course of the game. The answers had to be "right". The trip to Hymylä also reinforces the concept that riddles had to have a single answer unanimously accepted as correct by the riddling community.

Only one situation is known in Finland in which the answer to a riddle could be temporarily changed. This was when someone made the mistake of asking a riddle with a sexual answer in the hearing of children. Usually, however, the riddling would in this case be broken off and the subject changed: "Children were sometimes asked tricky riddles, but never any that could refer to something else. If a boy, or come to that a man, happened to ask something that could have been indecent, the other adults would butt in and even put an end to the riddling altogether." (SKS. Aino Hanhisalo AK 2:1.1966.)

## *Is it a case of guessing?*

I further wish to place under the magnifying glass two riddles the examination of whose variants reveals that the answer is not, however, arrived at by arbitrary means. The riddle "Mies tuvassa, tukka tuulessa."/"A man in the farm kitchen, his hair in the wind" (Kaivola-Bregenhøj 1977:25–27) has 136 variants in the archive collections. The answers fall into two main categories, one of which centres round the fireplace and smoke, the other round the farm kitchen and the supporting beam. The relationship between the riddle image and the answer is therefore either the relationship between a man and his hair = a fire and smoke or that between the farm kitchen and the supporting beam. In this case the riddle thus permits two interpretations of equal status. Both would appear to be equally logical to the riddlee who knows from his own living environment how a fireplace and a supporting beam fit in a peasant building. Alongside this riddle we may also take a second one with an almost identical image: "Mies mullassa, tukka tuulessa."/"A man in the earth, his hair in the wind." This riddle has 121 variants in the collections, and the answers concentrate on describing a turnip or some other root crop. The only answer diverging from this semantically uniform group of answers is "teeth", which is quite obviously "wrong" and temporarily improvised. The relationship between image and answer is in this riddle as follows: the relationship between the man and his hair = the relationship between a root crop and its tops. These two almost identical riddle images are kept completely separate apart from a few hybrid forms. The analysis is, however, not yet complete unless, in addition to the "man–hair" image we also allow for the adverbial expressions "in the farm kitchen" and "in the earth", which have to be taken literally in relation to the answer. This component, separating two images, may be thought of as giving the riddlees a clue to the answer. The adverbs of place in riddles often provide a clue, i.e. they should be taken at their face value.

These two riddles prove that the variation of image and answer is not arbitrary – at least not always – and that it is strictly governed by the semantic scheme (cf. Köngäs Maranda 1971a:192). Nor was just any answer fitting the image acceptable; only certain answers recur. When it comes to the answer, variation occurs in the form of either synonymous concepts (for example, a turnip, a turnip in the ground, a turnip growing), or semantic variants (root crops: a turnip, a swede). It seems in the light of these examples incredible that anyone could guess the answers (with the exception of teeth). In any case there was little leeway for guessing, and the riddlees knew from their competence and their familiarity with folklore what could be expected. Guessing in fact means that the person using riddles sifts through the images and answers in his mind and weighs up their compatibility. Both images and answers are relatively few in number in the riddle genre, so people would have been familiar with them even though they did not immediately recall them. Scholars would no doubt agree that "riddling is always closer to an academic test than to creative research" (Köngäs Maranda 1971a:196).

Guessing did not, therefore, by any means always lead to the right, i.e. an acceptable answer. Similar observations have been made by very many scholars. Riddles would, however, lose their vigour without the possibility inherent in the metaphor of two or more interpretations and sometimes even an arbitrary interpretation. "Contextual ambiguity" means that "during the riddling act the riddlee is not aware of the specific act of information upon which a riddle metaphor is based. That is, while the riddle agonists share a body of conventional information, only the riddler knows that, for example, eggs are being compared to houses." (Green & Pepicello 1979:12.) Only in exceptional cases is the riddle image a test of knowledge requiring a single answer – a number of suitable answers could in most cases be put forward. The answer to a riddle denotes a given cluster of properties, and any entity possessing the said properties will qualify as an answer (Lieber 1976:260–263). The riddler has in reality placed his authority at stake in making the question and will in most cases only accept the answer he had in mind. He dominates the situation and decides when to put an end to the game and the time for the answer to be given (Bausinger 1967). A large proportion of riddle metaphors thus become "frozen" images based on shared knowledge and with a known answer. The active riddlees and the rest of the audience will not, however, necessarily always accept the situation and will protest. Elli Köngäs Maranda has described a riddle occasion in which a correct answer was rejected: "I have recorded riddling situations in Malaita where heated discussions followed when a poser did not accept an answer that made sense. It is perhaps a psychological phenomenon worth noting that many riddle posers focus on the answer that they themselves have in mind, and they tend to reject perfectly suitable alternatives" (Köngäs Maranda 1971b:55). This illustrates how two different ways of solving the riddle metaphor may emerge in a riddling situation: the answer proffered by the riddlee really is founded on a creative guessing and deduction process, whereas the answer expected by the riddler is based on the conventional interpretation of the metaphor that does not tolerate any variation.

*Arbitrary and conventional answers*

Sometimes not even the correct answer during a riddling occasion satisfies the poser most obviously intent on humiliating the riddlee, as in: "---'What has four legs, a wagging tail, and barks?' On the face of it, this calls for a flash of triumph from the riddlee, for in the emotionally charged riddling session he is glad to be able to solve one. Therefore, he commonly hastens to answer 'A dog'. To which the riddler is then able to say, 'Oh, you've heard that one,' thereby making a statement about the simple-mindedness of the riddlee" (Abrahams & Dundes 1972:140). From there it is but a step to the situation in which every attempt by the riddlee, even if it is correct, is rejected. The following example comes from Monteros in Andalusia:

> Riddler: Where does woman have the most frizzy hair?
> Riddlee: (tentatively): In the cunt?
> Riddler: No, in the Philippines. Good. Now you can say: where she has it the most frizzy?
> Riddlee: (definitively): Of course, in the Philippines.
> Riddler: No. Where you told me before. (Brandes 1980:129–130.)

This is an example of a trick question that tends to make the riddlee look stupid, but more is known about the arbitrary relationship between the riddle image and the answer (for example, Sutton-Smith 1976:112 and Glazier & Glazier 1976:199). It is, however, overdoing things to conclude that "one goal of riddling is for the riddler to finally supply the answer to the riddlee(s) who has given up" (Pepicello & Green 1984:83). It is unlikely that riddling would be popular if it always ended up with one party being humiliated. The idea put forward by Pepicello and Green would seem to apply more to joking questions and other subgenres, which make up the bulk of their research material. In any case the roles of riddle poser and humiliated party change and a state of equilibrium is achieved.

The answer may also be so difficult or even arbitrary that it is impossible to deduce from the image (cf. Cole-Beuchat 1957:142). For example, the riddles presented in connection with rites may be obscure even to the native expert on the tradition in question (Harries 1971:386). My research into the nominativus absolutus formula showed that in the material of 106 riddles there were 23 whose answer could not be recognised by means of the rules for riddling (Kaivola-Bregenhøj 1978:106). One riddling test proved that the more difficult riddles are, the more heterogeneous are the wrong answers given. Riddles that were easy to solve, but which nevertheless did not yield the correct answer in the test, produced numerous identical wrong answers. (Garth 1935:342-345.) – The riddles most difficult to guess are those in which the answer describes a situation and the persons present, as in the following riddle of the Pangve tribe of Cameroon (Zurinskij 1989:46< Saarinen 1991:26): "There is a tree in the back yard whose fruits I never get a chance to eat. – A girl whispering with other men."

Users of tradition have also reported that the relationship between image and answer may remain incomprehensible to them: "--- It is a strict rule that riddles must be 'right', i.e. they may not be invented by the riddler himself unless he can invent such a good riddle (in poetic metre) that the others do not realise he made it up himself. Of many riddles, no more is understood than that a certain kind of object is alluded to. For example, the riddle: 'Hanhinlammas, hapsinsarvi, sillon villa vipsakki. – Hämähäkki. '/'Sheep of goose, horn of hair, it's got a woollen whipsack. A spider.' is wholly unintelligible to Veteli people. No one can explain why spiders are spoken of thus, but everyone knows what it means, and that is the main thing. In general it is impossible to guess riddles at the first hearing." (SKS. A. Salmela 60.1922.) The image and answer may become stabilised (Hamnett 1967:384) in an agreed form even when the metaphor is "easy" and would permit the invention of suitable solutions.

In a riddling situation people do not always deliberate very deeply, tending instead to recall an answer they know but have forgotten (Hamnett 1967:384, Haring 1974:197–198). In the Venda tradition "both riddle and answer were learned as a linguistic whole, and it is more important to know the riddle than to be able to puzzle out the answer or understand their content" (Blacking 1961:1, see also Haring 1974:198). Jack and Phyllis Glazier give an interesting account of an occasion among the Mbeere (Bantu) tribe at which a total of 93 riddles were posed. Only 47 of them were answered correctly at the first attempt, only nine riddlees attempted a second guess, and only three of their answers were correct. The Glaziers came to the conclusion that "correct answers are not reasoned out through deliberation". The riddle session proceeds at great speed, because "people acknowledge that, as one riddle participant lamented when she could not answer correctly, 'Someone who doesn't know, doesn't know'." They concluded that success in riddling depends on hearing riddles and remembering them. (Glazier & Glazier 1976:209.) On the other hand there are some cultures in which the riddlees may debate the answer for days on end before reaching an answer that satisfies the riddler. On examining accounts of Finnish riddling situations I found one case in which the answer was not given if no one guessed it: "We asked and begged for the answer, but they refused to tell us, just laughed and said you've got to guess it, we can't tell you. So we never heard the right answer to that riddle." (SKS. Aino Hanhisalo. AK 2:3. 1967.)

The old riddle literature often underlines the fact that riddles are a battle of wits and aim at developing mental agility. Field studies in true contexts do, however, clearly contradict this claim: riddles are not an intellectual exercise. The social contexts and functions of riddling have, on the other hand, changed since the days of the *Hervarar* saga. Anyone who does not know the answer to a riddle is not in any way encouraged to find it. Riddles have to be learned. Learning has a clear objective among, say, the Vendas, for displaying it brings prestige (Blacking 1961:5, Haring 1974:202).

The posing of riddles in test situations confirms the findings of field researchers. When asked to solve traditional Kazakh riddles, a test group of illiterate Kazakhs were able to answer 90 per cent of them. The same respondents fared much worse when faced with riddles that were less coloured by their own culture. A group of Russian riddlees also did well with riddles from their own culture, but when the Kazakhs were asked Russian riddles and the Russians Kazakh, each in their own mother tongue, the number of correct answers was slight. The ability to solve riddles does not therefore depend on language alone. Experiments with literate Kazakhs with a poor command of their own culture confirmed the theory that familiarity with culture-specific phenomena is more important than language in the solving of riddles. Bilingualism reduced the Kazakhs' ability to solve riddles associated with their own culture. Also taking part in the test were a group of Kazakh students and a group of illiterate Kazakhs. The students were not nearly as good as the illiterate group at solving riddles. General intelligence, familiarity with and command of language do not explain the ability to solve riddles. More important is a familiarity with the context and the ability to see analogies. (Grzybek 1987:251–257.)

Peter Grzybek underlines the importance of the ability to see analogies in the process of solving riddles. Various strategies are employed to form analogies. Sometimes the foremost strategies are logical, intellectual, linguistic and analytic, at other times associative, imaginative, synthetic and non-linguistic. The strategies are not, however, mutually exclusive and may complement one another. (Grzybek 1987:261.) The idea of strategies is in my opinion very pertinent, but I would at the same time stress that the ability to solve riddles draws on models assimilated along with cultural practices. It has in fact been suggested that "each solution can be valid as long as it is offered by a native speaker of the language who shares the cultural experience of the community and has an adequate familiarity with traditional knowledge" (Ben-Amos 1976:249–250). The hypothesis is both correct and false, depending on the perspective. When a given community begins riddling, it may accept a "wrong" answer so long as no one objects. The numerous unconnected answers given to my example riddle "Tuoppi tehty Tuonelassa, täällä vantehet valettu" were right-wrong answers of precisely this type. It is, however, obvious that traditional knowledge generally imposes limitations on this answering practice. On the other hand riddlers among the Edo people in Nigeria did not dare to suggest just any answer for fear of being humiliated. It was better to admit outright that they did not know the answer.

But what is the point of riddling if everyone knows the answer? This problem is in most cases solved by the fact that there are always different people present: there is always someone who has not heard the riddles before. It is, for example, known that in the Nordic countries the craftsmen travelling from farm to farm, the servant girls and farm hands would bring with them the variety needed by the riddling tradition to survive. It has also been pointed out that each time a riddle is asked, it is posed as if for the first time (Harries 1976:317). Despite the rules of the riddling game there is never any guarantee that the riddlee will know the "right" answer. There is thus always an element of excitement. Don Handelman (1996:42) gives an excellent description of this, saying: "The answer to the riddle image both leads elsewhere (the unusual relationship) and returns to the question in the image." An element of surprise is thus built into the answer, because the image can be interpreted in another way. The delight brought by recognising a semantic fit must, however, be stressed (Harries 1976): "The delight of the audience is to be so misled that when the answer is announced one has a sudden sense of a world order discovered or rediscovered" (Abrahams 1972:178). Sharing in the communal knowledge of riddles is a source of joy and reinforces the feeling of group belonging. Sometimes a riddle may be asked simply because everyone knows it, "not because anyone will be confused but precisely because everyone knows the answer and all can demonstrate their knowledge together" (Abrahams 1968:152). This may be just a form of "warming up" before going on to more difficult riddles, or a desire to teach the tradition to those less familiar with it. Indeed, in some cultures riddles are explained to children so that they are not left as outsiders (Cole-Beuchat 1957:142–144).

The conventional relationship between image and answer could be compared to the classical definition given by Ferdinand de Saussure of the linguistic symbol containing two elements, content and expression. In the linguistic symbol the relationship between expression and content is arbitrary. This does not, however, mean that the expression is dependent on the choice made by the speaker in question; it simply emphasises the fact that the expression is unmotivated in relation to the content, with which it has no natural relationship (de Saussure 1970:96–97). Comparing the riddle to the linguistic symbol, it follows that the relationship between image and answer is interpreted as unmotivated. Normally this is not, however, the case. When a successful riddle is created, the relationship between its image and its answer is strictly regulated by the semantic laws of the genre. The relationship between image and answer is then further motivated. But as a riddle becomes part of the repertoire repeated by a community, the motivated relationship between its image and answer may shift from the motivated towards a contractual one. The answer is then no longer always deduced from the image; it is known beforehand, and only this particular answer is accepted.

# 8 The future of riddle research

Riddles have in the past few decades ceased to be part of oral tradition. This does, however, apply only to true riddles, which are in Western culture beginning to represent the part of the genre that is going out of active use and found only in archives and on the pages of publications. The scholar interested in the guessing game tradition will quickly find material in the rapidly renewing topical folklore spread above all by the mass media. Riddling appears to have become channelled most strongly into two subgenres still clearly linked with the traditional riddle genres. By this I mean the joking question tradition and the numerous types of competitions performed or held by way of entertainment.

General knowledge quizzes would appear to be a direct continuation from the posing of riddles, for the first "wise men's clubs" were already going out over the air in, for example, Finland when riddling was still a living tradition. In these programmes a small group of men renowned for their general and specialist knowledge tried to answer the questions put to them. The programme became immensely popular and was later followed by many other quiz programmes. In the 1940s and 1950s the radio programme "Twenty Questions" was popular in many countries in Europe and North America. Nowadays in many countries quiz shows attract more viewers than almost any other TV programmes. Some of them concentrate exclusively on knowledge, others on quizzing – either facts or guessing – involving experimenting with the most fantastic of guessing tools. The verbal element has thus been supplemented by the visual. There is always a clear winner; in other words the "riddle" is solved, but it can also be solved by luck, though only in some programmes is the emphasis clearly on knowing. Whereas as late as the 1960s the "mastermind" on Finnish radio or TV was still a national hero, he or she nowadays goes away with goods, cruise vouchers and money.

The frantic need for joking characteristic of the times guarantees that one of the riddle subgenres, joking questions, is extremely expansive. The waves of joking questions witnessed in recent years have proved that almost anything can be dismissed by means of joking questions: the enemy in war or some other political opponent, immigrant workers, ethnic minorities, the pop musician who has strayed from the straight and narrow, AIDS, or the women's lib movement, to quote just a few examples. But the type of question also lends itself as a means of parody (for example, the parody on a sanitary towel advertisement familiar among schoolchildren: "Sucks blood and has wings but cannot fly? – Libresse goodnight.")

Jokes spread as both oral and written tradition. TV, radio and advertisements both provide topical motifs for joking questions and themselves draw on this joking tradition (Lipponen 1995:212). The dominant figure in, for example, Finnish schoolchildren's oral tradition has for many years been the dumb blonde ("Mitä blondi sanoi, kun huomasi olevansa raskaana? – Toivottavasti se ei ole minun."/"What did the blonde say when she found she was pregnant? – I hope it's not mine!"). This type of question is, however, common international property and is spread by, among others, computer networks.

The rapidly regenerating joking question tradition poses challenges of a new type for researchers to study the birth, life and death of tradition. What subjects are considered fit to be presented? The borders between good taste and ethics have been crossed innumerable times (for example, Biafra jokes), but are there still some themes too delicate to be joked about? In February 1994 the crisis in the former Yugoslavia was not mentioned at all in the Scandinavian young people's tradition. The following joking question in which both the question and the answer deliberately violate the linguistic rules is, however, known in Sweden (communication by Ulf Palmenfelt):

– Hur gammal kommer du ifrån?
– Tjugoslavien

("How old do you come from? – Tjugoslavien." This is a play on words including a slight mispronounciation. The word "tjugo" meaning "twenty" is twisted into the beginning of the Swedish word for Yugoslavia.)

Perhaps this war is too close to us, being brought into our living rooms by TV every day for years. In the Gulf War there were clearly two sides, both with a need for propaganda. Folklore was therefore enlisted as one means of satisfying this need, and it would be extremely interesting to know of the anti-American propaganda folklore circulating in Iraq. The situation in the former Yugoslavia is far more complex, because the opposing parties are engaged in a civil war in which all are both victims and guilty parties.

Although many researchers are keeping an active watch on the regeneration of the riddle tradition, basic study of the genre still contains many gaps waiting to be filled. One such gap is the identification, naming and closer analysis of the subgenres. The borders between genres in new oral tradition are nebulous, one reason being that a tradition product can be created by exploiting – either consciously or accidentally – other oral tradition.

One new subgenre inhabiting the no man's land between genres is the story-riddle. "It may be defined as a guessing game, in which the participants try to reconstruct a strange event, often with bizarre or morbid elements. The leader of the game gives some mysterious leads and then answers all questions only by "yes" or "no" until the others have solved the problem" (af Klintberg 1998:200–223). One of the earliest recordings of a story of this type appeared in the North Carolina Folklore Journal in 1974: "Here's the problem. A man was found in his room, hanged. The room was empty except for the man and the rope he used. Investigators found burns on the bottom of his feet. How did the man hang himself? Answer: he jumped off the block of dry ice." (Moore 1974:119.)

In the telling situation the answer is not, however, arrived at immediately, and the guessers have to acquire more information by asking questions. A guessing game can last for ages, and for it to be successful, the participants must finally be able to solve the problem. Some stories have local limitations, and only about 15 riddle-stories have spread internationally. Bengt af Klintberg (1998:200–233) points out that this subgenre has borrowed elements from older folklore genres (for example, neck-riddles) and popular culture (for example, detective stories and quiz shows). The genre has been studied most exhaustively by Olaf Brills (1996), who calls in the "Horror-Rätsel" and presents the 25 most common riddle-stories. From the 1990s onwards they have acquired a new life on the Internet and are now known all over the world. Unlike the popular joking question, the Horror-riddle permits serious consideration of the answer.

Identifying the subgenres will call for an active contribution from many scholars before the form, content, performance, use, distribution and functions of riddles of different types have been fully investigated. So far exhaustive studies have been made only of true riddles and neck riddles.

Despite the large number of subgenres explored by researchers in the past few decades, some large and interesting projects still remain to be attacked. One is the establishment of an international terminology covering all the subgenres of a genre and a type index of riddles. What sorts of true riddles and subgenres have been familiar to people at different times and in different cultures? And what about the position of riddling and riddle images in, for example, herding, agricultural, industrial and contemporary societies? Studies could likewise be made of the links between mentality and riddles. Riddle metaphors are culture-specific, but are they explained only by differences in material culture? The fragments of knowledge need drawing together.

This major project for the future is closely tied in with the problems of defining the riddle. The fact that many researchers are constantly reframing old definitions and creating new ones to suit their cultural requirements indicates the need for cooperation between riddle scholars. What sorts of ethnic genre definitions do we know, and is it possible or necessary to develop a global scientific definition on the basis of them that satisfies the demands of research? The definition should cover the needs manifest at various levels, such as contentual, stylistic, structural, semantic and pragmatic. Before a final definition is formulated, various research hypotheses should be subjected to further testing in the field for as long as there are still communities in which the use of true riddles and riddling in various forms are part of the active tradition.

The most ambitious and inspiring prospect is opened up by these in themselves challenging goals. It remains for future research to answer the question of the origin of riddles. And can we speak of one single riddle tradition with numerous cultural ramifications, or must we finally conclude that the genre has its origins in several different sources and their compounds? In what ways do different cultural circles depend on one another? And what about the links between the riddle and the other genres known within a culture – borrowed metaphors and shared contexts, for example? The basic ingredients for such investigations are to be found on the pages of *English Riddles* (Taylor 1951) and other comprehensive riddle collections, and having studied them, we would be far wiser about the different dimensions of the riddle genre.

The riddle researcher is at the moment to a great extent dependent on lucky discoveries, since it is, if not impossible, then at least extremely time-consuming to track down all the articles published. There is likewise a pressing need for an up-to-date bibliography. This basic analysis having been completed, the time would be ripe to compile a representative anthology of the ancient and contemporary research that remains sequestered behind linguistic walls and inaccessible to the English-speaking reader. Having a publishing forum of their own would in turn provide riddle scholars with an opportunity to engage in lasting dialogue and would draw many questions still waiting to be solved to the attention of the international community.

# BIBLIOGRAPHY

Aarne, Antti 1910. *Verzeichnis der Märchentypen. FF Communications 3*. Helsinki.
–1916. Arvoitusten tutkimisesta. *Suomalaisen Tiedeakatemian esitelmät ja pöytäkirjat.* 57–69. Helsinki.
– 1917. Vertailevia arvoitustutkimuksia. Tulta ja sauhua, harakkaa ja munaa merkitsevät arvoitukset. *Journal de la Société Finno-Ougrienne.* Helsinki.
– 1918–1920. *Vergleichende Rätselforschungen I-III. FF Communications 26–28.* Helsinki.
– 1923. Arvoitukset. F.A. Hästesko (toim.) *Suomalainen kansanrunous.* Helsinki.
Abrahams, Roger D. 1968. Introductionary Remarks to a Rhetorical Theory of Folklore. *Journal of American Folklore* 81:143–158.
–1972. The Literary Study of the Riddle. *Texas Studies in Literature and Language 14:* 177–197.
– 1980. *Between the Living and the Dead. FF Communications 225.* Helsinki.
– 1983. A Riddling on St. Vincent. *Western Folklore 42*: 272–295.
Abrahams, Roger D. – Dundes, Alan 1972. Riddles. Richard M. Dorson 1983. A Riddling on St. Vincent. *Western Folklore 42*: 272–295.
Abrahams, Roger D. – Dundes, Alan 1972. Riddles. Richard M. Dorson (ed.) *Folklore and Folklife*. Chicago.
Alster, Bendt 1976. A Sumerian Riddle Collection. *Journal of Near Eastern Studies* 35:263–267.
*Anglo-Saxon Riddles of the Exeter Book* 1963. Durham, N.C.
Anikin, V.P. 1975. On the Origin of Riddles. Felix J. Oinas and Stephen Soudakoff (eds.) *The Study of Russian Folklore*. The Hague, Paris.
Anttonen, Pertti J. 2000. Riddle Jokes in the Negotiation of a Love Relationship. Maria Vasenkari, Pasi Enges and Anna-Leena Siikala (eds.) Telling, Remembering, Interpreting, Guessing. A Festschrift for Prof. Annikki Kaivola-Bregenhøj on her 60th Birthday 1st February 1999. *Kultaneito III & Scripta Aboensia, Studies in Folkloristics 1. Joensuu*, 246–256.
Apollodorus 1967. *The Library*. London.
Aristotle. *The Poetics*. Oxford 1968.
– *On Rhetoric*, Bk III. Oxford 1991.
Barley, Nigel F. 1974. Structural Aspects of the Anglo-Saxon Riddle. *Semiotica* 10: 143–175.
Barrick, Mac E. 1964. The Shaggy Elephant Riddle. *Southern Folklore Quarterly 28*: 266–290.
– 1980. The Helen Keller Joke Cycle. *Journal of American Folklore 93*: 441–449.
Bascom, William R. 1949. Literary Style in Yoruba Riddles. *Journal of American Folklore 62*: 1–16.
– 1954. Four Functions of Folklore. *Journal of American Folklore 67*: 333–349.
– 1975. *African Dilemma Tales*. The Hague, Paris.
Başgöz, İlhan 1965. Functions of Turkish Riddles. *Journal of the Folklore Institute 2:* 132–247.
– 1972. Riddle-Proverbs and the Related Forms in Turkish Folklore. *Proverbium 18*:655–668.
Başgöz, İlhan – Tietze, Andreas 1973. *Bilmece: A Corpus of Turkish Riddles. Folklore Studies 22*. Berkeley.
Bauman, Richard 1970. The Turtles: An American Riddling Institution. *Western Folklore 29:* 21–25.
Bausinger, Hermann 1967. Rätsel-Fragen. *Rheinisches Jahrbuch für Volkskunde 17–18:* 48–70.
Beckwith, Martha W. 1922. Hawaiian Riddling. *American Anthropologist.* New Series

24: 311–331.
Ben-Amos, Dan 1976. Solutions to Riddles. *Journal of American Folklore 89*: 249–254.
–1992. Do We Need Ideal Types (in Folklore)? An Address to Lauri Honko. *NIF Papers No. 2*. Turku.
Bhagwat, Durga 1943. The Riddles of Death. *Man in India 23*: 343–348.
– 1965. *The Riddle in Indian Life, Lore and Literature*: 135. Bombay.
– 1984. The Riddle-Form in India. Ramesh Mathur and Masahiro Manabe (eds.) *Indian and Japanese Folklore*. Tokyo.
*The Holy Bible.*
Blacking, John 1961. The Social Values of Venda Riddles. *African Studies 20*: 1–32.
Boggs, Ralph Steele 1934. North Carolina White Folktales and Riddles. *Journal of American Folklore 47*: 289–328.
Bolte, Johannes – Polívka, Georg 1918. *Anmerkungen zu den Kinder – und Hausmärchen der Brüder Grimm 3*. Leipzig.
Brandes, Stanley 1980. Pranks and Riddles. Stanley Brandes (ed.) *Metaphors of Masculinity. Sex and Status in Andalusian Folklore.* Philadelphia.
Bregenhøj, Carsten – Johnson, Marie 1988. *Blodet droppar, blodet droppar! Skolbarns humor.* Helsingfors.
Brills, Olaf 1996. Horror-Rätsel – Erhebungen zu einer neuen Erzählgattung. *Fabula 37*: 1–2: 28-70.
Bronner, Simon J. 1988. *American Children's Folklore*. Little Rock, Arkansas.
Brown, Gillian – Yule, George 1983. *Discourse Analysis. Cambridge Textbooks in Linguistics.* Cambridge.
Brown, Waln K. 1973. Cognitive Ambiguity and the Pretended Obscene Riddle. *Keystone Folklore 28:* 89–101.
Bryant, Mark 1983. *Riddles Ancient and Modern*. London.
– 1990. *Dictionary of Riddles.* London.
Burns, Thomas A. 1976. Riddling: Occasion to Act. *Journal of American Folklore 89:* 139–165.
Bødker, Laurits 1964 in co-operation with Brynjulf Alver, Bengt Holbek and Leea Virtanen. *The Nordic Riddle. Terminology and Bibliography.* Copenhagen.
Child, F.J. (ed.) 1882–1898. *The English and Scottish popular ballads Vol. 1–5.* Boston.
Chomsky, Noam 1957. *Syntactic Structures.* The Hague.
Chyet, Michael L. 1988. "A Thing the Size of Your Palm." A Preliminary Study of Arabic Riddle Structure. *Arabica* 35: 267–292.
Cohen, Shlomith 1996. Connecting through Riddles, or the Riddle of Connecting. Galit Hasan-Rokem and David Shulman (eds.) *Untying the Knot. On Riddles and Other Enigmatic Modes.* New York.
Cole-Beuchat, P. D. 1957. Riddles in Bantu. *African Studies 16*:133–149.
Cong-Huyen-Tom-Nu, Nha-Trang 1971. Poetics in Vietnamese Riddles. *Southern Folklore Quaterly 35:* 141–156.
Davies, Christie 1990. *Ethnic Humor Around the World*. Bloomington.
Dorst, John D. 1983. Neck-riddles as a Dialogue of Genres. Applying Bakhtin's Genre Theory. *Journal of American Folklore 96*: 413–433.
Dundes, Alan 1963. Summoning Deity Through Ritual Fasting. *The American Imago 20*: 213–220.
– 1964. Texture, Text and Context. *Southern Folklore Quaterly 28*: 4: 251–265.
– 1971. A Study of Ethnic Slurs: The Jew and the Polack in the United States. *Journal of American Folklore 84*: 186–203.
Dundes, Alan – Georges, Robert B. 1962. Some Minor Genres of Obscene Folklore. *Journal of American Folklore 75*: 221–226.
Dundes, Alan – Vatuk, Ved Prakash 1974. Some Characteristic Meters of Hindi Riddle Prosody. *Asian Folklore Studies 33*: 85–153.
Dundes, Alan – Pagter, Carl P. 1975. *Work Hard and You Shall Be Rewarded. Urban Folklore from the Paperwork Empire*. Austin, Texas.
Dundes, Alan – Hauschild, Thomas 1983. Auschwitz Jokes. *Western Folklore 42*: 249–260.

Edmunds, Lowell 1984. The Sphinx in the Oedipus Legend. Lowell Edmunds and Alan Dundes (eds.) *A Folklore Casebook.* New York & London.

Edwards, Viv – Sienkewicz, Thomas J. 1991. *Oral Cultures Past and Present. Rappin' and Homer: 244.* Oxford.

Ellis, Bill 1991. The Last Thing... Said: The Challenger Disaster Jokes and Closure. *International Folklore Review 8*: 110–124.

*Eos* 1863:4.

Evans, David 1976. Riddling and the Structure of Context. *Journal of American Folklore 89*: 166–188.

Fauset, Arthur Huff 1928. Tales and Riddles Collected in Philadelphia. *Journal of American Folklore 41*: 529–557.

Fine, Gary Alan – Crane, Beverly J. 1977. The Expectancy Effect in Anthropological Research: An Experimental Study of Riddle Collection. *American Ethnologist 4:* 517–524.

Finnegan, Ruth 1970. *Oral Literature in Africa.* Oxford.

– 1977. *Oral Poetry. Its Nature, Significance and Social Context.* Cambridge.

von Frenckell, Ester Margaret 1947. *Offentliga nöjen och privata i Helsingfors 1827–1832. II* Helsingfors.

Freud, Sigmund 1960 (1905). *Jokes and Their Relation to the Unconcious.* J.Strachey (ed. and transl.) New York.

Ganander, Christfrid 1970 (1783). *Aenigmata Fennica. Suomalaiset arvotuxet, Wastausten kansa.* Helsinki.

Garth, Thomas R. 1935. Riddles as a Mental Text. *American Journal of Psychology 47*: 342–344.

Georges, Robert A. – Dundes, Alan 1963. Toward a Structural Definition of the Riddle. *Journal of American Folklore 76*: 111–117.

Gerd, Kusebai 1928. Über die Rätselabende bei den Wotjaken. *Ungarische Jahrbücher VIII.* Berlin und Leipzig.

Glazier, Jack – Glazier, Phyllis Gorfain 1976. Ambiguity and Exchange: The Double Dimension of Mbeere Riddles. *Journal of American Folklore 89*: 189–238.

Goldstein, Kenneth 1963. Riddling in Northeastern Scotland. *Journal of American Folklore 76*: 330–336.

Green, Thomas A. 1992. Riddle. Richard Bauman (ed.) *Folklore, Cultural Performances, and Popular Elements.* New York.

Green, Thomas A. – Pepicello, W. J. 1978. *Wit in Riddling: A Linguistic Perspective. Genre 11*: 1–13.

– 1979. The Folk Riddle: A Redefinition of Terms. *Western Folklore 38*: 3–20.

Grzybek, Peter 1987. Zur Psychosemiotik des Rätsels. Wolfgang Eisman und Peter Grzybek (hrsg.) *Semiotische Studien zum Rätsel.* Bochum.

Gustafsson, Anne 1980. "A Woman's in Her Nook with a Hundred Eyes in Her Head. – Siewe." Masculine and Feminine Metaphors in Finnish Riddle Tradition. *Nord Nytt 8*: 12–16.

Haavio, Martti 1955. *Kansanrunojen maailmanselitys.* Helsinki.

– 1959. "The Upside-Down World." Essais folkloriques. *Studia Fennica 10*: 209–221. Helsinki.

Hain, Mathilde 1966. *Rätsel.* Stuttgart.

Hamnett, Ian 1967. Ambiguity, Classification and Change: The Function of Riddles. *Man New Series:* 379–392.

Handberger, Maria 1995. *Katastroflore. En studie av vitsar och skämt som bildats runt Estonia och Mattias Flink.* C-uppsats i Etnologi. Uppsala universitet.

Handelman, Don 1996. Traps and Trans-formation: Theoretical Convergences between Riddle and Ritual. Galit Hasan-Rokem and David Shulman (eds.) *Untying the Knot. On Riddles and Other Enigmatic Modes.* New York.

Hanika-Otto, Liesl 1930. *Sudentendeutsche Volksrätsel.* Reichenberg.

Haring, Lee 1974. On Knowing the Answer. *Journal of American Folklore 87*: 197–207.

– 1985. Malagasy Riddling. *Journal of American Folklore 98*: 163–190.

Harries, Lyndon 1971. The Riddle in Africa. *Journal of American Folklore 84*: 377–393.
– 1976. Semantic Fit in Riddles. *Journal of American Folklore 89*: 319–325.
Hart, Donn V. 1964. *Riddles in Filipino Folklore.* Syracuse.
Hasan-Rock (later: Hasan-Rokem), Galit 1974. Riddle and proverb. The relationship exemplified by an Aramaic proverb. *Proverbium 24*: 936–940.
Hellberg, Elena 1985. Gåtor och gränser. *Tradisjon 15*: 87–96.
Herskovits, Melville J. – Herskovits, Frances S. 1958. *Dahomean Narrative: A Cross-Cultural Analysis.* Evanston.
Hiiemäe, Mall 1995. Eesti piltmõistattuste loomispõhimõtest. Mare Kõiva (toim.) *Lipitud-lapitud. Tänapäeva folkloorist.* Tartu.
Honko, Lauri 1980. Empirical Genre Research. Osmo Ikola (ed.) *Congressus Quintus Internationalis Fenno-Ugristarum Turku 20.–27. VIII 1980. Pars IV. Dissertationes symposiorum ad ethnologiam, folklore et mythologiam, archaeologiam et anthropologiam, litteras pertinentium.* Turku.
Huizinga, J. 1949. *Homo Ludens: A Story of the Play Element in Culture.* London.
Isbell, Billie Jean – Fernandez, Fredy Amilcar Roncalla 1977. The Ontogenesis of Metaphor: Riddle Games among Quechua Speakers Seen as Cognitive Discovery Procedures. *Journal of Latin American Lore 3:* 19–49.
Johnson, Ragnar 1975. The Semantic Structure of the Joke and Riddle: Theoretical Positioning. *Semiotica 14*: 142–173.
Jolles, André 1930. *Einfache Formen. Legende, Sage, Mythe, Rätsel, Sprach, Kasus, Memorabile, Märchen, Witz.* Halle.
Jones, Bessie – Haves, Bess Lomax 1972. *Step It Down.* New York.
Kaivola-Bregenhøj, Annikki 1974 a. Perinteellinen ja muuttuva arvoitus. Hannu Launonen ja Kirsti Mäkinen (toim.) *Folklore tänään. Tietolipas 73.* Helsinki.
– 1974 b. Formula Analysis as a Method of Classifying Riddles. *Studia Fennica 17:* 178–197.
– 1974 c. Arvoitusten mohdottomuuskuvastoa. *Kalevalaseuran vuosikirja 54*:169–184.
– 1977. Means of Riddle Expression. Leea Virtanen, Annikki Kaivola-Bregenhøj and Aarre Nyman (eds.) *Arvoitukset, Finnish Riddles. Suomalaisen Kirjallisuuden Seuran Toimituksia 330*: 58–76. Helsinki.
– 1978. *The Nominativus Absolutus Formula – One Syntactic-Semantic Structural Scheme of the Finnish Riddle Genre. FF Communication 222.* Helsinki.
Kinnunen, Eeva-Liisa 1988. Kertovatko naiset tuhmia juttuja? Naisten seksuaalisen työpaikkahuumorin tarkastelua. Irma-Riitta Järvinen, Jyrki Pöysä and Sinikka Vakimo (toim.) *Monikasvoinen folklore. Helsingin yliopiston kansanrunoustieteen laitoksen toimite 8.* Helsinki.
Klintberg, Bengt af 1972. Biafravitsar. *Trasdisjon 2*:61–72.
– 1978. Varför har elefanten röda ögon? Om absurda skämtgåtor bland skolbarn. *Harens klagan och andra uppsatser om folklig diktning.* Stockholm.
– 1980. Mexicans and Giraffes: Droodles among Swedish School Children. *Folklore on two Continents. Essays in honour of Linda Dégh.* Bloomington.
– 1983. Negervitsar. *Tradisjon 13*: 23–45.
– 1998. De mystiska ledtrådarna. Teman och motiv i en ny folkloristisk genre. *Kuttrasju. Folkloristiska och kulturhistoriska essäer.* Stockholm.
Knuuttila, Seppo 2000. Kymppitonnin arvoitukset. Maria Vasenkari, Pasi Enges and Anna-Leena Siikala (eds.) Telling, Remembering, Interpreting, Guessing. A Festschrift for Prof. Annikki Kaivola-Bregenhøj on her 60th Birthday 1st February 1999. *Kultaneito III & Scripta Aboensia, Studies in Folkloristics 1.* Joensuu, 261–271.
Kozumplik, William A. 1941. Seven and Nine Holes in Man. *Southern Folklore Quaterly 5:* 1: 1–24.
Krikmann, Arvo 1995. Lipitud-lapitud "kommunaari" king. Mõistatuset tänäpäevä koolpärimuses. Mare Kõiva (toim.) *Lipitud-lapitud. Tänapäeva folkloorist.* Tartu.
– 1996. The Main Riddles. Questions, Allegories and Tasks in AT 875, 920, 921, 922 and 927. Ülo Valk (ed.), *Studies in Folklore and Popular Religion Vol.1*:55–79. Tartu.
Krohn, Kaarle 1918. *Kalevalankysymyksiä. Opas Suomen Kansan Vanhojen Runojen*

*tilaajille ja käyttäjille ynnä suomalaisen kansanrunouden opiskelijoille ja harrastajille I–II.* Helsinki.

Kuusi, Matti 1954. *Sananlaskut ja puheenparret.* Helsinki.

– 1956. Arvoitukset ja muinaisusko. *Virittäjä 60:* 181–200.

– 1960. Seitsemän arvoituspähkinää. Jouko Hautala (toim.) *Jumin keko.* Helsinki.

– 1967. Johdatusta sananlaskuston formula-analyysiin. *Kalevalaseuran vuosikirja 47.* Helsinki.

– 1969. Southwest African Riddle-Proverbs.*Proverbium 12*: 305–311. Helsinki.

– 1974. Ovambo Riddles with Comments and Vocabularies. *FF Communications 215.* Helsinki.

Kvideland, Reimund 1983. Den norsk-svenske vitsekrigen. *Tradisjon 13*: 77–91.

Köngäs Maranda, Elli 1970. Perinteen transformaatiosääntöjen tutkimisesta. *Virittäjä 1970:* 277–292.

– 1971a. The Logic of Riddles. Pierre Maranda and Elli Köngäs Maranda (eds.) *Structural Analysis of Oral Tradition.* Philadelphia.

– 1971b. Theory and Practise of Riddle Analysis. *Journal of American Folklore 84*: 51–61.

– 1971c. "A Tree Grows": Transformations of a Riddle Metaphor. Elli Köngäs Maranda and Pierre Maranda (eds.) *Structural Models in Folklore and Transformational Essays.* The Hague.

– 1976. Riddles and Riddling. An Introduction. *Journal of American Folklore 352:* 127–137.

– 1978. Folklore and Culture Change: Lau Riddles of Modernization. Richard M. Dorson (ed.) *Folklore in the Modern World.* The Hague.

Laalo, Klaus 1998. Lasten arvoitusvitsit: kokeilevaa kielen tutkiskelua. Merja Karjalainen (toim.) *Kielen ituja. Ajankohtaista lapsenkielen tutkimuksesta.* Oulu.

Launonen, Hannu 1966. Varas menee aittaan... *Suomalainen Suomi 6:* 374–379.

Lehmann-Nitsche, Robert 1911. *Folklore Argentino I. Adivinanzas Ríoplatenses.* Buenos Aires.

Levin, Jurij I. 1973. Semantičeskaja struktura russkoj zagadki. *Trudy po znakovym sistemam 6.* Tartu.

– 1987. Die semantische Struktur des Rätsels. Wolfgang Eismann und Peter Grzybek (hrsg.) *Semiotische Studien zum Rätzel.* Bochum.

Lieber, Michael D. 1976. Riddles, Cultural Categories, and World View. *Journal of American Folklore 89*: 255–265.

Lipponen, Ulla 1988. *Kilon poliisi ja muita koululaisjuttuja.* Helsinki.

– 1992. *Usko, toivo, rakkaus. Tyttöjen runovihkoperinnettä.* Helsinki.

– 1995. *Jauhot suuhun. Arvoitusvitsejä ja kompakysymyksiä.* Helsinki.

– 1997. *Sika sumussa. Kuva-arvoituksia.* Helsinki.

– 1999. *Kaistapää. Kuvakirjoituksia ja piirrospähkinöitä.* Helsinki.

Lövkrona, Inger 1991. "Dä river å ravlar unner kvinnornas navlar..." Gåtor och erotik i bondesamhället. Jonas Frykman och Orvar Löfgren (red.) *Svenska vanor och ovanor.* Stockholm.

Manuel, E. Arsenio 1955. Notes on Philippine Folk Literature. *University of Manila Journal of East Asiatic Studies 4:* 137–153.

Mau-Tsai, Liu 1986. *Der Tiger mit dem Rosenkranz: Rätsel in China.* Berlin.

McDowell, John Holmes 1979. *Children's Riddling.* Bloomington & London.

– 1985. Verbal Dueling. Teun A. Van Dijk (ed.) *Handbook of Discourse Analysis,* Volume 3. London.

Messenger, John C. 1960. Anang Proverb-Riddles. *Journal of American Folklore 73*: 225–235.

Milner, George B. 1975. *Notes on Difference Between a Proverb and a Riddle.* Mimeo.

Moore, Danny W. 1974. The Deductive Riddle: An Adaptation to Modern Society. *North Carolina Folklore Journal 22:* 119–125.

Ohlert, K. 1912 (1979). *Rätsel und Rätselspiele den alten Griechen.* Berlin.

Olsson, Helmer 1944. Svenska gåtor 1. Folkgåtor från Bohuslän. Uppsala.

Oring, Elliott 1992. *Jokes and Their Relations.* Lexington (KY).
Pagis, Dan 1996. Toward a Theory of the Literary Riddle. Galit Hasan–Rokem and David Shulman (eds.) *Untying the Knot. On Riddles and Other Enigmatic Modes.* New York.
Palmenfelt, Ulf 1987. *Vad är det som går och går...? Svenska gåtor från alla tider i urval av Ulf Palmenfelt.* Stockholm.
Paris, Gaston 1877. *Préface to Eugéne Rolland. Devinettes et énigmas populaires de la France.* Paris.
Parry, Milman 1971. *The Making of Homeric Verse: The Collected Papers of Milman Parry.* Oxford.
Pepicello, W.J. – Green, Thomas A. 1984. *The Language of Riddles. New Perspectives.* Ohio.
Perttula, Pirkko-Liisa 1992. *Haisunäätä mikroaaltouunissa.* Helsinki.
Peterson, Per 1985. Gåtor och skämt. En undersökning om vardagligt berättande bland skolbarn. *Etnolore 4. Skrifter från Etnologiska institutionen vid Uppsala universitet.* Uppsala: Uppsala universitet.
Petsch, Robert 1899. *Neue Beiträge zur Kenntnis des Volksrätsels.Palaestra IV.* Berlin.
– 1917. *Das deutsche Volksrätsel.* Strassburg.
Peuckert, Will-Erich 1938. *Deutsches Volkstum in Märchen und Sage, Schwank und Rätsel.* Berlin.
Plaks, Andrew H. 1996. Riddle and Enigma in Chinese Civilization Galit Hasan-Rokem and David Shulman (eds.) *Untying the Knot. On Riddles and Other Enigmatic Modes.* New York.
Potter, Charles Francis 1950. Riddles. *Standard Dictionary of Folklore, Mythology and Legend II*: 938–944. New York.
Prasad, Leela1998. Bilingual Joking Questions: Ethnicity and Politics in Indian City Lore. Jawaharlal Handoo (ed.) *Folklore in Modern India.* Mysore.
Preston, Michel J. 1982. The English Literal Rebus and the Graphic Riddle Tradition. *Western Folklore 41*: 104–121.
Price, Roger 1953. *Droodles.* Los Angeles.
Puurunen, Seija 1992. Alttoviuluvitsit Freudin näkökulmasta. Julkaisematon opinnäytetyö. Sibelius-Akatemia.Helsinki.
*Pääskynen* 1871:5.
Raa, Eric Ten 1972. The Comparative Method in Social Anthropology and the Cross-Cultural Comparison of Riddles. *Paideuma 18*: 97–111. Wiesbaden.
Reeder, Roberta 1981. A Structural Analysis of the Russian Folk Riddle. *Semiotica 33*: 237–260. The Hague.
Roberts, John M. – Forman, Michael L. 1971. Riddles: Expressive Models of Interrogation. *Ethnology 10*: 4: 509–533.
Roberts, Leonard 1974. *Sang Branch Settlers: Folksongs and Tales of a Kentucky Mountain Family.* Austin.
Roemer, Danielle M. 1982. In the Eye of the Beholder. A Semiotic Analysis of the Visual Descriptive Riddle. *Journal of American Folklore 95*: 173–199.
Rolland, Eugène 1877. *Devinettes ou énigmes populaires de la France suivies de la réimpression d´un recueil de 77 indovinelli publié à Trévise en 1628.* Avec une préface de Gaston Paris. Paris.
Rudolph, Richard C. 1942. Notes on the Riddle in China. *California Folklore Quarterly 1*: 65–81.
Saarinen, Sirkka 1991. *Marilaisen arvoituksen kielioppi. Suomalais-ugrilaisen Seuran Toimituksia 210.* Helsinki.
– 2000. 'Arvoitus'. *Atlas Linguarum Europae I*: 6.Poligrafico, Roma.
Sadnik, Linda 1953. *Südosteuropäische Rätselstudien.* Graz – Köln.
Sadovnikov, D. 1901. *Zagadki russkago naroda.* St.Petersburg.
Santi, Aldo 1952. *Bibliografia delle Enigmistica.* Firenze.
Saussure, Ferdinand de 1970. *Kurs i lingvistik.* Budapest.
Schultz, Wolfgang. 1912. *Rätsel aus dem hellenischen Kulturkreise.* Leipzig.
Scott, Charles T. 1963. New Evidence of American Indian Riddles. *Journal of American*

*Folklore 76:* 236–241.
- 1965. *Persian and Arabic Riddles.* Bloomington.
- 1969. On Defining the Riddle: the Problem of a Structural Unit. *Genre 2*: 129–142.
- 1976. On Defining the Riddle: The Problem of a Structural Unit. Dan Ben-Amos (ed.) *Folklore Genres.* Austin.

Sein, Maung Than – Dundes, Alan 1964. Twenty-three riddles from Central Burma. *Journal of American Folklore 77*: 69–75.

Shulman, David 1996. The Yaksa's Questions. Galit Hasan-Rokem and David Shulman (eds.) *Untying the Knot. On Riddles and Other Enigmatic Modes.* New York.

Simmons, Donald C. 1956. Erotic Ibibio Tone Riddles. *Man 56.*

Simon, Gwladys Hughes 1955. Riddles from Ceylon. *Western Folklore:* 174–187.

Smyth, Willie 1986. Challenger Jokes and the Humor of Disaster. *Western Folklore 45*: 243–226.

Stein, Dina 1996. A King, a Queen, and the Riddle Between: Riddles and Interpretation in a Late Mizdrashic Text. Galit Hasan-Rokem and David Shulman (eds.) *Untyind the Knot. On Riddles and Other Enigmatic Modes.* New York.

Stewart, Ann Harleman 1983. Double Entendre in the Old English Riddles. *Lore and Language 3*: 39–52.

Stewart, Susan 1979. *Nonsense: aspects of intertextuality in folklore and literature.* Baltimore.

Straparola (1550–1553) 1834. *The Nights of Straparola.* Translated by W.G. Waters. Volume I. London.

Ström, Fredrik 1937. *Svenska Folkgåtor.* Stockholm.

*Stupid Jokes for Kids. Selections from the Big Fat Giant Joke Book.* New York 1991.

*Suomen Kansan Vanhat Runot I–XIV.* Helsinki 1908–1948.

Sutton-Smith, Brian 1976. A Developmental Structural Account of Riddles. Barbara Kirschenblatt–Gimblett (ed.) *Speech Play.* Philadelphia.

Sydow, C.W. von 1915. Om gåtor och gåtsystematik. O. Christofferson (red.) *Om Gåtor från Skytts härad i Skåne.* Folkminnen och folktankar 2. Lund.

Taylor, Archer 1931. The Proverb. Cambridge (Mass.).
- 1934. Problems in the Study of Proverbs. *Journal of American Folklore 47*: 1–21.
- 1938. Problems in the Study of Riddles. *Southern Folklore Quaterly 2*: 1–9.
- 1939. *A Bibliography of Riddles.* FF Communications 126. Helsinki.
- 1943. The Riddle. *California Folklore Quaterly II*: 129–147.
- 1944. American Indian Riddles. *Journal of American Folklore 59*: 1–15.
- 1948. *The Literary Riddle Before 1600.* Berkeley.
- 1949. The Varieties of Riddles. T.A. Kirby and H.B. Woolf (eds.) *Philologica. Malone Anniversary Studies.* Baltimore.
- 1951. *English Riddles from Oral Tradition.* Berkeley.

Toporov, V. N. 1987. Das Anagram in Rätseln. Wolfgang Eisman und Peter Grzybek (hrsg.) *Semiotische Studien zum Rätseln.* Bochum.

The Truly Tasteless Joke-a-Date Book 1994.

Valotka, Audrius 1992. *Informational Structure of the Riddles. Synopsis of the dissertation for a candidate's degree in philology.* Vilnius.

Ward, Donald 1976. American and European Narratives as Socio-Psychological Indicators. *Studia Fennica 20*: 348–353. Helsinki.

Wessman, V.E.V. (red.) 1949. *Finlands svenska folktidning IV. Gåtor. Skrifter utg. av Svenska Litteratursällskapet i Finland 327.* Helsingfors.

Williams, Thomas Rhys 1963. The Form and Function of Tambunan Dusun Riddles. *Journal of American Folklore 76*: 95–110.

Winograd, Terry 1981. What Does It Mean to Understand Language? D.A. Norman (ed.) *Perspectives on Cognitive Science.* Norwood, New Jersey.

Virtanen, Leea 1960. Arvoitus ja sen tehtävä. Jouko Hautala (toim.) *Jumin keko. Tietolipas 17.* Helsinki.
- 1970. *Antti pantti pakana. Kouluikäisten nykyperinne.* Helsinki.
- 1976. Ujo Piimä. Koululaishuumoria. Helsinki.

– 1977. On the Function of Riddles. Leea Virtanen, Annikki Kaivola-Bregenhøj and Aarre Nyman (eds.) *Arvoitukset, Finnish Riddles. Suomalaisen Kirjallisuuden Seuran Toimituksia 330.* Helsinki.
– 1988. *Suomalainen kansanperinne. Suomalaisen Kirjallisuuden Seuran Toimituksia 471.* Helsinki.
Virtanen, Leea – Kaivola-Bregenhøj, Annikki – Nyman, Aarre 1977. *Arvoitukset, Finnish Riddles. Suomalaisen Kirjallisuuden Seuran Toimituksia 330.* Helsinki.
Wolfenstein, Martha 1978. *Children's Humor.* Bloomington.
Volockaja, Zoja Michajlovna 1987. Struktur und Semantik von Rätseln des Gegenstandsfeldes "Natur". Wolfgang Eisman und Peter Grzybek (hrsg.) *Semiotische Studien zum Rätsel.* Bochum.
Wossidlo, Richard 1897. *Mecklenburgische Volksüberlieferungen I.* Wismar.
Wünsche, August 1896. Das Rätsel vom Jahr und seinen Zeitabschnitten in der Weltliteratur. *Zeitschrift für vergleichende Litaraturgeschichte, N.F.9:* 425/0456.

## ABBREVIATIONS USED IN THIS BOOK

ER -> Archer Taylor 1951. *English Riddles from Oral tradition.* Berkeley.
FR -> Leea Virtanen, Annikki Kaivola-Bregenhøj and Aarre Nyman (eds.) 1977. *Arvoitukset, Finnish Riddles.* Suomalaisen Kirjallisuuden Seuran Toimituksia 330. Helsinki.
SKS -> Finnish Literature Society (*Suomalaisen Kirjallisuuden Seura*)
SKVR -> Ancient Poems of the Finnish People (*Suomen Kansan Vanhat Runot*)

# Index

This index omits references to terms such as 'answer', 'culture', 'genre', 'riddle' and 'tradition' because of their frequent use in the text. They are, however, listed where they appear as or with a modifier: first cases where the word is preceded by a modifier (e.g. Finnish riddle), then cases in which the word itself is used as a modifier (e.g. riddle game). Countries are not listed as such but may appear in their adjectival form as modifiers (e.g. Chinese riddle).

Aarne, Antti 29–33, 40, 43, 139, 153
ABC book 15
aberration 132
Abrahams, Roger D. 25, 37, 42–43, 49–50, 56, 68–69, 94–96, 101, 110, 131, 137, 142,
activity
   game 119
   leisure time 119
*Adevineaux amoureux* 31
advertisement 164
advertising 24
*Aenigmata et griphi veterum et recentium* 76
*Aenigmata Fennica* 54, 79, 83, 115
*Aenigmatographia* 76
affinity 119
African Dilemma Tales 25
age 54
aggression 121
agility 160
   mental 108
Agni 11
Ahtisaari, Martti 23
allegory 141
alliteration 30, 128–129, 145, 149
ambiguity 22, 24, 46, 52, 55, 63, 111, 129, 131–132, 134–135, 158
amusement 23
anagram 129
analogy 45, 93, 110, 120, 161
   model 136
analysis 51
   comparative 34

   structural 40–41, 48
   genre 49
anecdote 28, 104
*Anglo-Saxon Riddles of the Exeter Book* 75
Anikin, V.P. 141
answer
   deducing the 159
   guessing the 47, 55, 107, 142, 159
   knowing the 36, 56, 101, 103, 107
anithesis 143
Anttonen, Pertti J. 82
approach, text-oriented 118
argument 122
Aristotle 41, 47
art 52
   verbal 29
*Arvoitukset, Finnish Riddles* 35, 136, 138–139
aspect, text-oriented 36
association
   country women's 15, 104
   farmers' 104
   small farmers' 15
   youth 15, 104
assonance 26, 129, 145
atmosphere 96
audience 105, 108, 120, 158
authenticity 135

Balder 13
ballad 69, 114
Bascom, William 25, 35, 40–41, 118–119
Başgöz, İlhan 34, 107

belief 28, 141
Biafra 20
*Bible* 15, 68
bibliography 35, 166
bilingualism 126, 161
*Bilmece: A Corpus of Turkish Riddles* 34
Blacking, John 35, 119–120
Boeotia 12
borrowing 139
Brandes, Stanley 102–103
Bregenhøj, Carsten 85
Brills, Olaf 165
Brown, Waln K. 90
Bryant, Mark 55, 75, 78
Burns, Thomas A. 94, 105–106, 114
Bødker, Laurits 35, 55

catastrophe 21, 126
catch 42, 52, 61
*Catechism* 15
category 45–46
  cognitive 36
  content 79
  emic 9
  linguistic 135
  opposing 136
Cervantes, Miquel 77
chain, thematic 110
Challenger 20, 22
charade 55, 77
charge, erotic 84
charm 28, 139
*Children's Humour* 86
*Children's Riddling* 110
Chomsky, Noam 45
Christian 13
Chyet, Michael L. 42, 145
circulation 29
circumlocution 103
class
  upper 102
  working 102
  class-consciousness 123
classification 40–41, 47, 49, 136, 145, 148
  genre 53
  c. criteria 54
cliché 28, 93, 116, 136, 141–142

closing 114
  opening 35, 114
clue 108, 109, 158
code, semantic 130
comedy 116
comment 40–41, 50, 97, 145
  political 124
communication 130
  cultural 29, 121
  oral 33
comparison 33
competence 130, 137–139, 158
competition 16, 52, 94, 97, 107–109, 114, 152, 163
  organised 106
  riddling 105

component 38, 144–145, 148, 150
  c. member 143
composition 16
conciliation 122
conflict, political 123
conformity 45
confusion 53
construction, binary 51
content 37, 47, 48, 55, 69, 72, 83, 124, 130, 134, 149, 162, 165
contest 106, 114
context 26–27, 29, 36, 47, 52, 60, 64, 75, 82, 92, 101, 118–119, 134, 139, 145–146, 155, 160–161, 166
  behavioral 93
  conversational 26
  cognitive 93
  cultural 14, 24, 53, 93, 111, 119, 139
  economical 139
  generic 42, 93
  linguistic 51, 92, 109, 119, 136
  narrative 69
  performing 5, 53, 82, 92–93
  situational 91–92, 94, 96, 109, 119
  social 51, 93, 94, 139
  topical 22
contradiction 131
  internal 42, 45, 47
contrast 147

conundrum 55, 112
cooperation 130
copulation 102
cotext → context, linguistic
courting 96
creativity 130
crises 122
    community 121
    personal 121
criteria 145
    morphological-syntactic 143
    stylistic 143
criticism 123, 125
    philological text 29
    source 30
culture
    material 10, 14, 139
    nonmaterial 10
    children's 86
    sub- 37
cursing 95
custom 139

Davies, Christie 18
death 122
debate 122
defeat 107
definition 38, 40–42, 47–48, 50–53, 153, 165
    genre 51
    structural 50, 153
    universal 51
deliberation 97, 101
description
    figurative 48
    literal 39, 48, 131
    metaphorical 39
    method of 110
devises
    expressive 24, 145–146
    onomatopoetic 129
    stylistic 27, 47, 128, 145
    witty 53
Diana, Princess 23
*Dictionary of Riddles* 55
discourse 49, 121
    riddle 45
disorientation 122

distribution 30, 34, 54, 118, 139, 165
double-entendre 91
"droodle" 62–64, 89
Duisenberg, Wim 68
Dundes, Alan 19–20, 35, 40–42, 48–50, 56, 68, 131, 135, 142, 145, 153

education 119
educational encounter 96
elections, the presidential 23
element 25, 38–41, 44, 56, 73, 130, 133–135, 138–140, 143
    basic 40, 42, 46–47, 49
    block 39–40, 48
    comparative 149
    descriptive 40–42, 49
    framing 39, 110
    image 41, 45
    metaphorical 48
    negative 40–41, 48
    non-oppositional descriptive 42
    oppositional descriptive 42
    positive 41, 48
    structural 143, 148
    supplementary 40
Ellis, Bill 20–21
embarrasment 82
enigma 41, 46, 56, 69, 108
*English Riddles from Oral Tradition* 34, 41, 48, 54–55, 79, 138, 166
entertainment 11, 24–25, 97–98, 102, 113, 118–120, 131, 141
entity
    behavioral 36
    syntactic 40
*Eos* 77
eroticism, folk 79
the Estonia shipwreck 21–22
ethics 130
ethnocentrism 36
etiquette 121
EU 23
euphemism 27, 141
euphony 128
Evans, David 93, 96–97, 119
event signal 92
exchange, verbal 97, 130

excercise, intellectual 97, 108
expectation
   false 80, 122
   scheme of 133
Expressen [newspaper] 19
expression 91, 135–137, 149, 158, 162
   conventions of 142
   crystallised 105
   enigmatic 63
   fix-phrased 9
   metaphorical 133, 136
   models of 56
   visual 87

fairytales 14
farce 115
feature
   binary 146
   contentual 29
   inherent 53
   linguistic 49
   semantic 136
   structural 29, 145
   stylistic 29
Fernandez, Fredy Amilcar Roncalla 142
*FF Communication* 30
fieldwork 29, 36, 37, 94, 118
fight, verbal 95
*Filipino riddles* 10
Finnegan, Ruth 50, 113
*Finnish Riddles* → *Arvoitukset*
focus list 93
folklore, small scale 141
*Folklore Argentino I. Advinanzas
   Ríoplatenses* 41
folkloristics 35
folk song 28
folktale 27–29, 69–70, 104–105, 114
forfeit 117
form 40–41, 118, 124, 130, 132, 141, 165
Forman, Michael L. 112–113
formula 24, 33, 51, 55–57, 61, 72–75, 83, 93,
   124, 141–148, 150
   antithetical 144–145
   closing 128
   joking question 143
   near / far 154

nominative absolute 146–147, 159
opening formula 51, 62, 90, 92, 109, 128–129
   f. analysis 142, 145, 149
   f. classification 143
   f. criteria 143
   f. element 144
   f. member 143, 145
   f. system 136
frame 115
   concluding 39
   introductory 39
f. element → element
framework
   cultural 119
   social 119
Frederik the Great 65
von Frenckell, Ester M. 77
Freud, Sigmund 102–103
fun 97
function 27, 29, 35–37, 40–41, 49–50, 82, 94,
   101, 108, 110, 118–122, 125–126, 134, 160,
   165
   cognitive 122
   common 45
   educational 126
   social 52
funeral 113

*La Galate* 97
game 92–93, 101, 103, 108, 117, 120–122, 129,
   134, 162–163, 165
   computer 67
Ganander, Christfrid 79, 115, 153
Gandhi, Indira 22
gathering, social 98
gay 17
gender 104, 119
generalisation 45
genre
   global 49
   ethnic 51
   expressive 96
   minor 142
   natural 50–51
   sub- 54–55, 57, 69, 93, 119, 122, 124, 134,
   153, 159, 163–165
   generic borders 25, 49

Georges, Robert A. 35, 40–42, 48–50, 131, 135, 153
Glazier, Jack and Phyllis 160
god, of thunder 28
Goethe, Johann W. 77
Goldstein, Kenneth 35, 96, 107, 120
Green, Thomas A. 50, 52–53, 132, 134, 159
greeting card 24
Grimm, Brothers 116
groups
    age 105
    gender 105
    occupational 101
    sex 101
    group's cohesion 102
Grzybek, Peter 161
guesser→riddlee
guessing 36, 95, 101, 153, 158

Hain, Mathilde 75
Halonen, Tarja 23
*Hamlet* 77
Hamnett, Ian 35
Handelman, Don 117, 162
Haring, Lee 42, 65, 137, 154
Harîrî, Al 76
Harries, Lyndon 28, 50–51
Hart, Don 35–36, 75, 118
Hasan-Rokem, Galit 27, 84
Hauschild, Thomas 19–20
Heidrek, King 13–14
Hedman, Marie M. 77
*Hervarar saga* 12, 69, 160
history 34
Holocaust 20
homophone 60, 129, 131
honour 109, 114
hooker 17
humiliation 109
    ritual 107
humour 20, 57, 72, 77, 86, 123
    black 20
    crazy 24, 131
    elephant 58
    in-group 60, 126
    neighbourly 74
    sense of 86, 122

    sexual 104
    sick 17
Hymylä 115–116, 157
    trip to 117–118

image 9–10, 14–15, 28, 35, 38–41, 43, 46, 53–56, 63, 68, 73, 93, 95, 108, 111, 128–129, 131, 133, 135–140, 146–147, 157–159, 165
    allegorical 134
    antithetical 130
    contrasting 130
    cosmological 28
    paradoxical 128, 130
improvisation 15, 148
incantation 117, 141
incongruens 58
industrialisation 14
initiation 122
insinuation, sexual 85
insult 104
interaction 36, 93, 120
Internet 59, 165
interpretation 131–132, 158
    Freudian 86
interviewee 36
interviewer 36
invariant 30
invention 153
inversion 45
irreality 133
Isbell, Billie Jean 142
jest 24, 54, 81–82
Jew 12–13
joke 24, 57, 60–61, 75 ,79, 82–83, 90–91, 125, 127
    "Auschwitz" 19
    Biafra 17–19
    catastrophe 20–21
    dumb blonde 59, 74
    East Frisian 19
    elephant 16, 57–58, 110
    erotic 82
    ethnic 16
    Jew 17
    Negro 17–18
    Polack 16 19
    president 23

Somali 17
viola player 19
Århus 19
joking question 9–10, 16, 18–21, 23–25, 52, 54, 56-58, 60–61, 63, 67, 74, 79, 83, 87, 122–126, 131, 134, 159, 16–163
Jolles, André 27
joy 92
juxtaposition 45

Kalevala
K. epic poetry 117
K. metre 15, 128, 149, 154
K-metric poetry 29, 115, 138
Kekkonen, Urho 23
kernel
  denominative 39
  descriptive 39
*Kilon poliisi* 67
af Klintberg, Bengt 17, 62, 165
knowledge
  test of 152
Knuuttila, Seppo 108–109
*Koran* 11
Krohn, Julius 29
Krohn, Kaarle 29–30
Kuusi, Matti 27, 46, 142
Kvideland, Reimund 19
Kymppitonni 108
Köngäs Maranda, Elli 10, 27, 35, 43–46, 51–52, 122, 128, 130, 135–136, 147, 158

Laalo, Klaus 134
language 22
  poetic 128, 130
  riddle 14–15, 45, 92, 128–132, 134–136, 139, 150
  shared 53
  specific 21
  vulgar 85
  l-specific 21
*The Language of Riddle, New Perspectives* 52
law
  epic 30
  transformation 30
  l. of opposites 30
  l. of thought and fantasy 32

legend
  urban 20
Lehmann-Nitsche, Robert 31, 34, 40–41
lesbo 17
level
  linguistic 134, 146
  semantic 148
  structural 49, 145
  stylistic 148
  surface 40, 49, 52
  syntactic 148
  textural 145
Levin, Ju. I. 50
library 15
Lipponen, Ulla 23, 57, 59, 64, 67, 71, 88–89
literature,
  old Norse 13
  oral literature 93, 139
*The Literary Riddle Before 1600* 35
logogriph 55, 77
lore
  children's lore 14, 23, 57, 65, 73, 84–85, 88–89, 120, 134
  sexual lore 85, 87, 102, 104–105
loser 106
lullaby 128
Lövkrona, Inger 80, 103

magazine
  children's 63, 77–78
  riddling 77
magic 94
*Mahabharata* 11
*Maqamat* 76
marriage 96
McAuliffe, Christa 20, 22
McDowell, John Holmes 110, 120, 150
meaning 36
  double 85
  educational 120
media, (mass) 15–16, 19, 87, 163
memory 130
*Mercure de France* 77
message 25, 134
Messenger, John C. 94
metaphor 14–16, 26–28, 31, 33–35, 41, 45–47, 50, 55–56, 72, 80, 93–94, 104, 111–112, 119,

124, 130, 135–141, 152–154, 158–159, 165–166
method
    "Finnish" 29
    historical-geographical 29–30, 32
    comparative research 29
metre, poetic 129
*Midrash* 13
milieu 29
    rural 119
    tradition 36
    urban 119
model 142–143, 145
    expressive 57, 141
    idea 142
    linguistic 142
    structural 93
Monroe, Marilyn 89
motif 27, 61–63, 74, 76, 102, 123
mould 141
movement
    temperance 104
    workers' 104
    youth association 104
motorcycle 16
myth 27, 123
    Boeotian 105
    mythological fantasy 27
    mythological metaphor 27
narrative 25, 71–72, 74–75, 96, 109, 111
Nazis 19
neck riddle → riddle
negation 132
*Neue Beiträge Zur Kenntnis des Volksrätsels* 39
news 67
newspaper 15
night vigil 96
*The Nordic Riddle: Terminology and Bibliography* 35, 55
norm 119
    linguistic 130
    breaking norms 83
novelties 10

Odin 13
Oedipus 12
*Old English Exeter Book* 76
Old Norse literature 13
*Old Testament* 11–13
Olrik, Axel 30
onomatopeia 45, 146
opinion
    amused 11
    ironic 11
opponent 106
opposition 40, 42–43, 131, 144
    antithetical contradictive 42
    causal contradictive 42
    privational contradictive 42
    semantic 42
order 122
origin 34, 47, 141, 166
Oring, Elliot 58

Pagis, Dan 52
Palmenfelt, Ulf 14, 59, 85, 164
parody 61, 68, 74–75, 122, 164
Parton, Dolly 89
pattern
    metric 35
    structural 49, 110
    stylistic 41
    p. of expectation 72
    p. of riddle 30, 141–142

people
    African 113
    African-American 17
    Altaic 141
    American Indian 36
    Anang of Nigeria 26, 94
    Bantu Soho 26
    Belgian 18
    Belomissian 141
    Biafra 20
    Canadian 18
    Chinese 17
    Dusun 35
    Edo of Nigeria 161
    English 18
    Ethiopian 20
    Filipinos 10
    Finnish 60, 134
    French 18

Iraqi 18
Irish 17–18
Israelites 12
Italian 17
Jewish 12–13, 17, 19–20
Lau 10, 27, 123
Mexican 17, 63
Mbeere 160
Newfoundland 18
Northern-Irish 125
Norwegian 18
Palestinian 22
Pangue of Cameroon 160
Philistine 12
Polish 16–17
Quechua-speaking (of Peru) 104
Sandawe 111, 113, 129, 140
Scandinavian 20
Somali 18
Sumerian 11
Swedish-speaking Finnish 60
people of Thebes 12
Udmurt 113
Venda 35, 37, 105, 113–114, 161
Wolof tribe 25
Pepicello, W. J. 50, 52–53, 132, 134, 159
performance 35, 105, 114, 119, 165
Petsch, Robert 39–40, 48–49, 51
Phicium 12
phrase 142
phrasing 26
*Le piacevoli notti* 76
play 129
player 92
poem 28, 30, 139
*On Poetics* 47
poetry 25
*Persian and Arabic Riddles* 49
politics, day-to-day 11
Potter, Charles Francis 122–123
power
 intellectual 152
 male 103
 social 152
 women 103
prank 101
Prasad, Leela 60–61

precedent 38 51
premise
 constant 44
 hidden 45
Price, Roger 62
press 62
problem
 arithmetic 110
 visual 78
prohibition 113–114
proposition 38
protest 83
protoforum 30
*The Proverb* 141
proverb 25–27, 29, 49, 92, 94, 98, 109, 113, 120, 128, 142
punishment 114–115, 117–118
puzzle 65–66, 70–71, 74–75, 77, 131
 arithmetical 25, 55–56, 74
 picture 87, 89
 pseudo 74
*Pääskynen* 77

question 38, 52–53, 57, 61, 68, 69–71, 74–75, 108–109, 120, 126, 128, 134, 138
 biblical 110
 catechetical 52
 clever 52, 55
 enigmatic 56
 joking → joking question
 obscure 117
 trick 74, 93, 131, 159
 quiz 67–68
 wisdom 28, 56, 68–69
 witty 55, 67, 72–75
quiz
 knowledge 163
 show 163, 165

Raa, Eric Ten 111, 129, 140
racism 17, 20
radio 15–16, 23, 62, 164
 local 16
rank, social 102
reality 135
 non-reality 135
rebus 64–65, 67

literary 55
recession 23
reference 109
    frame of 130
referent 10, 40, 42–43, 45, 56, 109, 132, 135–137, 153
relation, social 119
relationship, semantic 51, 149
relaxation 97
religion 104
respondent → riddlee
restriction 113
Reusner, Nicolaus 76
reversal 45, 135
revolution, technical 14
reward 114
*On Rhetoric* 47
rhetoric 122
rhyme 26, 30, 128–129, 145
rhythm 25
riddle
    African 50–51
    Anang 119
    Argentinian 31, 34
    Asiatic 34
    Bulgarian 27, 32
    Burmese 45
    character 129–130
    Cheremis 10, 132, 135, 146
    Chinese 130
    contemporary 54, 92, 122
    cosmogonic 27
    crazy 110
    descriptive 56
    English 144
    erotic 81
    Filipino 10
    Finnish 27, 46, 57, 112, 132, 135–136, 153
    folk 122
    French 34
    German 34, 144
    giraffe 63
    horror 165
    improper 104
    invented 108
    Iranian 22
    Iraqi 22
    Israeli 89
    Kazakh 161
    kernel 45–46
    Latvian 31
    literary 42, 75–77
    Lithuanian 31
    Macedonian 27
    metaphorical 42, 44, 57, 79, 135
    moron 85–86
    neck 52, 55, 68-69, 110, 165
    new 107
    non- 52
    non-erotic 103
    normal 39
    Northern-Irish 22–23
    obscene 102–103
    onomapoetic 41
    Ovambo 26, 46
    paradox 44
    parody 56, 72, 74
    pictorial 55
    picture 129
    pre- 54
    proper 56
    proverb 94, 119
    Quechua 133
    r. challange 121
    r. joke 84
    r. narrative 71
    r. of Samson 12, 68, 108
    r. of the Sphinx 12, 105, 108
    r. parody 24, 73
    r. poem 75
    r. poser → riddler
    r. process 50
    r. proverb 26
    r. section 110
    r. type 72
    Russian 32, 34, 129, 161
    Serbian 32
    sexual 41, 79–84, 91, 101–103, 114, 119, 122
    Slavic 148
    solving a 161
    story 165
    Swedish 129
    syllable 55
    Tambunan Dusun 118, 121

Ten'a 36
the Odin 12
true 9, 14–16, 24, 38, 42, 47–49, 52, 54–57, 63, 69, 93, 114, 119, 124, 132, 136, 151, 153, 163, 165
Turkish 28, 34, 144
Venda 119, 139, 160
Vietnamese 128
visual 61–62, 64-65, 67, 75, 79
Vote 31
waves of r.s 16
Yoruba 41 132
riddlee 36, 40, 44, 50, 52–53, 56–57, 61, 63, 68–72, 91, 93, 96, 105, 107, 110–111, 115, 117, 120–121, 130, 135, 137, 148, 152–153, 155, 157–160, 162
riddler 36, 45, 52, 56, 61, 63 ,69, 72, 80, 86, 93, 95–96, 105–106, 109, 114, 120, 131, 138, 152, 155, 158–159
*Riddles Ancient and Modern* 55
*Riddles in Filipino Folklore* 35, 118
riddling 15, 25, 35–37, 52, 56, 67, 69–71, 75, 82, 92, 94, 96, 103, 105, 114, 118–121, 130, 132, 135, 139, 141, 150, 157, 159, 161, 163, 165
  r. act 158
  r. battle 114
  r. community 111, 117, 154, 156
  r. discourse 110
  r. occasion 97, 100
  r. session 25, 55, 94, 97, 109–110, 130
  r. situation 25, 38, 82, 97, 108, 111, 117, 119, 152–153, 160
*Rig Veda* 11
rite 159
  death 96, 114
  initiation 84, 114
  r. de passage 152
ritual 94
  funeral 105
  r. practice 114
Roberts, John M. 112–113
Roemer, Danielle 88
role 120
  exhange 116
  game 101
Rolland, Eugène 34

rule 150, 159
  genre-specific 134
  strategic 105
  r. for making riddles 148
  r. of interaction 106
rumour 121
rune 142
aarinen, Sirkka 135
Sadnik, Linda 27
Sadovnikov, D. 34
Santi, Aldo 34
de Saussure, Ferdinand 162
saying 104
  metaphoric 26
scheme 132, 135, 141
  content 147
  linguistic 41
  semantic 146, 158
  structural 42, 50, 142
school
  elementary 104
  historical-geographical → method
Scott, Charles T. 37, 42, 49–50
script 93
Sein, Than Maung 48, 145
semantic fit 14, 46
sentence
  fixed phrased 26
  kernel 45
sequent 38, 51
sex 104
sexual
  s. act 102
  s. insinuation 104
  s. socialisation 104
Shakespeare, William 77, 89–90
shame 57, 92
  fear of 108
Sheba, Queen of 13
signans 44
signatum 44
simile 80, 141, 148
Simon, Gwladys Hughes 36, 111
situation 103, 137, 141, 158
  performing 46, 92, 93, 128
  spontaneus 97
  telling 165

Skov, Torben 64
"smut" 102
society, agrarian 14
Solomon, King 13
solution 40, 71, 111, 131, 136
Soma 11
song 96, 104
soap 16
soap opera 23
Socrates 61
speech 130
spoonerism 79, 90–96, 146
statement 128–129, 133, 135
status 101, 114
stereotype 16
   ethnic 61, 84
stimulus 118
story 25, 69, 72
   frame 108
   Oedipus 105
   Sphinx 105
   spooky 25
storytelling 25, 96
Straparola 76
strategy 52, 122
strife 105
structure 37, 40–41, 44, 50, 53–54, 91, 118, 132, 145
   basic 44
   cognitive 93
   deep 145
   logical 45
   morphological-syntactic 130, 149
   phrase 45
   semantic 132, 146
   stylistic 35, 39
   surface 40, 46, 132
   syntactic 146
   topic 93
structuralist 40, 49
Ström, Fredrik 55
style 48, 54, 118, 129–130
subject 110
succinctness 129
supremacy 105
Sutton-Smith, Brian 54, 86
von Sydow, C.W. 40

symbol 57, 69, 86, 111, 130, 132, 135, 162
Symphosius 76
*Syntactic structures* 45

taboo 17, 20, 84, 102
tale
   dilemma 25
*Talmud* 11
*Babylonian Talmud* 27
Taylor, Archer 10, 29, 30, 34, 36, 39–40, 47–49, 52, 54–56, 75, 79, 138–139, 141–142, 153
team 106
teasing
   erotic 82
technology 123
telephone 16
temperature 85, 101
Ten Grand [quiz] 108
tension 92
terminology 35, 38, 40, 46, 119, 165
test 67, 81
   t. of ingenuity 65
text 94
   isolated 93
theme 110
*Thousand and One Nights* 34
Tietze, Andreas 34
tolerance 122
topic 40, 42, 50, 145
tradition
   African 106, 113, 128
   Anglo-Saxon 41, 128
   catastrophe 19, 21
   Finnish 110, 128
   Hindi 107
   literary 105
   male 82
   Northern Ireland 123
   oral 69, 79, 83, 101, 105, 131, 163–164
   prose 142
   sexual 104
   Tambunan Dusun 55
   t. bearer 93
   t. milieux 36
   Turkish 113
   Udmurt 109
   workplace 82

Yoruba 119
transformation 45, 46, 142
triumph 92
Troubles [the Northern Ireland] 125
true riddle → riddle, true
truism 44
*The Truly Tastless Joke-a-Date Book* 17
Turtles, the 83–84
TV 15–16, 20, 62, 67, 72, 108, 163–164
TV series 23
type
   ideal 50, 52
   irreal 51
   real 51
   structural 51
   true riddle 79
   unstructured 51
   t. index 165
typewriter 16

*Ujo Piimä* 67
unit 40, 51
   basic 49, 143
   elemental 45
   minimum 40, 42, 49
*Universal Magazine of Knowledge and Pleasure* 77
use 27, 32, 34–36, 47, 54, 91–92, 94, 124–125, 130–131, 136, 139, 163, 165
user 29

Valotka, Audrius 146
value 24, 119, 122
variant 30, 33–34, 138–139, 153, 157
variation 33, 34, 40, 59, 74, 93, 132, 138–139, 154, 158–159
Vb [newspaper] 19
Vedic poetry 11

*Vergleichende Rätselforschungen I–III* 30
version 32
*Verzeichnis der Märchentypen* 30
victory 107
Virtanen, Leea 14, 67, 117
Virtanen et al. 103
vocabulary 129–130
Volockaja, Zoja Michajlovna 148
Voltaire 65

wake 94, 95, 101
war
   First World War 33
   Gulf War 22, 164
   Second World War 19, 23
"war of jokes" 19
WASP 17
wedding 146
   Turkish 106–107, 113
Wessman, V. E. V. 101, 104
wiev
   comparative 29
   structuralistic 29
winner 106
Williams, Fionnuala Carson 125–127
Williams, Thomas Rhys 35–36, 118
Winograd, Terry 93
wit 57, 74, 119, 131–132, 152–153
   test of 108
   verbal 9, 160
Wolfenstein, Martha 86
women, position of 104

Yaksa 11
Yudhisthira 11

"zen koan" 52

www.ingramcontent.com/pod-product-compliance
Lightning Source LLC
Chambersburg PA
CBHW080806300426
44114CB00020B/2848